FREEMASONRY

AN INTERPRETATION

By MARTIN L. WAGNER

Pastor of the St. Johns English Evangelical Lutheran Church,
Dayton, Ohio.

COLUMBUS, OHIO:
THE F. J. HEER PRINTING CO.
1912

Dedication

To the Church of Jesus Christ, pure only as she confesses the pure Faith of the Word of God, instructed by the doctrine of the blessed Apostles, walking in the true Light of the Truth of that Word and freed from all false religion, false and pernicious doctrines; and

To a Holy Ministry, earnestly contending for the Faith once delivered to the saints, into whose hands are committed the Mysteries of the Kingdom of God, and of which they are faithful stewards, this volume is Dedicated.

CONTENTS.

6 CONTENTS.

PREFACE.

I N this Interpretation of Freemasonry
the writer has been animated neither
by a spirit of curiosity nor of ani-
mosity, but by a sincere desire to ascertain, if possible, from the recognized and
official Masonic publications the true nature,
essence and doctrines of the institution, and
to present them to the reader in intelligible
and unveiled language. He has not in a
single instance knowingly read into the Masonic language what the context, ceremony
or historic allusions, in his judgment do not
warrant. He has been candid and honest in
his investigation, and if he has misinterpreted the ideographs and glyphs, and mis-
stated the doctrines of Freemasonry, it is
due to a misunderstanding of the nature of
the institutions which constitute the sources
from which it claims to have been derived.

In pursuing this task, he has not depended upon the so-called "exposures" of
the secrets and ritualistic work of Freema-

sonry. He has reached the conclusion that these "exposures," however sincere and honest in their efforts their authors may have been, do not, as high Masons contend, expose the essence of Freemasonry, but only exhibit the habiliments, the clothing, in and under which the real Freemasonry is concealed. This real Freemasonry is something beside and beneath the ritualistic form and the monitorial lectures. It is something which comparatively few Masons apprehend. "Modern Masonry," says Buck, "never possessed the true key for the interpretation of the secret doctrine". The institution is esoteric. It least does mean what it most does say and show. Its ritualistic ceremonies and monitorial lectures both reveal and conceal the secret ideas and doctrines, but very few of the craft discern them. This Masonic authorities as well as the ritual declare, and the writer has determined to discover if possible that secret doctrine which constitutes the essence of the institution and which is veiled under the terms and imagery of a builder's craft.

The essence of Freemasonry, that is its peculiar religious ideas, and doctrines, has survived from the periods of remotest antiquity until the present time, and continues with a persistence that is marvelous. It is diffused over the whole habitable portion of the globe. Like the mysterious force or energy in nature upon which it is based, the essence or data has been constant, but the forms in which it has found expression, have varied in the different ages and among different people. The marvel lies in this persistence. Crushed in one form it arises in another. Outlawed or exposed in one institution it evades detection by taking refuge under a different name, ritual and symbolism. Though the old "temples" in which it thrived in the past ages have either been destroyed, or fallen into decay, it erects for itself a new one, in which it propagates its doctrines. Like that mysterious life energy in nature, which perpetually dying renews itself in like, similar, yet different forms, so its peculiar religious ideas and doctrines dying with the decadence of the old sodalities reappear in like, similar yet different institutions and cults.

In its modern form, and organization, Freemasonry has had a checkered career, although it seems to defy all forces that tend to disintegrate institutions. Nor do we expect that this Interpretation will materially diminish its strength, curb its power, or check its progress. So long as there is unregenerate human nature, so long will the root of Freemasonry find a congenial soil, and keep alive the organization in some form. Exposure may check it and induce many of its followers, who have been lured by its pretenses, to repudiate it, but the thing itself doubtless will continue to live in some form. In 1826 when Wm. Morgan published his Exposure there were 50,000 Freemasons in the United States. On the strength of that exposure, 45,000 left the order, because they thought what Morgan made public was the essence of Freemasonry, whereas it was merely the form, the clothing, the cloak in which the real doctrine, was concealed and veiled. Continental Masonry was little if any affected by Morgan's exposure because the craft there discerned the deeper meaning of the ritual and monitorial Lectures, while comparatively few American Masons at that time, apprehended its true recondite teachings. These latter knew the *narrative,* but not the *doctrine*. Since then the order has grown rapidly in numbers, popularity, and in influence, so that at present there are about 1,500,000 Masons in the United States and a great number in foreign countries. It has become a world wide organization, so that it is literally true that "in its language men of every land converse".

There is a reason for this persistence of Freemasonry, for this rapid recovery from what was then thought to be its death blow, and for this rapid growth. Masons contend, and we believe the contention is well founded, that Morgan's Exposure does not expose the essence, the doctrines of Freemasonry. Unless there be given the key to Freemasonry, these exposures are of no material value. They present only the exoteric side of Freemasonry. To perceive the esoteric side, or the real teachings, the key for the interpretation of its ceremonies, allegories, and symbols is essential. These exposures by seceding Masons, exhibit only the trappings, in and under which the essence of Freemasonry, is concealed. This essence of the institution, the real Freemasonry, does not consist of the forms, grips, ceremonies, symbols, nor of the ritualistic ceremonial, nor of the monitorial instruction. The real Freemasonry lies concealed beneath these, and is as densely veiled to the Mason as to the profane, and the key to it, "not one Mason in ten thousand possesses, nor even suspects that it exists." "The true and real secrets of Freemasonry are not taught in the lodge at all." The facts upon which the ritual is based are old and have become obscure, or forgotten, or lost in the ritualistic accretions so that it is necessary for the Mason if he would understand Freemaonry, to recover that meaning. The large majority of the craft do not comprehend these facts because of the dense veils thrown around them. They see and learn only the outward forms, and the less the ignorant Mason knows, the more will he admire and believe.

What then is this thing which constitutes the mystic tie that holds its adherents in such a compact brotherhood? What is it that defeats all efforts to weaken it or to destroy it? It is the peculiar religion, which constitutes the essence, the life, the heart, the soul of this institution. The organization, despotic in its government, its oaths, horrible in their penalties, its ceremonies, impressively solemn, its secrets, mysteries in their nature are all designed to conceal and to protect from profane eyes, this religion. Religion is its mystic tie.

Religion has ever been and is even now the most powerful factor in human activities. In some form it has been the motor back of the commanders of the armies, and of statesmen that founded the great world empires of the past, that animated and upheld the most despotic governments, that fomented the bloodiest revolutions, that precipitated nations into sanguinary conflicts and that united alien peoples into almost indissoluble unions; that established the most arbitrary and despotic priest craft, enforced intellectual thralldom, and the tyranny of rulers. It has instigated, sustained and justified the most dastardly, atrocious, barbarous, and licentious acts in human annals, as well as the most liberal, just and pure. It has inspired the erection of the most stupendous, most elaborate, and the most costly structures as monuments to its power, and as shrines for its gods. It has produced the finest specimens of art, voiced the sweetest and holiest of song and inspired the loftiest flights of the intellect in all the realms of human knowledge. It has transformed human perverts into saints, and changed moral creatures into demons of lust, fury, and crime. It has enabled timid women and children to defy the threats of tyrants, and smile upon the terrors of dungeon, flames, and death. It has cemented brotherhoods and cults into unions which defeat the sagacity of statesmen, the erudition of jurists, the skill of marshals, the power of kings and the anathemas of popes, to destroy. Religion is without doubt the most powerful motor in man, and religion is the motor in Freemasonry.

Freemasonry in its chief and essential features, is a religion, and as such it has marks and elements which are peculiar to itself but which also differentiate it from Christianity. These vital and essential elements in this religion are not spiritual facts and spiritual mysteries, but carnal and psychical, the facts of life and the mysteries involved in the generation and reproduction of life, and from their nature appeal most powerfully to man. They relate to the living principle in man and to his dominant passion namely the desire to procreate. They therefore excite the passions, awaken the emotions, impress profoundly his mind, and engage most deeply his thought. The institution fascinates the imagination and charms the disciple with these mysteries of life with which it deals and professes to unfold. It is hard to conceive of anything more exquisitely fitted to appeal to the natural man and incite him to fidelity than is this institution, because it deals not with the spiritual side of his nature, but with the carnal and psychical, and makes the gratification of those carnal desires a sacred privilege and a solemn duty. It is a religion which makes the mystery of procreation the *objective fact* upon which it rests; the mysterious life generating principle in man the object of adoration and worship; the generative acts the pattern for its rites and ceremonies; the generative organs the basis of its symbolism, and the passions the inspiring spirit.

The peculiar charm and fascination which Freemasonry has for its disciples is to be accounted for on this intimate connection between the religious ideas which it holds and inculcates, and the functions of sex in the reproductive processes. It conceives of the divine nature as residing in man, and that it is especially active and expressive in the sexual passion; and that the gratification of this passion is pleasing to the deity and is the duty of the Mason. It aims to make passion, therefore, sacred by making its gratification a moral and religious duty.

On its theological side, Freemasonry is a sort of pantheism, the deity being the generative principle, the reproductive power which pervades all animated nature. And as this power inheres in man, it is viewed as "incarnate in humanity in toto," thus establishing man's union and unity with the divine nature. In the deification and worship of this generative principle, Freemasonry makes the dominant carnal passion the *subjective fact* upon which this religion is based. The two constituent elements of this Masonic religion are the idea of the divine nature in man, and man's cooperation with the divine nature in the reproduction of life. This generation of human beings through sex agencies, is the "great work" of Freemasons, which it characterizes as "building a temple for the indwelling of the Great Architect of the Universe." Upon this "temple every Freemason is enjoined to labor." With desire as its moral law, the generative principle as its deity, the procreative instinct for its animating spirit, humanity for the temple of its god, and the origin and destiny of the human soul for its mystery, Freemasonry appeals most powerfully to the natural man.

It is contended by some that Freemasonry is unworthy of serious notice and investigation, and that it will eventually decay, and lose its charm and influence. In this opinion we do not concur. It is a sex-cult, and like its prototypes and predecessors, will always have a large and influential following. Sex cults always have had a strange fascination for mankind. The ancient ethnic religions were sex cults, and more or less secret. So long as public sentiment frowns upon indecencies, excesses, and sexual uncleanness, such cults can not exist except under esoteric forms. Their existence depends upon secrecy. If then these

2

secrets of Freemasonry become known to the general public surely all decent and self respecting men who have been lured into the lodge under its veiled pleas of morality will leave it because of shame. They will confess their deeds, and burn their books. But so long as carnal minded men deify passion and worship it in secret, so long will there be men who will defend this religion and who will worship at its shrines.

Over against this ancient religion modernized and veiled, under a new name, and taught in the language and imagery of a builder's craft, we as followers of Jesus Christ, must oppose the Mysteries of the Kingdom of God, the facts, the claims, the doctrines of His Gospel. We hold that Christianity is the pillar of society, the only safeguard of the nations, the parent of social order, the ground of that Truth, which alone is able to curb the passions, to teach men to love Truth, to practice charity, and to guarantee to each individual his inalienable rights. Christianity can not ignore its rivals and enemies, who hold down the Truth in unrighteousness. It must enter their dark chambers and bring to light the "hidden things of darkness." It must not only point out the "cunningly devised fables whereby men lie in wait to deceive," but also set forth its testimonies over against all other claimants for man's service, devotion, and worship. In the facts, acts and teachings of Jesus Christ, and the Truth involved in them, the religious sentiment in man finds its steadfast anchor, its fullest, purest, highest and most symmetrical development and expression. Freemasonry with its boastful claims to antiquity, universality and sublime morality, can not offer any valid reason why it should not be investigated, compared with Christianity, and tested in the light of history and of the Word of God. We must oppose the Mystery of the Incarnation of the Son of God over against the mystery of procreation; of spiritual entities and facts over against the psychical mysteries of these cults; spiritual regeneration over against carnal generation.

The most dangerous antagonists of Christianity in its earliest days were the worship of Isis, under various modifications as Demeter, Cybele, Diana, or as the power of fertility; and Mithraism, the worship of the

generative power under the aspect of light.
The enemies of Christianity clothed these
ideas in the language of the New Testament
and of the Church. This was the secret of
their power and influence. By skilfully veiling their pagan ideas under the terminology
of Christian doctrine many who thought
themselves serving the Lord Jesus Christ
were led unconsicously into the pagan cults.
And this is the method of Freemasonry. It
clothes its pagan ideas in the garb of Christian truth, and in architectural imagery, and
by means of these "cunningly devised
fables," fascinating allegories, and pretended deference to the Word of God, it leads
thousands of Christians into this organization under the impression that they are worshiping and serving the Almighty Jehovah,
and makes it so difficult to expose its ero-
neous doctrines. It is hard to reach error
when it hides under the garb of the Truth.
Can the Church of Christ then ignore with
safety these antagonists, who profess such
reverence for Truth, but set it aside as the
errors of a deluded people, and substitute
for it the lie that has debauched its millions.
Research, exposure and testimony are essen-

tial to unmask this form of error, for hiding under the garb of Truth it can not be reached as candid error can.

The writer offers this Interpretation as his testimony against this modern effort to hold down the Truth in unrighteousness.

The authorities and works consulted in the preparation of this book so far as their language is quoted, or their statements are utilized, are indicated in the text.

INTRODUCTION.

THE author of this book has undertaken a most difficult and a most important work. Masonry, with its numerous offsprings is a powerful factor in our civilization. It is influencing our civic, our social, our family, our moral and our religious life far more than is generally realized. The whole secret society system with its countless lodges and their organizations, is an outgrowth of Masonry. All the secret societies, even the so-called minor orders, have assimilated and incorporated more or less of the fundamental principles of Masonry. A comparison of their various rituals with the rituals of Masonry demonstrates this fact.

Our author has elected to write this elaborate, scholarly and exhaustive work on Masonry. What he claims and charges against that system applies with more or less force against the whole secret society system.

The importance of the study of this subject can scarcely be overemphasized. The whole system is a giant evil. We firmly believe that it is the greatest foe that the Church has to contend against. It insidiously undermines and overthrows the very foundations of evangelical Christianity. Its tendency is to make men indifferent to doctrine and hostile to the positive teachings of Revelation as embodied in the Church's creeds and catechisms. In proportion as men understand, accept and assimilate the teachings of the lodge, in that proportion do they become indifferent if not hostile to an earnest evangelical Church. Masonry practically puts all the so-called sacred books of the east on an equality with the Bible. This cannot help but lower the estimate of the Bible. It necessarily robs it of its unique, divine, inspired character. It encourages the dangerous and damaging idea that the Bible is to be regarded and treated like any other human production. We have long since felt that the secret society system, with Masonry at its head is responsible in a large measure for the rationalistic negative criticism of the Bible that is threatening ruin to the Church of Christ.

It is high time that earnest believers in Christ and His Word should seriously study and understand the fundamental principles of Masonry and kindred man made organizations. It is too late in the day to say that no one can know these fundamental principles unless he is a member. The literature on the subject is voluminous. The rituals can all be bought at a nominal price. Any one who will, can inform himself on the subject. It is next to criminal for a minister of the gospel to be ignorant on the subject. No earnest and consecrated minister who will read the Rev. Mr. Wagner's book and the books to which he refers can be a Mason or a friend of Masonry. Mr. Wagner knows what he says. He has studied the subject for years. He knows more about it than thousands of Masons do. Many of these are good men, personally, and are Masons because they have never understood the underlying religious principles of the lodge. Such men leave the lodge when they learn what its real and fundamental religious teachings are. And they ought to be willing to be shown.

We believe that the Rev. Mr. Wagner has written a powerful book. His basic contention is that Masonry is a religion. He shows that its religion is based on heathen cults and mythologies. It has borrowed much from the Greeks, more from the Hindoos, considerable from Egyptians, Persians, Arabians and others. It is a religion of nature. It is largely pantheistic. It deifies man. Like the ancient nature cults it puts a high estimate on the procreative powers of man. It deifies them. It builds a mystic symbolic cult around the procreative powers and their physical organs. The author claims and argues that the Masonic religion is permeated with phallicism.

Whether he establishes this claim the writer of this is unable to say. He would fain hope that the author claims too much. At any rate the author of this book comforts himself with the hope that thousands of Masons do not see these disgusting things in the symbolism of their system. If the author's contention on this point is true the world ought to know it. And it is high time that respectable Masons should examine the religion and the cryptic meaning of its strange secrets and ceremonies.

In the estimation of the writer of this the strongest part and the part that every one can understand, is the closing part of the book.

This shows up the ethics of Masonry. Here there is proof, demonstrated proof, that the ethics of Masonry is abominable, vile and unworthy of a decent and an honest man. Again we can only charitably hope that Masons, as a class, have not seriously examined the true inwardness of the ethical system of their order. But there is no excuse for such ignorance. Serious and manly men ought to know what their order teaches. They ought to know that by belonging to the order they sanction its teachings. They ought to know that their example invites others to accept these teachings.

Surely it is high time for true believers in Christ and His Church to earnestly examine this world power and to ask themselves what it has to do with the startling apostasy of the masses from the Church, with the impurity and selfishness of the spirit of the age and with so much coldness, unbelief and laxness in the Church itself.

Is Masonry a part of the final apostasy?

G. H. GERBERDING.

PART I.

Freemasonry a Religious Institution.

(29)

CHAPTER I.

IN whatever aspect we may view the Masonic institution it presents to us a very complex and intricate organization, which makes it no easy task to reduce its symbols, emblems and ceremonies, and the ideas they are designed to express, into a consistent and intelligible system. If we enter a lodge room when all is in readiness for "work," or for "refreshment," we are surprised at the number and variety of the material objects employed in its initiations. We are deeply impressed with the solemnity of the ceremonies, and our curiosity is aroused by the vague expressions and repeated "allusions" occuring in the language employed, especially in the rites, lectures and charges. But upon closer observation we discover that all these things have a specific meaning, and that they are employed in an orderly manner for each separate degree and initiation. There is order in this apparent chaos of ceremony, symbol and speech.

That the reader who is not familiar with Freemasonry may have a reasonably clear idea of the matter we purpose to examine and interpret in this work, let us take a glimpse of the institution, of the objects which it employs, the sciences which it utilizes, and the ceremonies which it performs, by means of which it teaches its peculiar ideas of religion, of ethics, and of government. We therefore, first of all propose to take our reader into the lodge room and portray to him the things that are there seen, done and heard. Space, however, will not permit a full portraiture, for that would require a volume. We call attention chiefly to the essentials.

The regulation form of the room in which the lodge of Masons assembles for its peculiar work, is that of an oblong rectangular solid, whose longest dimensions are, at least theoretically, east and west. The ceiling of this room is blue and decked with stars. The floor is a mosaic pavement with an indented tessel. In the center of this rectangular floor, at least in some countries, there is traced the outlines of a blazing star. On the floor in the east, south and west sides of the room are elevated platforms, the one in the east being the highest of the three. This is a brief description of the lodge room, in its general form and outline. Attached to it and connected by doors are two ante-rooms, one of which is the preparation room, in which the candidate is prepared for his ordeal of initiation.

The officials of the lodge are the worshipful master, who presides, the junior warden and the senior warden, who respectively occupy the east, south and west platforms above described. To the right and left of the master are the senior deacon and the secretary respectively, and on the right of the senior warden in the west is the junior deacon. Besides these there are the stewards, who carry out the directions and orders of the master, a treasurer, and a tyler.

In the center of the room stands the Masonic altar. To its east, south and west sides are placed tall candles or lights, forming the "triangle of lights," within which the altar stands. On the top of this altar rest a book,

3

usually a Bible, the square, and a pair of compasses, and in some countries, also a sword.

The several objects with which the lodge room is supplied, and which have their place and use in the respective ceremonies of initiation, are grouped in different classes and given special designation. The square, the compass, and the holy book constitute the "furniture" of the lodge. Their presence is absolutely essential. The three columns, real or mystic, and representing the three officials, are the "supports" of the lodge. The holy book, square and compass constitute the three "great lights" of Masonry, while the sun, moon and the master of the lodge constitute the "lesser lights," represented by three burning tapers at the altar. The "work tools" of the first degree are the twenty-four inch gauge, and the common gavel; in the second degree the plumb, square and level, and in the third degree, all the implements of operative Masonry, but more especially the trowel. The "ornaments" of the lodge are the mosaic pavement, the indented tessel and the blazing star. The "jewels" are the square, level and plumb, the rough ashler, the perfect ashler and the trestleboard.

The second degree has several objects peculiar to it alone. They are the two columns, surmounted by globes, the winding stairs, with its series of three, five and seven steps, the five orders of architecture and the letter G.

In the third degree there are certain objects which serve as emblems, namely the pot of incense, the beehive, the book of constitutions, the sword pointing to the naked heart, the anchor, the ark, the forty-seventh problem of Euclid, the hourglass, the scythe, the setting maul, the sprig of acacia, the spade and the coffin.

In addition to these there are other objects that figure in its symbols, such as the all seeing eye, the point, the circle, straight lines, triangle, the apron, collar and swords. There are mystic names, grips, signs, approaches, points of fellowship, points of entrance, postures, raps, and pass-words. There are frequent references to biblical characters, such as Solomon, Hiram Abiff, Hiram King of Tyre, the saints John, and others.

The institution makes use of the five senses, of which seeing, hearing and feeling are the most important. It has disquisitions on the seven virtues, brotherly love, relief, truth, temperance, fortitude, prudence and justice, which it professes to teach and enjoin.

The liberal arts and sciences also play a part in the rites. Grammar, rhetoric, arithmetic, geometry, music and astronomy are all brought into requisition, but of all these geometry is the most noble.

From this brief description the reader will perceive that the institution of Freemasonry is a very complicated organization; that its component parts of fact, fable and fiction, of theology, philosophy and science, of symbolism, ritualism and ceremonialism, of hieroglyphs, ideograph and art speech, of government, ethics and religion, are most cunningly and intricately interwoven, and presents such a medley of contradictions and combinations of opposites, that it is a bewildering task to separate them and trace each to its true source and determine its specific Masonic meaning. Upon closer examination it presents to our view a series of substitutions and duplications that renders an analysis very difficult, and a systematic classification of its elements almost impossible. The student who seeks to discover its real sentiments and doctrines is repeatedly baffled by this complexity in its constitution, which puzzles, confuses and misleads him in its maze of traditions and facts. For this reason few students, either within or without this organization, have been able to thread its labyrinthine chambers and discover its true nature and secret doctrines. It is so constituted that he who seeks to unravel or to unfold its mysteries is almost certain to be frustrated in his endeavors.

If we take a view of its teachings, the institution is a veritable kaleidoscope. Its mirrors are science, philosophy and religion. Its elemental contents are the doctrines and speculations of the ancient cults, with a mixture of Jewish and Christian terms. In it can be seen, according to the angle of light and the viewpoint of the observer, an endless variety of mathematical, ethical, philosophical, architectural and religious elements, combined into fascinating forms and tints, that mystify and charm the observer. In this religio-ethical color scheme are tinges of Brahminism, Judaism and Christianity; of Mithraism, Essenism, Gnosticism and Kabbalism; of Platonism and Pythagorism; of Deism and Pantheism and the essential tenets and rites of the Egyptian, Phrygian, Grecian and Canaanite mysteries and cults. All these are present and others not necessary to enumerate, and are combined into beautiful and ever changing religious mosaics as the viewpoint of the observer changes, or the work of the lodge unfolds.

Question the members of this institution what all this paraphernalia and solemn ceremony mean, what peculiar views of religion, or ethics, or philosophy these are intended to set forth, they reply that that "is a secret concealed among them which has never been found out" and "cannot be divulged except to those who are bound by irrevocable ties to the institution," and that they dare not communicate it to others. Question them as to the institution itself and they reply, "Freemasonry is a system of morality veiled in allegory, and illustrated

by symbols." Inquire as to the methods of
instruction the reply is, "Freemasonry consists of a course of ancient hieroglyphical
and moral instruction taught according to
ancient usages by types, emblems and allegorical figures." (Rit. p. 23).

If we consult the encyclopedias and dictionaries, we find the institution defined in
its outward form, or in its social and fra-
ternal aspect, and not as to its doctrines and
methods of instruction. The definitions
given by Masonic writers as to the essential
features and distinctive doctrines of the organization are frequently couched in Masonic terms, so as to be unintelligible to the non-
Mason, for these Masonic definitions are designed to mislead the non-Mason. They
define Freemasonry in its exoteric, and not
in its esoteric aspect. These the initiated
but not the uninitiated will understand.
Not until one comprehends the peculiar
language and catches the hidden meaning
of Masonic terms and discerns the allegorical
methods of instruction and the symbolic
illustrations, can he get the full import of
Masonic definitions and explanations. To
render Masonic accounts and definitions in-

telligible, we must translate them into terms whose value and meaning are known to all.

The institution viewed as to its method of communicating its doctrines, and of concealing them from the uninitiated is predominantly esoteric and in a relative degree, secret. Esoterics is a science, a method of instruction designed for and understood by the specially initiated alone, by which secret or mysterious doctrines are communicated in language which expresses one thing but really means quite another thing. Esoteric language usually least does mean what it most does say. In an esoteric organization, the secret or mysterious doctrines are not intelligible to the general body of disciples, but only to the discerning few, who have the wit to perceive the real doctrine intended to be conveyed. And so Freemasonry is an esoteric organization. It is so constituted that its doctrines shall be understood by the especially initiated alone, and are neither communicated nor intelligible to the majority of its disciples. Its real doctrines are concealed under an array of objects, symbols, emblems and ceremony, and in order to safeguard them from the eyes and the understanding of the non-Mason, it expresses them in the imagery and technical terms of operative masonry and architecture, of geometrical science, and in the language of Holy Scripture. These expressions have some real or assumed resemblance in sentiment to the ideas and doctrines intended to be communicated, but in their natural sense do not convey the essence of Freemasonry. They are the cloak under which the real doctrines of the institution are concealed. These esoteric forms are spurious Freemasonry while the secret doctrines and sentiments concealed under these constitute the genuine Freemasonry.

This secret doctrine, whatever it may be, "veiled in allegory and illustrated by symbols," is the essence of the institution, its life, soul and spirit. It is so deeply veiled, hidden and concealed beneath such a vast array of other matter, that comparatively few Masons discern it, or suspect that it exists. The institution employs the so-called liberal sciences, the orders of architecture, the five senses, the speculations of philosophers and the characters and some incidents in Old Testament history, historic and legendary lore to aid in concealing more completely this secret doctrine, and to confuse, puzzle, bewilder and defeat the efforts of the non-Mason to discover it. But while these veils conceal the secret doctrines, they also in a sense reveal it, but not one Mason in ten thousand discerns that revelation. The ritual, lectures and monitors set forth the essence of Freemasonry, but one must read between the lines to discern it.

Because of this esoteric character Freemasonry, like the Sphynx, has been the riddle among modern institutions. As that unique image, embodying in its composite form of man, beast and bird, the dominant types in which the life of Nature expressed itself, was designed to conceal and to reveal the philosophical thought of that age, namely, the unity of the life of Nature and that that life is the Divine Nature, and by its gaze to the sunrise indicated the source from which that life was viewed as emanating, so Freemasonry conceals and reveals in its constitution, rites and symbols, its unique conception and doctrine of the Divine Nature; and by its constant "looking to the east," indicates from whence this doctrine is derived. The key to the mystery of the Sphynx is the philosophical thought and religious conceptions held by the people of the age that produced the Sphynx, namely, that the life of Nature is not only a unity, but that it is the Divine Nature which they worshipped and adored. Its gaze to the sunrise indicated the source of that life, the sun, the great Osiris. The key to the mystery of Freemasonry is its peculiar notion of the Divine Nature which it worships and adores as the Great Architect of the Universe.

Notwithstanding the fact that the institution on its exoteric side presents to our view a medley of contradictions, and a combination of opposites, appearing to be very self-contradictory, it is, however, on its esoteric side, a very self-consistent, symmetrical and harmonious system. On this side "it is a wonderful structure, well proportioned in its dimensions, symmetrical in its design and remarkably well adapted to its purpose."

Freemasonry as defined by Sickels, "is a moral institution established by virtuous men, with the praiseworthy design of recalling to our remembrance the most sublime truths in the midst of innocent and social pleasures, founded on liberality, brotherly love and charity" (Ah. Rezon. p. 13). "Freemasonry is an institution, not as the ignorant and uninstructed vainly suppose, founded upon unmeaning mystery, for the encouragement of Bacchanalian festivity and support of good fellowship; but an institution founded on eternal reason and truth, whose deep basis is the civilization of mankind, and whose everlasting glory is supported by those two mighty pillars — Science and Morality." (A. R., p. 13). "Freemasonry," says Hemming, "according to the general acceptation of the term, is an art founded on the principles of geometry and directed to the service and convenience of mankind. It is a science that inculcates the principles of purest morality, though its lessons are for the most part veiled in allegory and illustrated by symbol." The ritual says, "Freemasonry consists of a course of ancient hieroglyphical and moral instruction taught according to ancient usages by types, emblems and allegorical figures." Buck says, "it is a summary of human wisdom, clear, concise and simple, such as nowhere exists in the world." It is "an impressive system in which the most profound lessons of divine truth are taught in images of poetic form." Mackey says: "It is a science which is employed in the search after the divine truth and employs symbolism as its method of instruction." (Ency. 210).

Taking these definitions, which are all from Masonic sources, and studying them, we find that the Masonic institution contains a system of government, a system of ethical principles, a system of religious and theological doctrines, a system of religious ceremonies, a system of symbols, ideographs, hieroglyphs and art speech, by means of which it communicates its religious, theological and ethical ideas to its disciples; and that these ideographs, allegories and art expressions least do mean in this institution what they most express in their ordinary sense. The secrets not only involve certain mysteries in the processes of Nature, but also the peculiar doctrines of the institution, relative to moral duties, to individual rights, to Masonic rights, to the deity, Nature, man, and immortality. These secret teachings and tenets taken as a whole, constitute its body of doctrine, but the essence and foundation of them all are its peculiar views on religion, as those views involve the belief in deity, in the soul, and in immortality.

The reader must bear in mind that the Freemasonry published in the monitors, dictionaries, rituals and periodicals, is not the genuine article. That is exoteric Freemasonry. It has been exposed, analyzed and dissected repeatedly. On its face exoteric Freemasonry is a series of contradictions. Gadicke says: "The ceremonies, customs, moral explanations and symbolical interpretations and figures cannot be the real Freemasonry." (Masonic Library, 191). If the entire ritual with its rubrics were published, it would not be an open publication of Freemasonry. The secret doctrine lies latent in it, but only those who have some knowledge of it, could discern it. Hence those Masons who know say that the real Freemasonry has never been disclosed.

The Masonic institution then is a composite. It has a system of organization for the government of the craft. This government is rigidly despotic. It has a system

of doctrine or body of divinity, which it
vigilantly protects and conceals from profane eyes, and which it designates as the
"Divine Truth." It has a system of communicating this secret doctrine in art speech,
by means of symbols and in mimic ceremonies. It clothes this secret doctrine under
forms or in narratives, which mean something very different. It is an esoteric institution in almost every feature of its many-
sided nature. Its body of divinity or religious doctrines are its heart and soul. For
the concealment of this religion all the other
features are employed.

In order then to render Freemasonry intelligible to our readers more than a simple
definition is necessary. It must be dissected
and analyzed, and its several elements examined in their true and in their assumed
light and in their relation to each other in
this organization. Its several aspects must
be studied in detail and each part in its particular setting in this complicated system,
and the hidden meaning made plain. This
is the task we have set before us in this work.
We purpose to look at it from its several
viewpoints, and keep before us the distinc-

tion between the essence of Freemasonry and the cloak under which it conceals itself. That cloak is of many colors, nicely blended, exquisitely fitted to cover and to conceal its secret parts, and to fascinate and attract the beholder.

THE EVOLUTION OF FREEMASONRY. The first three degrees known as the Entered Apprentice, the Fellow Craft and the Master Mason degrees are the only degrees universally recognized by the craft as Freemasonry. These, taken in their entirety in symbolism and meaning, constitute the root and stock of Freemasonry and contain its sap and essence. Out of these, as the foundation and root, all the various rites with their higher and side degrees, have been evolved.

Freemasons have not been content with this genuine or ancient craft Freemasonry, and have exercised their ingenuity to expand and adapt it to the various nationalities and religions with which it has come in contact, that is, to conform it to the religion of the country into which it has come. These higher degrees differ somewhat from the original in their externals, but contain the fundamental principles of ancient craft

Masonry, and exhibit it under a different symbolism.

These higher degrees have been arranged into groups or series called Rites, such as the York Rite, the Scottish Rite, the Egyptian Rite, etc., while the Freemasonry set forth in these Rites is designated as York Rite Masonry, Scottish Rite Masonry, etc., indicating the particular aspect in which the Freemasonry is viewed.

The Freemasonry of the first three degrees is viewed in several aspects. It is "Blue Lodge Masonry" when viewed as to the color scheme of the lodge in which it is conferred, and the degrees are the "Blue Lodge degrees." It is "Symbolic Masonry" when viewed as to the method of instruction, "Genuine Freemasonry" when viewed as to the essence or doctrine, or the "divine truth" it aims to set forth; "Ancient Craft Masonry" when viewed as to its source and origin, "Speculative Freemasonry" when viewed over against operative masonry, and "spurious or exoteric Freemasonry" when viewed as to the ritualistic, symbolic and ceremonial forms by which it is taught.

All the degrees above the third are "spu-

4

rious Freemasonry," that is, they have been grafted upon the original stock. These degrees have been invented by Masons, imposters and pretenders for various purposes, and a number, though by no means all of them, have been incorporated for obvious reasons into the institution, but always designated as spurious Freemasonry. They aim to express in a variety of symbolic forms the different ethical, philosophical, political and religious elements which the institution has drawn from ancient sources, to show for it a unity and harmony with the religion of the country in which Masonry is found, to conceal more effectually its true nature and to set forth in new and peculiar symbolic and ideographic forms the fundamental principles. It employs this variety of symbolism as a method of instructing its members in the "divine truth" for which it is searching, and which it professes to have discovered, and to prove that this "divine truth" lies at the basis of all religion, and that therefore all religions are essentially alike.

CHAPTER II.

FREEMASONRY is essentially a religious institution, and it is in this aspect that we shall interpret it in this work.

Nowhere is definition more difficult than in the sphere of religion, but for our purpose it is not necessary that we give a definition that is in every particular comprehensive and exact. "In the wider sense the term refers to all the aspirations of man after God, but in its narrower sense it refers to the realization of these ideas or conceptions, after which man has struggled. In the wider sense it is applied to all foreshadowings of the communion of man with God; as where the existence of a Supreme Being and man's obligation to serve Him, are acknowledged. In the absolute sense, it is man's cheerful recognition and joyful service of a Supreme Personality, based upon the consciousness of reconciliation and a community of interests with Him. The term is

(51)

popularly used to designate the various modes or systems which profess to lead man to communion with God. The communion of man with God is religion subjectively so-called. The statement of the principles underlying this communion is religion objectively so-called."

Religion, though a communion with God and of a decidedly subjective character, is also a life, and as much a social as an individual affair. Reciprocal contact between individual and individual is the general condition of its development, and thus originate common forms of the religious consciousness, and the common forms of its expressions in the outward religious life. Religious ceremonies, places for religious services, articles with which to perform the rites, and symbols for the expression of religious ideas, are the natural growths out of the religious consciousness and life.

Freemasonry, according to all accepted definitions, both of itself and of religion, is a religious institution, and viewed as to its essence and inner principles, is a religion. We cannot conceive of it as anything else, although there are many both Masons and non-Masons, who deny this religious character. As a religion it has its subjective and objective sides. It has its peculiar religious experiences, beliefs, practices, and above all its peculiar conceptions and doctrines concerning the nature of the divine. Like all recognized religions it has all the paraphernalia of religion, images, symbols, ceremonies, prayers, temples, altars, priests and worship. It has its own peculiar divine objects to which it pays divine honors and as we can not conceive of a religion without its rites and ceremonies, so we can not look upon these temples, altars, priests and rites of Freemasonry without the conviction that they are the outward expressions of a religious idea and system. Let us briefly notice this Masonic paraphernalia in detail.

. 1. *Freemasonry has its own revelation.—* Religion and revelation are correlative terms; that is the relation in which man places himself to deity in religion, presupposes the relation in which deity has placed himself to man in revelation, so there can be no religion without a revelation, either genuine or spurious, upon which it is based. This revelation, in the opinion of its adherents, is the deity's message to them, and the source of their faith and the warrant for their practices. It is preserved either in the traditions of its priests, in the ceremonials, or recorded in permanent form which record becomes the Sacred Book of that particular religion. The writers are regarded as the spokesmen of deity, and their statements as his oracles. These sacred books become the rule of faith, of worship, and of life to the disciples.

Each of the so-called great religions has its sacred books or peculiar revelation upon which it is based, and which are important factors in their respective religious systems. Pre-eminent among these is Christianity, which has the canonical scriptures of the Old and New Testament, which it holds as the sole revelation of God's will, and of human redemption and salvation, and the only rule of faith and sole authority in religious questions. To these Christianity appeals for an explanation of its existence, and as a warrant for its authority, faith and work. It accepts these writings not because they have been placed in the canon, but because Christ is set forth in them, as the way, the truth and the life. It rejects all other so-called revelations as spurious because they have not Christ in them. Christianity as a religion rests upon the revelation or manifestation of a Person, who is human and divine, who is the Savior of man and of whose nature, history, work and office the Bible is the authoritative, genuine and inerrant record.

Judaism has its sacred books. They are the Old Testament scriptures. Judaism rejects the New Testament and the Savior and Salvation set forth therein because it claims that Jesus Christ of Nazareth is not the Messiah promised and set forth in the Old Testament.

Islam has its revelation. In a general way it receives the Christian scriptures as a religious book, but it gives the pre-eminence to the Koran, by which the others are to be judged. The utterance of the Koran is final in Islam. Its creed is "there is no God but Allah, and Mohammed is his prophet."

And so with other religions. Parseeism has its Zend Avesta. Brahminism its Vedas, Mormonism its Book of Mormon, and Christian Science its Science and Health.

A revelation of some kind is an essential prerequisite to a religion. Even in the lower forms of religion, as Animism, Totemism and Fetichism, the worshipper believes that in these sacred objects the deity is present and speaks to him. The belief that the divine is immanent in nature is the foundation of all religious symbolism and the worship of material objects.

Freemasonry is no exception to this principle, that is, that a religion presupposes a revelation. In one sense Freemasonry has more sacred books than any other religion for it tacitly accepts, receives and incorporates into its system all the sacred books of all religions. But it accepts them only as *symbols* of the will of God. The revelation upon which Freemasonry as a religion is based is not a book written on parchment, but is the universe itself, in which it claims deity has revealed himself in a sufficiently perspicuous manner so as to be known and served acceptably by his intelligent creatures. Nature, the material universe, is the revelation which is the correlative to the religion of Freemasonry. It regards all revelations which may be found in the sacred books of any religion, as re-publications of this primal, adequate and unerring revelation in Nature.

The sole revelation which Masonry recognizes as absolute and from which it derives its peculiar religious ideas, rites and warrant, is Nature or the Universe. Pike says that "the Universe is the uttered word of God," the "thought of God pronounced." (Morals and Dogma, p. 206). "The permanent one universal religion is written in visible nature and explained by the reason and is completed in the analogies of faith." Buck says, "God never manifested himself to be seen of men. Creation is his manifestation." (Mystic Masonry, p. 134). In the Masonic religion God is conceived of as an omnipotent, eternal, boundless and immutable principle, coeval and coextensive with space, in all, through all and above all, divinity immanent in Nature, alike the external cause and result, each without beginning or end, and each alternating forever. (See Mystic Masonry, p. 149). According to Masonry the deity is clothed in the universe. Garrison says, "God created and must continually support the temple of the universe, which he not only forms but in which he also dwells as its eternal, all-pervading, ever present spirit.'' (Fort, p. 464). All the more recent Masonic writers whom we have consulted agree that the universe is the sole revelation God ever made of himself. Nature then is the book in which Freemasonry finds the divine will expressed. Its sentiments are well expressed by Philo, namely, that Nature is the language in which God speaks. The human voice is made to be heard, but the voice of God to be seen, that what God says consists in acts, not in words.

This book of Nature, Masonry claims, is sufficiently perspicuous for all of man's religious and moral guidance. It teaches him all he needs to know concerning his duty to his God, his neighbor, his country, or to himself. No additional revelation is considered necessary; that all these duties are clearly discerned from that uniform mode of the operations and processes of Nature called natural laws. In this permanent revelation of Nature the will of God is discoverable to us by the light of reason without the assist-

ance of a supernatural revelation. These
natural laws become the moral law in
Masonry, "the will of God relating to human
actions, grounded on the moral differences
of things, and because discoverable by
natural light, are obligatory upon all mankind." Mackey's Juris., 502). The universe is then above all others, the sacred book
of Masonry, the only genuine revelation of
the divine will, and is pre-eminently the
revelation upon which the Masonic religion
rests. It is the trestleboard upon which the
Great Architect has drawn his designs.

"Masons are taught to regard the universe
as the greatest of all symbols, revealing to
men, in all ages, the ideas which are eternally revolving in the mind of the Divinity,
and which it is their duty to reproduce in
their own lives and in the world of art and
industry. Thus God and geometry, the material worlds and the spiritual spheres, were
constantly united in the speculations of the
ancient Masons. They consequently labored
earnestly and unweariedly, not only to construct cities and embellish them with magnificent edifices, but also to build up a temple

of great and divine thoughts, and of ever
growing virtues for the soul to dwell in."
(Sickel's Ah. Rez., 197).

2. *Masonry has its own temples.* — A
temple is an edifice erected and set apart in
honor of some deity and used for his service
and worship. In every prominent city of
our land there is found a building which is
called the Masonic Temple, erected and dedicated to the service and worship of the Great
Architect of the Universe, the Masonic
deity. These buildings in their arrangements and design are peculiar to Masonry.
They are the outward and unmistakable
mark of an inner religious life and service.
In their religious use these temples are distinctively Masonic, and as emphatically set
forth a distinct religious system as the
temple at Jerusalem set forth Judaism
or those of the ancients set forth the
worship of the deities to whom they
were dedicated. The construction of these
Masonic temples is begun with services in
honor of the Great Architect of the Universe, and when completed are dedicated to
his worship with elaborate religious ceremonies. They are sacred edifices, devoted

to the service and promulgation of a specific religion, whose name and designation is Freemasonry.

3. *Freemasonry has its altars.* — An altar is a table or pedestal upon which gifts and sacrifices are offered to some deity, and at which supplication and solemn covenants are made. It is especially a mark of religion, an evidence of religious service and worship. In sacred edifices it marks the "holy place" and is generally so situated that it is visible from all points in the sanctuary. The Masonic altar stands in the center of the lodge indicating that the religious acts there performed are the central things in the Masonic religious system.

The Masonic altar is specifically marked as such. Generally we find the distinctive symbols of Masonry engraved upon its sides, and always do the square and compass and the "book of the law" rest upon its top. It stands within the "triangle of lights," another specific Masonic mark. It is therefore an altar that is distinctively Masonic, and a mark of religion which is Masonic.

At this altar the candidate for Masonry kneels, and at it he solemnly swears alle-

giance to the institution, promising "ever
to conceal and never to reveal any of the
secret arts, parts, or points of the hidden
mysteries of Masonry, which may have been
heretofore, shall be at this time, or any
future period communicated to him." He
then calls upon the Masonic deity to witness
his oath and covenant, and binds himself by
horrible penalties to be faithful to this Masonic covenant. This covenant from the
Masonic viewpoint is paramount to all
others which a Mason may enter. It can
never be repudiated nor laid aside. Says
the ritual, p. 30, "We obligate them by
solemn and irrevocable ties to perform the
requirements of, and avoid the things pro-
hibited by Masonry." "No law of the land
can affect it, no anathema of the church can
weaken it." (Webb, Mon., 240).

4. *Masonry has its religious symbols
and emblems.*—"An emblem comprises a
larger series of thought than a symbol which
may be said rather to illustrate some single
special idea. All esoteric societies have
made use of emblems and symbols, such as
the Pythagorean Society, the Eleusinians,
the Hermetic Brethren of Egypt, the Rosi-

crucians and the Freemasons. Many of
these emblems it is not proper to divulge to
the general eye, and a very minute difference may make an emblem or symbol differ
widely in its meaning." (Kenneth Mac-
Kenzie, Royal Masonic Ency.).

"A symbol is a complex thought clothed
in a sensuous form." In religion, symbols
are sensuous emblems of spiritual acts and
objects. The cross as a Christian symbol
signifies that Jesus Christ bore in his own
body on the tree, our sins, and that he has
made everlasting atonement for them. It
signifies that on it, the Lord of Glory died
for man, the creature's sin. It is a reminder
of the purchase price of our redemption and
a banner proclaiming the victory of Christ
over sin, death and the grave. While it was
for ages before our era a symbol of immortality, or of "life to come," among the pagan
nations, it has become emphatically a Christian symbol from the stress the Christian
writers laid upon the vicarious sufferings of
Christ.

Islam has its symbol, the Crescent. It
signifies the Turkish power and the religion
permeating and upholding it. And so almost

every religion has its symbols, which set forth some prominent phase or conception thereof, or some doctrine thereto peculiar.

Masonry, too, has its unique religious symbols, which are held sacred by Masons, and who make them prominent factors in their worship and covenants. The chief symbols are the holy book, the square, the compass, the all seeing eye, the letter G, etc. The commonly used tools of the stone masons, have also become emblems, jewels and symbols in the craft.

The square and compass were employed by operative masons, but Freemasonry incorporated them into its speculative system, and makes them the symbols of moral and religious principles and sacred objects. They occupy a very high place, as is evident from their presence everywhere in the system. They are inscribed upon its altars and engraved upon its jewelry. They are as prominent among Masons as the scarab beetle was upon the amulets and religious symbols of the ancient Egyptians.

Besides these symbols, Masonry also has a number of emblems and jewels, which have a moral and religious signification in the order, all of which show that Masonry is a religion.

These symbols are reverenced and adored by Masons, especially in their religious services in the lodge. They are used in the Masonic devotions as devoutly as the Romanist counts his beads and adores the crucifix. They are employed to impress the candidate in his initiation, to enforce the obligation and Masonic fidelity to brethren, and to secure favors, positions, and honors in social, political and commercial spheres. Their use is as prominent in the moral and religious life of the Mason as are the rosaries, images and crosses in that of the Romanist. He appeals to these symbols to prove his sincerity and honesty in his business transactions, employing them as sacred representations of things which his religious scruples regard as inviolable.

And these symbols are peculiarly and exclusively Masonic. In some states they have legal protection making it a misdemeanor for a person not a Mason to use them or wear them even as an ornament.

5. *It has its confession of faith.*—In the Christian system there is an objective faith,

5

unique and peculiar, which is the pure Christian religion. The rule of that faith is the Bible, the word of God. That faith received, accepted and believed, makes an individual a Christian. The confession of that faith marks the individual as a Christian.

So also there is an objective and unique faith in the Masonic system. The reception, acceptance and belief of that faith makes men Masons. The confession thereof marks them as Masons. The rule of that faith is the universe. (See Sickels, p. 84). The moral and religious truths which Masons profess to discern in, and derive from the book of nature, constitute the objective faith of Masonry. That objective faith it sets forth in allegory and symbol, but keeping it deeply veiled. Its symbols, rightly understood and masonically interpreted, set forth that faith, and that faith accepted by an individual makes him a Mason. To this creed or faith Masonry requires assent from every one who would pass the threshold of its lodge. In this it is inexorable.

This confession of faith in the Masonic deity is its religious test, the test which determines whether the candidate is willing and qualified to receive, accept and live the Masonic religion. With the change of his faith, there is also a change of his religion, if words mean anything, and there is any consistency in language.

What Masons believe is indicated in the following: "The creed of a Mason is the belief in God, the Supreme Architect of the heaven and earth, the dispenser of all good gifts and the judge of the quick and the dead." (Craftsman, p. 356). "Masonry does not attempt to interfere with the peculiar religious faith of its disciples, except so far as it relates to the belief in the existence of God, and what necessarily results from that belief." (Mackey Juris. p. 38). "The person who desires to be made a Mason must be a man believing in the existence of a Supreme Being, and of a future existence." (Sickels Ah. R. p. 19). "The foundation upon which Masonry rests is the belief and acknowledgement of a Supreme Being." (Id. p. 59). "The creed of a Mason is brief. It is a creed which demands and receives the universal consent of all men. It is a belief in God, the

Supreme Architect of heaven and earth."
(Mackey Lex. p. 100). Pike says, "Masonry
propagates no creed except its own most
simple and sublime one taught by nature
and reason. There has never been a false
religion in the world. The permanent and
universal revelation is written in visible
nature and explained by the reason, and is
completed by the wise analogies of faith.
There is but one true religion, one dogma,
one legitimate belief." (Inner Sanctuary,
1:271). This creed differentiates the Masonic god from the Christian's God.

This confession of faith in this Masonic
deity carries with it the repudiation of all
former faith and religious belief not in
harmony with it. "There is not only to be
a change for the future, but also an extinction of the past, for the initiation is as it
were a death to the world and a resurrection
to a new life." (Mackey Rit. p. 123). This
means the extinction of the religious life,
faith and hopes of the past profane life.
From the Masonic statements, there is no
evasion of this conclusion. The ceremony
of initiation is religious. There is a demand
for faith in a specific deity, who is not

Jehovah, but the Masonic deity, and that fact requires a change in religious views before the ceremony can proceed. It is a demand that his former faith, if not in harmony with the Masonic faith, be renounced, repudiated, and extinguished, not openly but tacitly, and supplanted by a faith in "that God whom Masons worship and reverence." It is a distinctively Masonic confession of the Masonic faith in the Masonic god. And this initiation is also to be a resurrection to a new life, that is a new religious and moral life, and to become alive unto the Masonic religious life, requires death unto the former religious life.

6. *Masonry has its own priests.*—A priest is a religious official, whose duty is to perform specific religious acts. Masonry has its priests of various degrees. "The master of the lodge is its priest." (Webb, Monitor, p. 231). If a chaplain is appointed he simply represents the master in the devotions of the lodge. These officials offer the prayers to the Masonic god, the Great Architect of the Universe, and also have part in the public religious exercises in which the lodge may engage.

The chaplain, an appointive office, is generally a minister of the gospel who has been hoodwinked into the lodge, but the services he conducts in that capacity, are Masonic and not Christian. He wears the insignia of his office, addresses the prayers to the Masonic deity, and invokes special favors upon the lodge. The religion expressed or the service conducted is emphatically Masonic, and he who conducts it, is for the time being a Masonic priest.

7. *The religion administered by these religious officials is Masonry.*—It can not be anything else. The prayers are those provided by Masonic authorities; they are couched in unmistakable Masonic language, and they express decidedly Masonic sentiment. The hymns are Masonic, and the scripture passages read are expurgated of all Christian sentiment, so as to make them Masonic. Such passages are taken with slight but necessary modification, says Mackey. (Ritualist, p. 272). The modification is necessary in order to make them agree in sentiment with the Masonic religion.

8. *Masonry has its own peculiar re-*

ligious forms.—Religious ceremonies are proofs of religion. They are the outward forms in which the inner life or the religious sentiment finds expression. As such they signify and mean something. In some cases impressive and elaborate ceremonies are employed to inspire the devotee with awe, to impress him with the solemnity of the transaction, and to intensify his sense of obligation and duty to deity, and to his fellowmen. Without some form of ceremony, religion would be useless. Rites and ceremonies from the very nature of religious notions are essential to its power and influence over man. A purely abstract religion can not exist. To be effectual religion must be presented in a concrete form, in befitting and expressive ceremony.

It must be evident to the most indifferent observer that Freemasonry has its own and peculiar religious rites, services and ceremonies. These are the "forms of words" and "the forms of needs" in the institution. They are designed and used on the one hand, to impress profoundly the candidate for initiation, and on the other to strengthen the Mason in his peculiar faith. These cere-

monies are the outward signs of a distinct
inward religious life, which is Masonry.
They are designed to beget within the Mason
the belief that Freemasonry deals with the
most sacred things with befitting solemnity;
that the lodge is a most holy place, and "that
its floor is holy ground." (Sickels A. R., p.
85). The candidate is made to feel that the
"all seeing eye" is looking down upon him,
and that he is about to be ushered into the
very presence of deity. The whole procedure
in the lodge whether opening working," "refreshment" or "closing" is a religious ceremony, intensely and exclusively religious,
more so than many services conducted in a
Christian church. It is worship, ceremony,
service, religion throughout, and therefore
the conclusion is irresistible that Freemasonry is a religion.

The Masonic initiation is purely a religious ceremony. It is as much so as is confirmation or baptism in the churches, or the
solemnization of marriage, or the ordination
of a minister of the gospel. It is a ceremony
in which a solemn agreement is made and in
which the Masonic deity is recognized as a
party to the covenant, and whose help is

implored. In this act certain duties are set forth and recognized, obligations are assumed, solemn promises are made, and the god of Masonry is called upon to witness and confirm the same. The only difference between the purpose of the ceremonies of the church and of Masonry, is in the kind of religion practiced and set forth. If the church is a religious institution, Masonry is also.

The initiation proper is preceded by the instruction of the candidate as follows: "Mr. J. H., the institution of which you are about to become a member is by no means of a little and trifling nature, but of high importance and deep solemnity. Masonry consists of a course of ancient hieroglyphical and moral instruction, taught according to ancient usages by types, emblems and allegorical figures. Even the ceremony of your gaining admission within these walls is emblematic of an event, which all must sooner or later experience. It is emblematic of your final exit from this world to the world to come. You are doubtless aware that whatever a man possesses here on earth, whether it be titles, honors, or even his own reputation will not gain him admission into the celestial lodge above, but previous to his gaining admission there, he must become poor and penniless, blind and naked, dependent on the soverign will of our Supreme Grand Master; and in order to impress these truths more forcibly upon your mind, it is necessary that you be divested of your outward apparel and clad in a garment furnished you by the lodge." (Ritual, p. 23-4). This explanation has an intensely religious flavor. Everything is symbolic. The entrance into the lodge, even to its minor details, is emblematic of his entrance into heaven. The lodge here is a type of the lodge above. The Grand Master here represents the Grand Master in heaven. The titles and honors here, earthly titles, count for nothing, but the honors, titles and secrets bestowed by the lodge count for everything in the lodge above. The garment furnished by the lodge symbolizes the Masonic righteousness which will admit him into the lodge above. All this is religious ceremony.

After further preparation and questioning, the initiation proper begins. To the question, "Who comes here?" the senior deacon replies for the candidate "A poor blind candidate, who is desirous of being brought from darkness to light, and receiving a part of the rights, lights and benefits of this worshipful lodge erected to God and dedicated to the holy Sts. John, as many a brother and fellow has done before him." (Rit. p. 25). The candidate, after further instruction is ordered to kneel at the altar and attend prayer, when the lodge is called up and the following prayer is offered: "Vouchsafe thine aid Almighty Father of the Universe to this our present convention; and grant that this candidate for Masonry may dedicate and devote his life to thy service, and become a true and faithful brother among us. Endue him with a competence of thy divine wisdom, that by the secrets of our art, he may be better enabled to displace the blots of birth, love relief and truth, to the honor of thy holy name. Amen. So mote it be." (Rit. p. 26-27; Sickels A. R. p. 55). Then a confession of faith is demanded of the candidate, and the ceremony goes on, every step being a religious act, culminating at the altar where the oath is taken and the covenant entered into, which, according to Masonic teachers, is the highest obligation a man can assume here on earth.

The initiation is positively religious, a religious allegory. In a general way, the stripping of the candidate and putting on the garments of the lodge, is emblematic of his conversion to Masonry, that is putting off the vices of the profane life and putting on the virtues of Masonry, the exchange of the polluted and profane worldly honors for the sacred honors of Masonry. This initiation is his regeneration fitting him for the celestial lodge above. He is ushered neither barefooted nor shod into the lodge, to symbolize that he is on holy ground. He is hoodwinked to symbolize that he is in spiritual darkness, and needs the glorious light of Masonry in order to be able to love relief, seek truth and subdue his passions. He receives solemn instructions at the south, the west, and the east as to his duties. This is the symbolic pilgrimage and symbolizes life and soul troubles. (See Sickles A. H. 56.). He is solemnly obligated to keep secret and sacred that which is committed to him in the lodge then and thereafter, and as an evidence of his sincerity of intention kisses the holy book, and is then freed from his cabletow, and by the removal of the hoodwink, is brought to Masonic light, amidst clapping of hands and stamping of feet. This is the shock of entrance and symbolizes the throes of the new birth, the birth into Masonry.

At the door of the lodge the candidate confesses his ignorance, blindness and servitude to his passions. At the threshold of his induction he confesses his faith in the Masonic deity. Within the lodge all is religious ceremony. The "divestment" and "reinvestment", the "decalcation" and "perambulation", "salutation" and "obligation", the "induction" "pilgrimage" and "ceremony", "prayers" and "lectures" are all religious and have a religious signification. After his covenant "he is received as a brother among them." He is received and fellowshipped by the fraternity, is regarded no longer polluted and profane, and is then symbolically "placed" as a stone in the temple. He has been regenerated, purified and placed. All these are religious acts and ceremonies. It is too patent to be denied.

Thus far we have had in mind the first degree only. The ceremonies in the higher degrees are more intensely religious than in the first degree. They advance until they become "sublime and ineffable". These ceremonies are all designed to set forth a peculiar religion and that religion is Masonry.

In the third degree, the climax of the ceremony is the mock murder and resurrection of Hiram Abiff, the "Christ" of Masonry. This is made as solemn as the farcical nature of the thing will permit. But it is a religious ceremony, a resurrection service, by which the candidate becomes entitled to eternal life. In a sense it is in Masonry what the resurrection of Christ is in Christianity. "Few candidates may be aware that Hiram whom they have represented and personified is ideally and precisely the same as Christ. Yet such is undoubtedly the case. This old philoposphy shows what Christ as a glyph means, and how the Christ state results from real initiation, or from the evolution of the human into the divine." (Mystic Masonry p. 248).

9. *Masonry has its authorized rituals or book of forms.*—A ritual is a book containing a prescribed order or form for reli-

gious services. Rituals are external marks
and evidences of the exercise of religion.
Masonry has its authorized rituals and
forms of service. They are in evidence in
the lodge room, and in ther public services,
such as dedications, installations, and burials. In the rituals these services are prescribed and the details indicated by appropriate rubrics. This stamps Masonry as a
religion, as much as the die stamps the
precious metal as coin. Masonry is the most
ritualistic of all secret religions. It has its
forms for everything, initiations in the various degrees, dedications of public buildings,
either civil or Masonic, laying of corner
stones, installations, burials, baptisms for
infants and youths, and what not. And these
prescribed forms are faithfully adhered to.
No departure from them is permissible.
These rituals are necessary in order to prevent this Masonic religion from becoming
corrupted by omissions or additions, for
every ceremony must be "in due form".

10. *It has its own peculiar worship.*—
The members of the Masonic fraternity
exercise themselves in their Masonic religion
according to the forms of service prescribed

by the order. They take part in these services, and do it heartily. They are as devout and reverent in the lodge, as is the Christian in his worship in the sanctuary. There are set prayers, distinctively Masonic, which are solemnly and reverently said. There are responses in the religious services in the lodge, which they ardently repeat. There are genuflexions, postures, and attitudes, all emphatically religious and distinctively Masonic, which they cheerfully assume, and there are hymns and odes, also Masonic, which are joyously sung. These exercises would be very incongruous in a church because the religion they express is foreign to that which a Christian church teaches. It also has a distinctive burial service for its dead. It is for those only who die in the Masonic faith. Only third degree Masons are entitled to Masonic burial. To hold this service for one who is not a Mason, would be from the Masonic viewpoint, sacrilege of the highest kind. And only Masons take part in the burial service. It is not for the lips of the "profane." It is the exercise of a purely Masonic religion by men who have been made Masons in due form. It has a baptismal service for infants and for youths. It has in some countries a marriage and communion service. It has all the external and essential marks of religion. Whatever else may be found in Masonry, science, philosophy, history or ethics, the dominant factor in the institution is religion. Freemasonry is a religion.

11. *Freemasonry has its own distinctive deity whom it worships and adores.*—This subject is treated in Chapter XI.

CHAPTER III.

FREEMASONRY IS RECOGNIZED AS A RELIGIOUS INSTITUTION.

IT would seem unnecessary to offer evidence that Freemasonry is a religion, when its own officials, authorized representatives and spokesmen, recognize, declare and concede its essentially religious character. But as there are both Masons and profane who deny this religious nature of the institution when objection to it is offered on the ground that it is a religion, another gospel, and claim that it is a purely moral and social organization, it will not be amiss to show out of their own mouths, that Freemasonry is a religion. Even on the assumption that it is a moral and social organization, it can still be shown to be essentially a religion, because of the intimate and interdependent relations that exist between morality and religion. To characterize it as a moral institution describes only one feature of its many sided nature. Religion is its chief and dominating factor, the soul and life of the organization. Buck in his diagram illustrating the derivation of modern Freemasonry, makes it one part science, one part philosophy and two parts religion. (See Frontispiece in Mystic Masonry).

1. *Its religious character is conceded by competent authorities.* a. The testimony of non-masonic and ex-masonic witnesses.— "Masonry is a sort of religious sect, a kind of church. It has a religious creed. It has a religious test for admission of members, it has a religious ritual. It has its hymns and religious readings and hortations. The lodge is opened in the name of the Almighty. In the prayers prescribed for the opening of the lodge, occur these words: 'In thy name we have assembled and in thy name we desire to proceed in all our doings'." (Prof. David McDill, D.D.).

"Masonry claims to be a religion which effects forgiveness of sin, a new spiritual birth, a life of holiness acceptable to God, a happy death and eternal salvation, and, that this is accomplished in every local member of the lodge, whether he is a Christian, Jew, Mohammedan or Buddhist without any conditions or qualifications, except those made by the lodge." (Edmund Belfour, D.D.).

"Masonry is a religion. If it is not why should it have temples, altars, official rituals, with hymns or odes, prayers, consecrations, and benedictions? Why have high priests, chaplains, written and authorized forms for opening and closing its meeting, for corner stone laying, and dedications, for installations, for the burial of its dead and what not? Why the grotesque imitations and caricatures of the church's forms, even to its sacraments?" (Prof. G. H. Gerberding, D.D.).

We might multiply the citations from eminent ministers of the gospel, of almost every denomination, expressing their convictions that Masonry is a religion. In fact the most learned men of the church, irrespective of denominational affiliation, who have given this question any attention, with one voice, testify that Masonry is a religion. These men representing not only the church, but also occupying professor's chairs in seats of learning, men whose business it is to deal with religion and questions of religion, are from that fact, competent judges; and from the Masonic publications, its lexicons, rituals, encyclopedias and apologetic literature, enough of Masonry can be learned in order to judge of its nature and character. Surely the testimony of these men has weight.

With the testimony of these learned Christian men agrees that of those who were at one time honored members of the Masonic fraternity, but for sufficient reasons left it, and in not a few cases, exposed it. We have conversed with a large number of this class of seceding Masons, all of whom assigned as the reason for their repudiation and renunciation of Masonry, that it is a religion; that it conflicts and interferes with their views and duties as Christians; that it teaches moral and religious precepts which their Christian conscience could not approve and practice without jeopardizing their souls; that its aim and tendency is to undermine their faith in the Lord Jesus Christ as their personal Saviour; that it alienates their affections and support from the church, and destroys their faith in the Bible as the word of God. Their common sense as well as their moral sense taught them that as a religion, Masonry is incompatible with Christianity; that it is another religion, and being unable to serve two masters, they were driven to renounce Freemasonry with its hidden things, in order to have peace of mind and a good conscience toward God. From the testimony of these devout Christians, who firmly expected to obtain more light when they united with the fraternity, we are persuaded that Freemasonry is a religion. These men learned these things, came to these convictions while active members of the craft and sought earnestly its secret arts by which they might learn truth, practice relief, and above all to subdue their passions. Finding it a religion which sought their support and loyalty over against that of their Lord Jesus Christ, they renounced its hidden works, and repudiated its claims. Upon the testimony of seceding Masons, Freemasonry is a religion.

b. Masonic testimony.—But our intention is to adduce the testimony of Masonic witnesses, for out of the mouth of two or three of these our proposition is established beyond question.

Webb says, "Freemasonry is the most moral institution that ever existed." (Mon., p, 37). Sickels says, "Masonry teaches the most sublime truths and points out to its disciples a correct knowledge of the Great Architect of the Universe, and the moral laws he has ordained for their government." (Mon., p. 7-8.). Pierson declares that Masonry "embodies all that is valuable in the institutions of the past, embraces within its circle all that is good and true of the present, and thus becomes a conservator as well as a depository of religion, science and art." (Trad. of F. M., p. 14). "Genuine Freemasonry is a pure religion, and in the earlier period, Freemasonry may be identified with religion." Pierson with many other Masonic writers makes the claim that the Mosaic religion was an initiation into mysteries, and identifies the fig leaf aprons of Adam and Eve with the Masonic apron. Steinbrenner claims that "Masonry is not only a perfect code of morality, but that it also enforces a system of intellectual culture (Orig. and Hist. of F. M., p. 15), that it can and will educate the pious man to that higher religion, that religion in which all men can agree, which indeed embraces the lower religions of creed and sects." (Id. 13, 14). "As there is a natural right, which is the source of all positive laws, so there is a universal religion covering all the peculiar religions of the world. We profess this universal religion, and consequently we welcome those who profess a particular religion, which is but a part of it." (Orig. and Hist. of F. M., 14). "Freemasonry is so interwoven with religion as to lay us under obligations to pay that rational homage to the deity which at once constitutes our duty and our happiness." (Sick. Ah. R., 123).

"The religion of Masonry", says Mackey, "is a pure theism, upon which its different members graft their own peculiar opinions, but they are not permitted to introduce them into the lodge." (Lex. p. 402). "The truth is", says the same writer, "that Freemasonry is undoubtedly a religious institution, its religion being of that universal kind in which all men agree, and which was handed down through a long succession of ages from that ancient priesthood who first taught it, and embraces the great tenets of the existence of God, the immortality of the soul, tenets which by its peculiar symbolic language, it has preserved from its foundation, and still continues in the same beautiful way to teach. Beyond this for its religious faith we must not, we can not go." (Jurisprudence, p. 93). "Speculative Freemasonry is the scientific application and religious conservation of the rules and principles, the implements and materials of operative Masonry to the veneration of God, the purification of the heart and the inculcation of the dogmas of a religious philosophy." (Ency. 730).

"Masonry is a religious institution, its ceremonies are a part of a really religious worship." (Mackey's Ency. p. 60). "All the ceremonies of our order are prefaced and terminated with prayer because Masonry is a religious institution, and because we show thereby our dependence on and our faith in God." (Mackey Lex., 369). "Masonry is in every sense of the word, except one, and that its least philosophical, an eminently religious institution. It is indebted solely to the religious element which it contains for its origin and continued existence, and without this religious element it would scarcely be worthy of cultivation by the wise and good." (Mackey's Ency., p. 640). "Inculcating religious doctrine, commanding religious observance and teaching religious truths, who can deny that it is eminently a religious institution." (Mackey's Ency. 594). "If it does not constitute a religion, it is at least religion's handmaid." (Mackey's Lex. Art. Order). Buck says, "Masonry is not only a universal science but a world wide religion, and owes allegiance to no one creed, and can adopt no sectarian dogma." "Masonry is the universal religion only because and only so long as it embraces all religions." (Mystic Masonry, p. 113, 114). "The system of Masonry, as in its original inception, still claims to be a system of religion in which all men can unite." (Pierson, Trad. 372). Dermot says he "believes the Royal Arch degree to be the root, heart and marrow of Masonry." Concerning this degree Hutchison says: "As Moses was commanded to put off his shoes from his feet, on Mount Horeb, because the ground whereon he stood was sanctified by the presence of divinity; so the Mason who would prepare himself for this exalted stage of Masonry should advance in the naked paths of truth, be divested of every degree of arrogance and approach with steps of innocence, humility and virtue, to challenge the ensigns of an order whose institutions arise on the most solemn and sacred principles of religion." Oliver says, "Masonry, according to our definitions, forms the sum and substance of religion in its universal acceptation." (Star in East, p. 6), and that "Religion is the pedestal of Freemasonry." Morris says, "the essentially religious character is shown under the head deity." (Dict. art. God). Grand Inspector Cunningham says Freemasonry is a pure religion. General B. F. Butler says, "Masonry is a religion of the highest and noblest type," and Albert Pike says, "Masonry is a religion, for every man before becoming a Mason must express his belief in deity, and in the continued existence of the intellectual portion after death. The trouble with ministers of religion is that they want us to believe too much, while the Ingersolls want us to believe too little." (Address at Harpers Ferry, Sept. 11, 1879). We might adduce further testimony from both non-masonic and masonic authorities in evidence that Masonry is a religion and that the organization is a religious institution, but we deem it unnecessary. It is so viewed by its enemies and by its friends. When its religious character is denied, as it is at times, it is for the purpose of evading the force of the argument that can be marshalled against it on that ground. But as a rule, it is viewed by Masons as a religion, and as "a good enough religion for them."

2. *Efforts have been made to identify Freemasonry with Christianity.* That eminent Masons believe that Masonry is a religion is shown by the efforts made by them to prove its identity with Christianity. Among the most prominent of these that have come to our notice are the Rev. George Oliver, Mr. Hutchinson, Mr. Arnold and Mr. Towne. These men were doubtless misled by the apparently Christian character and symbolism of some of its degrees. The Rev. Dr. Oliver in his work "The Star in the East" attempts to show that Masonry is Christianity. But, as one of his reviewers has said, "his assumptions in this work are monstrous falsehoods." His contradictions and labored efforts show very clearly that either he does not know what Masonry is, or what Christianity is, or he deliberately attempts to deceive his readers. After dis-

coursing on the Royal Arch degree, which he declares to be purely religious, he closes a paragraph thus: "If this be not religion, if this be not Christianity, what is it?" We reply, that it is religion, but it is not Christianity. In his Antiquities he assumes the practical identity of the religion of Freemasonry with the religion of the Bible.

Mr. Arnold says (Rationale and Ethics of F. M., p. 189), "Masonry marches in the same path with Christianity today; it seeks to exorcise the foul spirit of selfishness, to make men love each other as brethren and bear one another's burden. Masonry seeks to restore unity and brotherly love. Masonry is friendship, love and integrity." "We wish to say of our honored institution, the loving spirit of Christ presides over all its arrangements and inspires all its operations. Other associations are good, but their operations are limited. Freemasonry has a wider influence and power, and far greater facilities for accomplishing its benevolent purposes. We do not hesitate to say that we regard Freemasonry as the truest expression of the mind and thought of Christ, this age is destined to witness. Christianity is its central idea, and at the same time the foundation and corollary of our temple. Nay, Masonry is Christianity, Christianity applied to life, made actual in the arrangements of society; Christianity realized in man's relation one with another." "The soul which animates our order inspiring all its members, and controlling all its acts, is the spirit of love. And certain we are that one cannot be a good Mason without being a better man, a better citizen, and a better Christian. Christianity is the central idea of the institution. The sentiments of religion pervade all its arrangements. There is no religious organization, no Christian church, more vigilant in watching over the conduct, or more strict in its discipline of its members. (Id. 196-198). Inwood says, "Masonry is the excellency of Christianity, and every Mason is if he is in reality a Mason, a true Christian; or at least he is in reality truly religious according to his profession, whether Jew or Christian." (Masonic Library, 47). With such assumption and assertions, do these men endeavor to prove that Masonry is Christianity.

Buck contends that Jesus was chief

among ancient Masonic brethren, and prince among the Magi of his age. In becoming so he was aided by the Wise Men of the East, with whom he probably spent the eighteen years between his interview with the doctors of the law in the temple, and his public appearance as a teacher. They taught him the genius, the landmarks and the mysteries of Freemasonry. As a result he gained sagacity and power, becoming a perfect and upright man and Mason. Buck evidently holds the opinions in common with other Masonic writers, that Christianity originated from ancient Freemasonry. (See his "Mystic Masonry," and his "Genius of Freemasonry, and The Twentieth Century Crusade"). If in the opinion of eminent Masons, Christianity and Freemasonry are identical, then Freemasonry is a religion, or else Christianity is not a religion.

These Masons who have thus attempted to establish the identity of Freemasonry with Christianity, do so under the conviction that Masonry is a religion, and possessing the same essential religious elements as Christianity. But they are not sustained in their opinion as to the identity of Freemasonry and Christianity, by the more eminent Masonic authorities as is evident from the following: "Freemasonry is not Christianity, nor a substitute for it. It does not meddle with sectarian creeds or doctrines, but teaches fundamental religious truth." (Mackey, Ency., p. 64). "Hutchinson, and Oliver have fallen into a great error in calling the master Mason's degree a Christian institution. If Masonry were simply a Christian institution, the Jew and the Moslem, the Brahmin and Buddhist, could not conscientiously partake of its illumination. But its universality is its boast. In its language citizens of every nation may converse, at its altars citizens of every nation may kneel, to its creed disciples of every faith may subscribe." (Mackey's Ency., p. 162). "The Jews, the Chinese, the Turk, each reject either the New Testament, or the Old, or both, and yet we see no good reason why they should not be made Masons. In fact Blue Lodge Masonry has nothing whatever to do with the Bible. It is not founded on the Bible; if it was it would be Masonry; it would be something else." (Mackey's Ency., 207).

This testimony shows very conclusively that while Freemasonry is not Christianity, it is, however, a religion.

3. *It is recognized by the state as a religion, and virtually is the state religion.*— It is a fundamental principle in our system of government that church and state, religion and civil affairs be kept entirely separate; that before the law every religion has equal rights and every citizen be assured of the free exercise of his religion so long that in so doing he does not interfere with the inalienable rights of others. It is not the function of the state to administer religion of any kind, but to leave that to the religious bodies that may exist. The state can not consistently give any recognition or preference to one religion, to the exclusion or detriment of another. Its duty is to maintain a strict neutrality on all these matters, to see that neither religion is aided or abetted by the civil authorities, but that justice be meted to each and all alike.

The state as such, in our system of government, can not have a religion, if consistent with its design and constitution. It is to guarantee the free exercise of religion, but

7

never to propagate, foster, aid or abet it. Its function is purely civil. But it is a question whether this has been and is the case in the practical workings of the government. If the official acts of the state officials are the acts of the state in these matters, we are led to the conviction that the presumption, that the state has no religion, or that we have no state religion, is no longer sustained by the facts. The state has gradually and perhaps unconsciously but no less really acquired a religion which it recognizes to the exclusion of all others in certain state functions, and which has become as intimately and organically though not formally perhaps, connected with the government, as are the state religions of England, Germany and Italy, with the governments of those countries. This religion is not Christianity, but Masonry. In support of our assertion we submit the following for the reader's consideration.

When public buildings such as court houses, state houses, United States government buildings, city buildings, exposition buildings, public library buildings and public monuments are erected, almost invariably religious services are connected with their inception and dedication. The corner stone is laid with a religious ceremony and in accordance with a religious form. There are hymns, religious readings, prayers and addresses, setting forth certain religious principles. When the structure is completed, there is a dedication service, also intensely religious. If these religious services are not conducted by men representing the government, they are however endorsed and approved by the civil authorities, and these ministers or priests of this religion are selected by them and therefore are to all intents and purposes the acts of the government, and the religion set forth is the state religion. We do not see how this conclusion can be evaded.

The religion thus publicly acknowledged and ministered by the state in these state and federal functions is Masonry. The Masonic lodge is regularly opened in the lodge room, then it proceeds in regular order to the building or site where the specific service is to be conducted, and after the service is over, the lodge returns to its room and is regularly closed. (See Sickels, p. 281).

The acts are therefore wholly and purely lodge acts. The officials, federal, state or municipal, as the case may be, are expected to attend the service, and it is by their act, invitation or consent that the lodge officiates. The men who officiate are the priests of Masonry. The form of service is that prescribed by the order for such occasions. The prayers are offered to the Great Architect, the Masonic deity. The addresses are pregnant with Masonic precepts, doctrines and tenets. The whole service is emphatically and exclusively Masonic. And these public buildings being dedicated by Masons for the state, it is but natural and logical that this religion, with its peculiar tenets concerning citizenship should become a prominent factor in the administration of the civil functions, within such edifices. There seems to be a tacit understanding by virtue of this Masonic service, that the government of the State of Masonry, and the religion of Masonry shall also be recognized, represented, administered and maintained in these buildings. This is evident from certain expressions in the service. The closing passages in the invocation is, "and grant us all a supply of the corn of nourishment, the wine of refreshment, and the oil of joy." These are the "wages" the Mason receives, the rewards for Masonic fidelity. These are veiled expressions and have a concealed meaning, and the natural and logical inference is that in these buildings the Masons will always receive that which these expressions mean. In the Grand Master's address the opening sentence is: "Be it known unto you that we be lawful Masons, true and faithful to the laws of our country, and engaged by solemn obligations to erect magnificent buildings to be serviceable to the brethren." This plainly says that these Masons erect these buildings and make them serviceable to their brethren. In other words, in these edifices Masons shall always receive their wages, the institution be nourished, and the joys of a favored class of citizens be experienced. These, it appears, are some of the "secrets which Masons have concealed from the eyes of all men, which cannot be divulged, and which have never been found out." In short the whole service (See Sickels A. R., 281) for the laying of the foundation stone of a public building, when read carefully, and in the light of Masonic teachings, means that the Masonic religion and its adherents shall have a pre-eminent place in the administration of affairs in that building. It commits the state to a formal recognition of Masonry, and makes it the state religion.

The religious services connected with the corner stone laying or with the dedication of these public buildings, are conducted by Masonic officials. If these officials happen to be clergymen, as is sometimes the case, they do not act in that capacity, but as ministers of Masonry. The clerical office is laid aside for the time, as well as all distinctively Christian features in the service, and the Masonic elements are emphasized. The religion proclaimed and set forth by them is not Christianity, but Masonry. The whole service is in the hands of Masons, and approved by the civil power, and thus tacitly at least Masonry is recognized as the state religion.

By these acts the state recognizes Masonry as a religion, and as the religion of the state. The impression made upon the reflecting citizen is, that this is the official religion of our country. No functions of this character occur but that the Masonic priest or chaplain, is as much in evidence, as the representative of the state church in similar functions in foreign lands. The foreigner in our land is led to believe from these things that Masonry is the state religion of the United States. If it is not already so in fact, the trend of public practices indicates that it will not be many years until it is a fact.

In countries where there is an established religion, adherence to it is a necessary qualification for office. A citizen's religion determines largely his eligibility to a place of public trust. In this country, while we have no legally established religion, we do have what in effect amounts to substantially the same thing. Masonry has become so powerful, so thoroughly organized, so thoroughly insinuated into the political life of our country, that adherence to it has become practically a prerequisite to appointment or election to office. If it does not in every case dictate the nomination of the candidates, it does succeed in bringing them into its fold after their election, thus making them adherents of the state religion. There are over one million Masons in the United States all voters, and these are a powerful factor in influencing those in office. Being a secret organization and governed by principles which are designed to exalt the order and its members, there is practically nothing to frustrate their designs. They have placed in the executive chairs, in the Congress and Legislatures, in the offices of trust and profit, and upon the bench, its devotees, and thus for all practical purposes have made Masonry the religion of the state. We doubt whether any ecclesiastical power controls more completely the government of any country through the established church, than does Masonry the federal, state and municipal governments of our land. Freemasonry is to all intents and purposes, and in its practical effects, the state religion in our country.

The Zion News, a Masonic paper, says, "The public has no right to know that any man is a Mason. That he has a right to conceal the fact for business and other reasons, or for no reason at all; that it is one of the secrets of Freemasonry that no one has a right to reveal but himself.'' Freemasonry is not only a religion, but it seems to be making efforts to become the favored religion in our land, and thus to supplant all others by becoming the state religion of our country.

And Freemasonry seems to become more bold and ventures more and more into the open. Dr. Buck in his recent work ''The Genius of Freemasonry and the Twentieth Century Crusade'', claims that the republic was founded by Masonry, that it framed the Constitution and is the source of all that has been good in its politics, while all the evil has come from lack of adherence to Masonic ideals. He charges cowardice or treason on all Masons who refuse to use their controlling influence in the churches, and their two million votes in the nation, in wiping out summarily, the religious world power, clericalism. He declares that ''America today is not only facing the most momentous issue in her history, but the issue is one that can not long be evaded.'' As continental Freemasonry aims at the overthrow of clericalism, and of blind adherence to creeds, so American Freemasonry also evidently aims at the same end, with the ulterior purpose of enthroning itself in the seats of government, and force itself upon the public as the state religion.

4. *Freemasonry claims to be the supreme religion.*—Masonry in its modern form has followed the universal course of false religions. First it asked simply to be tolerated; next it claimed equality; and lastly it arrogates its superiority over Christianity. According to its accredited teachers, it is the supreme religion, the universal religion, the original and primitive religion of which all other religions, not even excepting Christianity, are perversions, or subordinate parts.

To summarize from passages before quoted and which also bear on this point, the Masonic writers state that Masonry teaches the most sublime truths, points out a correct knowledge of the Great Architect of the Universe, and the moral laws which he has ordained; that it embodies all that is valuable and good; that it is a perfect code of morality; that it educates man to the higher religion; that it is a religion of the highest and noblest type; embraces all the peculiar religions of the world; and that it is the religion that can absolutely purify the soul here on earth.

Pike says, "Masonry teaches and has preserved in its purity, the cardinal tenets of the old primitive faiths, which underlie and are the foundation of all religions." (Morals and Dogma, p. 324). Buck says, "Masonry is not only a universal science, but a world wide religion, and owes allegiance to no one creed, and can adopt no sectarian dogma as such, without ceasing thereby to be Masonic;" that "Masonry is the universal religion only because and only so long as it embraces all religions. Neither persecution nor misrepresentation can ever destroy it." (Mystic Masonry, pp. 113, 114). It is plain that in the opinions of these high Masons, it is the supreme religion.

Its supremacy as a religion is assumed in its teachings concerning the Masonic covenant. Masonic authorities with one accord say "It is the covenant that makes the Mason", and that "no law of the land can affect that covenant, no anathema of the church can weaken it". This covenant is

a religious transaction and agreement. It
is entered into in the initiatory service, and
from the Masonic viewpoint effects a moral
and spiritual regeneration of the initiate,
which makes him thenceforth and forever a
Mason. He can never unmasonize himself.
He may renounce and repudiate his covenant, but he remains a Mason none the less.
"Once a Mason, always a Mason." In the
ceremony of initiation the candidate is
solemnly informed that these obligations
"once taken can never be repudiated or laid
aside." It is plain from these statements
that Masonry arrogates to itself preroga-
tives which neither the individual's inalienable rights, nor the state, nor the church can
affect or weaken. It exalts itself above each
and all of these; so that when a man covenants with Masonry, he enters into a compact which not only binds him forever, but
also transcends any other relation or covenant he may enter. Even the power of
Jesus Christ, King of kings and Lord of
lords, can not according to Masonic teachings break that covenant, nor absolve the
Mason from it.

Its claims of supremacy as a religion is

shown by its position on the moral law. Christianity teaches that the moral law as set forth in the decalogue, is the highest law given to man. It is God's revelation and forms the basis and rule of all moral actions. It has never been superseded by any subsequent revelation, nor supplanted by anything which man has been able to discover.

But Masonry teaches differently. It has its own moral law, which, according to its teaching, supersedes and transcends the decalogue. This moral law of Masonry is an entirely different thing from the moral law of the Bible. Mackey says: "Every Mason, say the old charges of 1722, is obliged by its tenure to obey the moral law. Now this moral law is not to be considered as confined to the decalogue of Moses, within which narrow limits ecclesiastical writers technically restrain it, but rather as alluding to what is called the lex naturae or the law of nature. The universal law of nature is therefore the only law suited in every respect to be adopted as the Masonic code." (Jurisprudence, 502). The moral law of Masonry transcends the moral law of the Bible. "The ten commandments are not obligatory upon a Mason as a Mason, because the institution is tolerant and cosmopolite, and can not require its members to give their adhesion to any religious dogmas or precepts except those which express belief in the existence of God and the immortality of the soul." (Mackey, Ency., 205). The authority of Masonry supersedes the ten commandments and it deliberately sets them aside as of no more authority than a syllabus and as of no binding force over its disciples. It claims to be the supreme religion.

This claim of the superiority of Masonry over other religions, is shown in its judgments upon them, and especially in its contempt for Christianity. It assumes to sit in judgment upon the divine claim of Christianity, and brushes it away as though it were a cobweb. It impeaches the authority of the Bible, and ridicules its distinctive doctrines. It denies and repudiates the historic and biblical Christ and reduces Him to a glyph and a figment. It charges the church with falsely interpreting the Bible and perverting the true teachings of Jesus. It changes the truth of God into a lie, and exalts its lies to the position of

"Divine Truth". There is nothing sacred or pure in the scriptures unless so pronounced by its infallible dictum. In its view "the Bible is a pseudo-revelation", in which the natural sense is not the sense intended by its writers. Sotheran says, "There is no institution that has done so much, and is yet capable of such great undertakings in the future for humanity, religion and political government as Freemasonry". It now proposes to sweep all opponents off the field and establish itself as the religion founded upon science and eternal reason. The Deist, Pantheist and Theosophist all are given welcome in its ranks, but the Christian must renounce his errors ere he can be a brother true, and a perfect man.

The following extracts from Masonic authorities betray this spirit of arrogant supremacy on the part of Freemasonry. "The sacred books of all religion, including those of the Jews and Christian, were and are no more than parables and allegories of the real secret doctrine transcribed for the ignorant and superstitious masses." "Salvation by faith and the vicarious atonement were not taught, as now interpreted, by

Jesus, nor are these doctrines taught in the exoteric scriptures. They are later and ignorant perversions of the original doctrines. In the early church, as in the secret doctrine, there was not one Christ for the whole world, but a potential Christ in every man. Theologians first made a fetich of the impersonal, omnipotent divinity; and then tore the Christos from the hearts of all humanity in order to deify Jesus, that they may have a God-man peculiarly their own." "All the ancient Mysteries had the true doctrine, and the early Christians had it. Masonry uncontaminated by the disciples of Loyola, had and has it also."

"Humanity in toto, then is the only Personal God and Christos is the realization or perfection of this divine Persona, an individual conscious experience. When this perfection is realized the state is called Christos with the Greeks, and Buddha with the Hindoos." "If the Christ state can be attained by but one human being during the whole evolution of the race, then the evolution of man is a farce and human perfection an impossibility."

"It also has been shown that every act in

the drama of the life of Jesus, and every
quality assigned to Christ, is to be found in
the life of Krishna and in the legends of all
the sun gods from the remotest antiquities."
"Drop the theological barnacles from the
religion of Jesus, as taught by him, and by
the Essenes and Gnostics of the first centuries, and it becomes Masonry. Masonry
in its purity, derived as it is from the old
Hebrew Kabbala as a part of the great universal wisdom religion of remotest antiquity, stands squarely for universal brotherhood of man." (Mystic Masonry, pp. 119,
130, 138, 139, 140).

Buck contends that in early Christianity
as well as in the Hebrew religion, there were
secret and open doctrines, the secret for the
initiate, and the open for the profane.

"The Bible with all the allegories it contains, expresses in an incomplete and veiled
manner only, the religious science of the
Hebrews. The doctrine of Moses and the
Prophets, identical at bottom with that of
the ancient Egyptians, also had its outward
meanings and its veils. The Hebrew books
were written only to recall to memory the
traditions, and they were written in symbols

8

unintelligible to the profane. The Pentateuch and the prophetic poems were merely elementary books of doctrine, morals and liturgy, and the secret and traditional philosophy was only written afterward under a veil still less transparent." (Morals and Dogma, 475).

"Few Christians are perhaps aware that such was the case with Christianity during the first two or three centuries." (Mystic Masonry, 60), that is, that it had its secret and non-secret doctrines. "This in its purity, as taught by Christ himself, was the true primitive religion as communicated by God to the Patriarchs. It is no new religion, but the reproduction of the oldest of all, and its true and perfect morality is the morality of Masonry, as it is the morality of every creed of antiquity." (Morals and Dogma, 541). "Christian dogmas", says Pike, "have for Freemasons but the import of changing symbols, veiling the one permanent truth, of which Masonic science and acts are a progressive revelation and application." (Id., 516).

This view of Buck and Pike that Jesus was a Mason and taught the fundamental

principles of Freemasonry, is held and advocated by a number of Masonic writers. We
summarize what T. K., the writer of a recent
Masonic volume entitled "The Great
Work", has to say on this matter. In this
book the lineage of Freemasonry is traced
back to the Great Parent School of India.
This writer says: "The life and ministry of
Jesus repersents another effort of the great
school to convey its message of light and life
to the world. To this great school Jesus
went for His spiritual preparation. In it
He spent the years of His special preparation. From it He went forth to preach the
gospel of peace and the kingdom of love.
For the cause it represents He labored and
suffered and died; that the records of the
great school contain a detailed history of the
life of Jesus, of His education and preparation for His work in the world, and of the
purposes to be accomplished thereby; that
these records are not open to the public, but
only to those who are duly and truly prepared, worthy and well qualified, and who can
establish the right to such confidence."

He asserts that the ethical teachings of
Jesus, in so far as they have been accurately

stated in the gospels, are identical in spirit and in principle with those of the great school, that He was but echoing the ethical philosophy of the ages as it had been wrought out and crystallized within the secret body of the great school of the masters; that Jesus was made priest after the order of Melchizedek, the mystery of which can be understood by those who are familiar with the great school of the masters, that His name is familiar to the members of the great school as one of its most illustrious high priests; that when He refused to tell the chief priests and scribes by what authority He came among them and performed such wonders, He was but following the policy of secrecy and silence in strict conformity with which the great school has proceeded through the ages and will continue to do until secrecy, silence and obscurity are no longer necessary to protect it from the selfish obtrusions of men.

It is such claims as these that Masonic writers are putting forth to show that the church does not have the true doctrine of Jesus, that she has either misunderstood and misinterpreted the gospel or is a deliberate deceiver and falsifier, and that Freemasonry is the legitimate organization founded upon the teachings of Jesus, and is therefore the supreme religion.

This claim of the supremacy of Freemasonry over Christianity, as being the original, universal and supreme religion, is set forth in every modern Masonic book and is discernible on almost every page of the ritual. It is expressed in the pompous ceremonies, the names of its officials and degrees, and in the gaudy regalia. Masonry is not only a religion, but it claims to be the supreme religion, of which all other religions are corruptions and perversions, having lost their primitive doctrines, which were, in the Masonic contention, what the essence of the Masonic religion is.

The real spirit of Freemasonry in its attitude toward Jesus Christ as confessed by the Church is expressed very clearly in a speech of Senator Delpech, of France. "The triumph of the Galilean has lasted twenty centuries. But now he dies in his turn. The mysterious voice announcing to Julian the Apostate the death of Pan, today announces the death of the impostor God who promised an era of justice and peace to those who believe in him. The mendacious God is now disappearing in his turn; he passes away to join in the dust of the ages the other divinities of India, Egypt, Greece and Rome, who saw so many deceived creatures prostrate before their altars. Brother Masons, we rejoice to state that we are not without our share in this overthrow of the false prophet." (Quoted in Cath. Ency.).

CHAPTER IV.

FREEMASONRY PROFESSES TO DO THE WORK OF RELIGION.

THE objective aim and purpose of religion is to please God by rendering Him proper honor and to glorify Him as God. The subjective aim and purpose is to purify the worshiper in all his many sided natures, to sanctify him in body, soul and spirit, here in this life, and for happiness in the life to come; to bring him into communion with the divine nature and into participation in the divine life. Freemasonry claims to do this very thing. It claims to honor God, to exalt Him and magnify His name, and to render Him acceptable worship. It claims by the secrets of its arts and esoteric truth to purify the individual and fit him for admission into heaven. Its spokesmen are serious and positive in their assertions as to the saving and regenerating power of Masonry. It proposes to take the man, divest him of his vices, and to implant in him a moral and spiritual energy, which will transform him until there is nothing lacking in him for a fit temple for the indwelling spirit of God, and finally to admit him into the celestial lodge above. That Masons are serious in this claim can scarcely be questioned.

1. Freemasonry regards all men outside of its ranks, of whatever religion, as profane, helpless, vicious, and unfit for its honors, privileges and truths, and therefore also unfit for heaven. Sickels says: "The entered apprentice is the type of unregenerate man, groping in mental and moral darkness, and seeking for light which is to guide his steps and point him to the path which leads to duty and to Him who gives to duty its rewards." (Ah. R., 51). "The rite of induction is intended, still further, to represent man in his primitive condition of helplessness, ignorance and moral blindness, seeking after the mental and moral enlightenment, which alone can deliver his mind from all thralldoms and make him master of the material world." (Ah. R. 55.) Mackey says of the candidate for initiation: "There he stands without our portals, on the

threshold of his new Masonic life in darkness, helplessness and ignorance. Having been wandering amid the errors and covered over with the pollutions of the outer world he comes inquiringly to our doors seeking the new birth and asking a withdrawal of the veil which conceals divine truth from his uninitiated sight. There is to be not only a change for the future, but also an extinction of the past; for the initiation is as it were a death to the world and a resurrection to a new life." (Ritualist pp. 22-23). "In the ancient mysteries the aspirant was always kept for a certain period in a condition of darkness. Hence darkness became the symbol of initiation. Applied to Masonic symbolism, it is intended to remind the candidate of his ignorance which Masonry is to enlighten; of his evil nature which Masonry is to purify; of the world in whose obscurity he has been wandering and from which Masonry is to rescue him." (Mackey's Rit. Art. Preparation, p. 44).

2. Masonry has its rites and ceremonies which it claims will regenerate profane man, enlighten him, and fit him for the celestial lodge above. Sickels says: "The rite of

induction signifies the end of a profane and vicious life, the palingenesia (new birth) of corrupted human nature, the death of vice and all bad passions and the introduction to a new life of purity and virtue." (Ah. Rez. 54). "In Egypt, Greece and among other ancient nations, Freemasonry was one of the earliest agencies employed to effect the improvement and enlightenment of man. Cicero tells us that the establishment of these rites among the Athenians, conferred upon them a supreme benefit. Their effect was to civilize men, reform their wild and ferocious manners, and make them comprehend the true principles of morality, which initiate man into a new order of life, more worthy of a being destined to immortality." (Ah. R. 57). These rites are intended to embrace all the circumstances of man, moral, social and spiritual, so that the whole man is regenerated. "The mental illumination, the spiritual light, which after the new birth is the first demand of the new candidate, is but another name for divine truth, the truth of God and the nature and essence of both which constitute the chief design of all Masonic teaching." (Mackey's Rit., p.

38). The result and effect of this initiation is Masonic regeneration. The candidate becomes a Mason, a new creature. In that ceremony of initiation, there is imparted to the candidate a moral and spiritual potency which he did not before possess, and which makes him a new order of man, a Mason. "To initiate is to regenerate." "It is the covenant that makes the Mason," are aphorisms of Masonry. Referring to the emblems of the first degree, Sickels says: (Ah. R., p. 64). "These all have exclusive reference to the leading idea of the ceremony, namely, the release from moral, spiritual, and intellectual darkness." "The rite of illumination indicates the triumphant conclusions of man's conflicts, sacrifices and trials; announces that he has found that Light for which he has so persistently sought, that Truth which alone can give dignity to his life, freedom to his spirit, and repose to his soul, and which is the grand recompense for all his journeyings, labors and combats." After the candidate has been initiated into the first degree and has become pure and innocent, he is given the white lambskin apron, which "is his badge as a

Mason, a sign of his purification and innocence." It is to be laid upon his coffin and buried with him, and entitles him to eternal reward. (Id., 67). The placing of the candidate in the north east corner of the lodge signifies "that he is now a perfect and upright man and Mason, the representation of a spiritual corner stone on which he is to erect his future moral and Masonic edifice." (Id., 69). "Masons erect a structure in which the God of Israel shall dwell forever." All this is plain in its meaning. The Masonic ceremonies are regarded as able to reform, renew and regenerate the profane man, and make him a pure, perfect and upright Mason. That Masons believe this is beyond question. Buck says: "In the third degree the candidate impersonates Hiram, who has been shown to be identical with the Christos of the Greeks, and with the sun-gods of all other nations. The superiority of Masonry at this point over all exoteric religions consists in this: All these religions take the symbol for the thing symbolized. Christ was originally like the Father. Now he is made identical with the Father. In deifying Jesus the whole of humanity is bereft of Christos as an eternal potency within every human soul, a latent Christ in every man. In thus deifying one man they have orphaned the whole of humanity. On the other hand, Masonry, in making every candidate personify Hiram, has preserved the original teaching, which is a universal glyph. Few candidates may be aware that Hiram, whom they have represented and personified is ideally and precisely the same as Christ. Yet such is undoubtedly the case. This old philosophy shows what Christ as a glyph means, and how the Christ state results from real initiation, or from the evolution of the human into the divine. Regeneration is thus given a meaning that is both apprehensible and attainable both philosophical and scientific, and at once ideal and practical." (Mystic Masonry 247-8).

"That the Christ life and the power that made Jesus to be called Christos, master, whereby he healed the sick, cast out devils and foretold future events, is the same life revealed and attained by initiation in the greater mysteries of antiquity, is perfectly plain. The disrepute into which the divine science has fallen, has arisen from its abuse and degradation. Masonry in its deeper meaning and recondite mysteries possesses this science, and all genuine initiation consists in an orderly unfolding of the natural powers of the neophyte; so that he shall become the very thing he desires to possess." (Mystic Masonry, 94). Masonic initiation, which is a religious ceremony, is an act by which the ignorant, vicious, profane worldling is transformed into a man having new ideas, new knowledge and new spiritual attainments and powers hitherto unpossessed, which make him a Mason. It is a process by which this new order of man, called a Mason, is evolved out of the ignorant, profane, passionate, polluted man; a process by which radical moral and spiritual transformations are effected, *ex opera operato.* (See Sickels A. R., pp. 30, 51, 54, 63, 64). In a certain sense initiation is in Masonry what regeneration is in Christianity. This resultant state claimed to be produced by initiation is the work of religion. Masonry is a religion because it claims to do effectively the work of religion.

3. It proposes and claims to save the human soul. Freemasonry not only claims

to possess regenerating power, but also to
carry on the work, thus begun, to completion, culminating in the entrance of the soul
into heaven. On this point we will let Masons be the spokesmen. "On the night of
his initiation," says Mackey (Manual, p.
41), "commences the great task which is
never in his future Masonic life to be dis-
continued, of erecting in his heart a spiritual temple for the indwelling of God."
"An adhering Mason aims by a uniform
tenor of virtuous conduct, to receive when
his alloted course of life has passed, the in-
appreciable reward from his cherished
Grand Master, 'Well done thou good and
faithful servant.'" (Mackey Lex., p. 450).
"Speculative Masonry is the application
and sanctification of the working tools and
implements, the rules and principles of
operative masonry, to the veneration of God
and the purification of the heart. The speculative Mason is engaged in the construction
of a spiritual temple in his heart, pure and
spotless, fit for the dwelling place of Him
who is the author of purity." (Mackey Rit.,
39). "The common gavel is an instrument
made use of by operative masons to break

off the corners of rough stones, the better to fit them for the builder's use; but we as free and accepted Masons are taught to make use of it for the more noble and glorious purpose of divesting our hearts and consciences of all vices and superfluities of life, thereby fitting our bodies as living stones for that spiritual building, that house not made with hands, eternal in the heavens." (Mackey's Rit. 37). This language of the ritual is quoted by almost all the leading Masonic writers. "Freemasonry teaches that a master Mason has all that the soul requires. We now find man complete in morality and intelligence, with the stay of religion added to insure him of the protection of the deity, and guard him against ever going astray. These three degrees thus form a perfect and harmonious whole nor can we conceive that anything can be suggested more which the soul of man requires." (Sickels' Man., p. 97-8. Ah. R. p. 189). "Speculative Masonry," says Towne, "according to present acceptation, has an ultimate reference to that spiritual building erected by virtue in the heart, and summarily implies the arrangement and perfection of those holy and sublime principles by which the soul is fitted for a meet temple of God in a world of immortality." (Spec. Freemasonry, p. 63). "In advancing to the fourth degree, the good man is greatly encouraged to persevere in the ways of well-doing even to the end. He has a name which no man knoweth save he that receiveth it. If therefore he be rejected and cast forth among the rubbish of the world, he knows full well that the master Builder of the universe, having chosen and prepared him a lively stone in that spiritual building in the heavens, will bring him forth in triumph while shouting grace, grace to the Divine Redeemer. Then the Freemason is assured of his election and final salvation. Hence opens the fifth degree where he discovers his election to, and his glorified station in the kingdom of his Father." "With these views the sixth degree is conferred, where the riches of divine grace are opened in boundless prospect." "Then he beholds in the eighth degree, that all the heavenly sojourners (i. e. Freemasons) will be admitted within the veil of God's presence, where they will become kings and priests before the throne

9

of His glory forever and ever." (Id., pp. 79-81). With many other words and arguments does this eminent Freemason endeavor to show that Freemasonry does as much and identically the same for the soul as does the gospel of Jesus Christ. He even claims that Solomon organized the institution by inspiration from God. (Id., p. 187). Masonry claims the power to conduct its disciples to heaven. "The ceremony (initiation) instructs, but it does not transform. To transform means to regenerate, and this comes by trial, by effort, by self-conquest, by sorrow, disappointment, failure, and a daily renewal of the conflict. It is thus that man must work out his own salvation." (Mystic Masonry, 175). "Freemasonry is the subjugation of the human that is in man, by the divine, the conquest of the appetite and passions, by the moral sense and reason; a continual effort, struggle and warfare of the spiritual against the material and sensual. That victory, when it has been achieved and secured, and the conqueror may rest upon his shield and wear the well earned laurels, is the true Holy Empire." (Mystic Masonry, 245).

"In the ceremonial of the third degree the last grand mystery is attempted to be illustrated in a forcible and peculiar manner, showing by striking analogy, that the Master Mason can not be deemed perfect in the glorious science until by the cultivation of his intellectual powers he has gained such moral government of his passion, such serenity of mind, that in synonymous apposition with mastership in operative art his thoughts like his actions, have become as useful as human intelligence will permit; and that, having passed through the trials of life with fortitude and faith, he is fitted for that grand, solemn and mysterious consummation by which alone he can become acquainted with the great security of eternity. Unlike the entered apprentice and fellowcraft, the Master Mason can learn nothing beyond the third degree; his hopes therefore, with his thoughts and wishes, should be directed to the grand lodge above, where the world's Great Architect lives and reigns forever. The ceremonial and the lecture beautifully illustrate this all engrossing subject, and the conclusion we arrive at is that youth properly directed leads us to honorable and virtuous maturity; and that the life of man regulated by morality, faith and justice, will be rewarded at its closing hour by the prospect of eternal bliss." (Dr. Crucifix in Ah. R. 170). "If we with suitable true devotion maintain our Masonic profession, our faith will become a beam of light and bring us to those blessed mansions where we shall be eternally happy with God, the Grand Architect of the Universe." (Sickels A. R. 79).

These extracts from recognized and trustworthy Masonic authorities show the unanimity of sentiment among Masons, that Masonry can save the soul, purify the life and fit man for entrance into heaven. Every candidate is made to say that his reasons for joining the craft are that he "may learn to subdue his passions, love truth and practice relief". Throughout the whole course of the progressive work of Masonry, the teachings are that it will give standing before God, and perfect the life both here and hereafter.

That Masons are confident that its religious precepts are able to make the individual perfect and pure is evident from the fact that it has a specific name for such. An

'Acacian' is a "Mason who by living in strict obedience to the obligations and precepts of the fraternity, is free from sin." (Mackey). Oliver says, "When the Master Mason exclaims 'my name is Cassia,' it is equivalent to saying, I have been in the grave. I have triumphed over it by rising from the dead, and being regenerated in the process, I have claim to life everlasting." (Cyclopedia of Freem., p. 48). And "so also the master's degree inspires the most cheering hope of the final reward which belong alone to the just made perfect." (Mackey Lex. 298).

Christianity claims to do no more for the salvation of the soul than does Masonry, but of course in a different way and upon a different basis. The aim of the two is the same, namely, to fit the soul for heaven. If Christianity is a religion, Masonry is also, and if Masonry is not a religion, Christianity is not.

PART II.

—

Freemasonry Is An Esoteric Religious Institution.

(135)

CHAPTER V.

DO FREEMASONS GENERALLY PERCEIVE THE REAL
MEANING OF THE MASONIC LANGUAGE AND
CEREMONIES, AND APPREHEND THE
DOCTRINES OF THE INSTITUTION?

"The narrative of the doctrine is the cloak. The
simple look only at the garment, that is, upon the
narrative of the doctrine. More they know not. The
instructed however, see not merely the cloak, but
what the cloak covers."—*Zohar III* :152.

TAKING into account all the facts in the
case we think that beyond controversy Freemasonry is a religious
institution. That it holds and
teaches a secret religious doctrine which
involves the deity, nature and man, and that
this secret religious doctrine is both concealed and expressed in its theistic terms, in
its ceremonies, and in its symbols and
emblems. The official definitions of the
institution plainly imply it; the art speech,
allusions and lectures bespeak it, and the
standard Masonic writings declare it.
Whether that doctrine is true or false we

do not now inquire. We simply contend that there is in this institution a hidden religious doctrine which is the heart and essence of Freemasonry.

The Masonic ritual has many elements which have come down from antiquity, and connect the modern institution with the cults of the ancients not so much in form as in doctrine. The myths and legends which appear in the ritual and are woven around the rites, are attempts either to explain, or to justify, or to conceal, or to commend this doctrine to its disciples, while the biblical narratives and allusions are designed to give it the sanction of the holy scriptures. These features indicate that the secret doctrine of the ancient cults have passed down into Freemasonry, but so veiled under the narratives of the ritual as not to be readily discerned. Its professed "divine truth" is veiled and concealed to the uninitiated sight.

Besides this internal evidence the testimony of all the more prominent Masonic writers is to the effect that there are secrets in the institution which have not been divulged, that these secrets are concealed in the rites and in the symbols, ideographically expressed, but not discerned by the majority; that these secret doctrines constitute the substance of its religious teachings, and are the heart, life and soul of the institution, and that if once discovered by or disclosed to the profane, the organization would fall. Their testimony is that the existence of Freemasonry is dependent upon the preservation of its secrets from the eyes and from the knowledge of the profane. We believe Masons are sincere in these representations, and we too are confident that were the secret religious doctrines of Freemasonry generally known the institution would surely fall, for such doctrines as we apprehend them, and institutions founded upon them, can not exist except under the cover of absolute secrecy, and a disguise impenetrable to the uninitiated.

But we are also convinced that very few Masons know what Freemasonry is, especially in its fundamental religious aspect, and it is for their enlightenment as well as for the information of the non-mason that we pursue this task. We would ask our Masonic readers for a suspension of judgment until they have calmly considered what we have to offer. We do not pretend to a superior knowledge of Freemasonry, but desire to give the craft members and all others who care to read this work the results of years of diligent study of this institution, and put into their possession the key that successfully and consistently unlocks every symbol and ceremony.

In support of this contention we cite the testimony of some of the most eminent Masons, and of others upon whom certain Masonic writers place great reliance. Buck expresses his opinion that not one Mason in ten thousand understands the real key to Masonry; that there is a large and increasing number of Masons who are satisfied that there must be other and profounder meanings behind the ritual and ceremonies of the lodge; that the greater part of modern Masons are dealing with symbols, the key for the real interpretation of which they never possessed, or even suspected that it ever existed; that it remains for the future to determine whether any considerable number of Masons really desire to possess in fuller measure the living truth which the dead letter text conceals, and that modern Masonry never possessed the true key for the interpretation of the secret doctrine. He asserts that it is in the ancient symbols of Freemasonry that its real secrets lie concealed and that these are as densely veiled to the Mason as to any other, unless he has studied the science of symbolism in general, and Masonic symbolism in particular. He defines Masonry as a system of morals illustrated by symbols and something more, and beneath them there is a science and a philosophy concealed in the symbolism of the square and compass. He declares that Masonry has no secrets in its ritualism, nor in its monitorial lessons, but that the secrets lie in the ancient symbols, that the candidate is debarred from possessing the secrets solely by his inattention to the hints everywhere given in the ritual of the lodge, or by his indifference to the subject; that if Masonry has made only a superficial use of these hoary secrets and their deeper meaning is still unknown to the craft, it is equally unknown to all others, except as the result of genuine initiation. (See Mystic Masonry, pp XXXV, XXXVI, XXXVII, 87, 242, 255, 266).

The testimony of Heckethorn is as follows: "In the first three degrees nothing but the exoteric doctrines are revealed." (Vol. 2:19). "That the figures and schemes for the presentation of the knowledge and properties of nature are preserved in Masonry, but not the pseudo-Masonry of the majority of craft members; that the truest Masons today are found without the lodge." He declares that "the members of the first three degrees of Freemasonry are not initiated in the grand so-called secrets of Freemasonry. Only in the royal arch degree are they informed of it." (Vol. 1:99).

Hartman, evidently a Mason, says, "Fortunate is the Mason or priest who understands what he teaches. But of such disciples there are only a few. The systems in which the old truths have been embodied are still in existence, but the spirit has fled. Doctors and priests see but the outward form, and few can see the hidden mystery that called these forms into existence. The key to the inner sanctuary has been lost by those who have been entrusted with its keeping, and the true password has not been rediscovered by the followers of Hiram Abiff." (Magic, Black and White, p. 62).

Albert Pike, than whom there is no higher Masonic authority, says: "The lessons and ceremonies of the blue lodge degrees have come to us from an age when symbols were used, not to reveal but to conceal, and are now corrupted by time and disfigured by modern additions and absurd interpretations." (See his Morals and Dogma, p. 106). "Masonry jealously conceals its secrets and intentionally leads conceited interpreters astray. Part of the symbols are displayed to the initiated, but he is intentionally misled by false interpretations. The initiated are few though many hear the Thyrsus. The meaning of the symbols is not unfolded at once. We give you hints only in general. You must study out the recondite and mysterious meaning for yourself. It is for each individual Mason to discover the secrets of Masonry by reflection on its symbols and a wise consideration." (Quoted in Cath. Ency. art. Masonry). He also came to the conclusion that certain Hermetic philosophers had a hand in the organization of the Free and Accepted Masons, and that if they embodied in its symbolism more than appears on the surface, and far deeper truths than the superficial student discerns, it was evidently designed that future generations should discern and use these profound secrets; that the evidence in this direction is not only conclusive but overwhelming; that it is in the province of Masonry to elect if it chooses, that its symbols shall have only a superficial meaning in the lodge; that Masonry not only nowhere denies this deeper meaning to its symbolism but that many writers have admitted it and have expatiated upon it, but that very few seem to have been able to discern its real meaning and that they have generally failed because of their sectarian bias.

Mme. Blavatsky, whose writings are held in high regard by certain Masons, states that there is abundant material in the imperial libraries of St. Petersburg to show that at the end of the eighteenth and beginning of the nineteenth centuries many Freemasons went to Tibet and were initiated in unknown crypts of Central Asia, and returned with a rich store of information as could not be secured elsewhere in Europe.

(See The Secret Doctrine, Vol. 1, p. XXXVI).

Sickels says that "the ritual has enshrined within it in symbol and allegory certain great and essential moral truths" (A. R., 275), and expresses it as his conviction that "the mass of the brotherhood do not understand the beautiful and truth glowing ritual, and the sublime symbolism of the institution; that it requires close application and untiring diligence to ascertain the precise nature of every ceremony which our ancient brethren saw reason to adopt in the formation of an exclusive system;" that "before we can, in any degree, appreciate Freemasonry, or understand the significance of its mysteries, we must go back to the past, and question the founders of the order. We must learn in what necessities of human nature, and for what purpose it was created. We must discover the true genesis of our rites, and become familiar with the ideas which the Fathers intended to shadow forth through them, and impress upon the mind. It is not enough for us to accept the letter of the ceremonial, and perform it blindly, interpreting its meaning in whatever way or fancy or imagination or convenience may dictate. We should know what the ancients meant to say through it; what truth each rite and each symbol represented to their minds. Our rites will be of little value to us if we, accepting the symbol, have lost the sense. It is our duty then to make Freemasonry the object of profound study. We must consult the past. We must stand by the sarcophagus of the murdered but restored Osiris in Egypt; enter the caverns of Phrygia, and hold communion with the Cabiri; penetrate the College Faborum of ancient Rome, and work the mystic circle of Sidon. In a word we must pursue our researches until we find the thought that lay in the minds of those who created the institution and founded our mysteries. Then we shall know precisely what they mean." (Ah. R. pp. 14, 53, 56). Preston concedes it as a fact that many of those initiated fail to get the real secrets. (Masonic Library, p. 230). Oliver says that "to publish an account of the ceremonies of the lodge however wrong it may be, does not communicate the secrets of Freemasonry; that every one is not acquainted with the true secrets of Masonry who have been initiated into the order; that it is in the emblems that the secrets of Freemasonry are chiefly concealed". (Masonic Library, 162, Antiq., pp. 23, 129).

This testimony supported by other high Masons not here cited, establishes it as a fact that there is a secret doctrine in the ritual and symbols of Freemasonry which very few members of the fraternity discern or apprehend.

If then such eminent Masonic authorities as those above cited, declare that few Masons understand Freemasonry, or discern its true meaning, or get its thought, the reader will not regard the writer presumptious when he expresses the same opinion. The exposures published by different seceding Masons, do not disclose this secret doctrine any more than do the authorized rituals. The doctrine is there, but not made plain to the reader. It still remains expressed in allegory and cipher. The language is ambiguous, and the real hoodwink is never completely removed from the eyes of a large majority of the members of the craft. They are never brought to the true light of Masonry. They fail to see the light, because their eyes are bedimmed with other things, especially things drawn from the holy Bible. They have not the wit to discern. They see the garment, but not the thing the garment conceals. They get no inspiration in the lodge, but become the foremost of those who appear in dress parade, or feast at the banquets, thinking that these are the chief things in Freemasonry.

Another reason we would assign why we are sure few Masons get the thought of Freemasonry is the method employed for imparting its religious ideas.

Masonic writers all agree that the doctrines of Freemasonry are presented to the Mason not in an open, direct and dogmatic manner, but in a veiled form either in allegory, or by means of hieroglyphs, ideographs, ciphers, symbols, and in ambiguous language of which misleading interpretations are purposely given so that if the Mason apprehend the real meaning it is solely through his own wit and power of discernment. "It should be borne in mind" says Buck, "that in modern Freemasonry there is always an exoteric portion given out to the world, to the uninitiated, and an esoteric portion reserved for the initiated, and revealed by degrees according as the candidate demonstrates his fitness to receive, conceal, and rightly to use the knowledge imparted." (Mystic Masonry, 69).

That the institution may be perpetuated from generation to generation, and its integrity be maintained, it is imperative that its essential secret doctrine be communicated from the Mason to the neophyte in a manner that makes it secure from discovery by the uninitiated. This is effected by means of symbols and art speech which are made to carry under disguise a complete system of the Masonic ideas of the deity, nature and man. This teaching must be by symbols, for only by these can the doctrine be promulgated Masonically. All explanations that are given of these symbols are designedly misleading interpretations the more completely to defeat the interpreter, to hide their Masonic meaning and to prove the candidate's ability to catch the Masonic doctrine.

The sectarian bias so frequently assigned by Masonic writers as the reason why so few Masons catch the thought of the symbolism and ritualism, are their preconceived notions of it. These notions are based either upon the exoteric explanations which they have heard, or upon the opinion that Freemasonry is in harmony with their own religious ideas. It is this persistence of opinion and their proclivity to interpret it from their own subjective viewpoint, that blind them to the real thought of Freemasonry. Ragotzsky says, "Freemasonry has been of old and will forever remain the requirement of a Freemason to possess a pair of clearly seeing eyes."

The neophyte comes to the lodge ignorant of its nature, religious character and methods of instruction, and therefore disqualified to discern the Masonic ideas conveyed by these mimic rites, symbols and art speech. He does not know that a double meaning is attached to these symbols and art speech, so that the most ordinary language is made to carry a deep religious and ethical meaning, which very few apprehend. He puts his own interpretation upon them for he understands them only from his viewpoint and knowledge, and in the sense of the exoteric language which purports to explain their meaning. It therefore follows that in a large majority of cases a vast difference exists between his notion of Freemasonry, and the real objective Freemasonry. He takes the symbol for the thing symbolized, and holds that as Freemasonry which is not Freemasonry but only its garment, for "he who does not see the meaning, does not see the thing." He is prone to understand these mimic rites, symbols and art speech in an ethical sense, geometrically or figuratively expressed, rather than in their Masonic sense.

This principle of the right of individual interpretation Masons say is imperative "so that concord may be maintained in the institution." "The exercise of religious freedom is admitted and proclaimed to be the inalienable possession of each individual Freemason," says McKenzie. It is a necessary principle the more completely to conceal the real objective Freemasonry from those whose intellectual, moral or religious qualifications unfit them to be entrusted with the real doctrines and to leave them under the hallucination that they understand it and have its secrets. To all such the symbols are dead letters and the ceremonies a dumb show. All are alike instructed, but only the discerning few catch the hidden doctrine, those who believe that Freemasonry means far more than the ceremonies and moral precepts indicate.

This method for the communication and promulgation of the Masonic doctrines is so cunningly devised that it baffles on the one hand those who have professed to expose it and give a rational explanation of its symbols and ceremonies, and on the other, the majority of those who are loyal to the institution, in catching its real sentiments. While "it is devised to defeat conceited interpreters", it also defeats the average Mason in discerning the true meaning. The tendency of those who study Freemasonry is to take the ritualistic language and the symbols at their ordinary value, while a more correct and fruitful principle is that its language and symbols least do mean what they most do say and show. Freemasonry is a system of cunningly devised fables whereby it deceives all except the discerning few whose wit and wisdom enable them to perceive the deeper meaning, and who alone of all those admitted into the order become the true Masons.

The peculiar theological and religious ideas which Freemasonry holds and aims to inculcate while positively non-Christian, are expressed in terms of Christian theology, not to express the Christian ideas or to show their harmony with Christian thought, but to give them a Christian coloring the more effectually to deceive, mislead and hoodwink the neophyte, the conscientious member, and the non-Mason into whose hands Masonic literature may come, and also to intensify the task of the Mason to learn the real sentiments. Thus the biblical and Christian appellations of God are employed to denote the Masonic deity, who is specifically known as the Great Architect of the Universe. It employs the terms regeneration, illumination, resurrection, justification, and other terms of Christian theology to express not the Christian ideas, but under which to hide the Masonic religious operations. These terms have a peculiar and a specific Masonic meaning, and in studying this institution we must not permit ourselves to be misled by this use of Christian theological terms, as many a Mason is misled by them to believe that Freemasonry is a Christian institution.

Because the peculiar Masonic religious doctrines are not taught in a dogmatic manner in the lodge, but by symbols, emblems and mimic rites; because the religious offices of the officials are veiled in the allusions to the offices of the sun in the east, the south and in the west; because of the poor blind candidate continually searching for light, and for more light, and the sorry plight in which he repeatedly finds himself, the meaningless talk about the honor and dignity of the apron and of those who know how to wear it, and scores of other things, the candidate can not and does not catch the thought intended to be set forth. Outwardly these things are a medley of contradictions, a confusing series of substitutions, so that he does not discern the hidden religious ideas which are esoterically expressed and unfolded in an orderly and systematic manner. He does not perceive the peculiar religion set forth by the entire symbolism of the lodge, a religion that astonishes us with the sublimity of its conceptions, but shocks us with its grossness, rudeness and obscenity. He looks with

wonder upon the pillars, the stairs, the furniture, the emblems, the weeping woman, the
scythe and the coffin, not knowing that these
are the visible objects which give sense to the
allegories that are related, and index fingers
which point out to him who has the
wit to see, the way to the hidden secrets and
doctrines of Masonry. It is therefore only
the few who get the meaning, those who have
the intellectual grasp of the mysteries with
which Freemasonry deals, and therefore the
majority of the craft members do not succeed
in really passing the veils.

Another reason we would advance in support of our contention that Freemasons
generally do not know what the hidden doctrine is, lies in the fact that some of the profoundest subjects that have ever attracted
and engaged the intellectual powers of man,
some of the profoundest mysteries of nature,
some of the most abstruse speculations in
which the human mind has been engaged
for ages, are the subject matter involved in
the Masonic symbolism, namely the mystery
of life, its generation, its continuation and
its cessation. It is in this sense, or with
reference to these matters, that the ritual

says the greatest and best of men have been patrons and members of the craft. But while Masons know no more of these mysteries than do others, they constitute the basis of their meditations and symbolism. But these mysteries and the knowledge concerning them can only be apprehended by those whose mental training has fitted them for it. It is therefore not only probable, but reasonably certain that the majority of Masons never get the real thought expressed and conveyed by the symbols and ceremonies. Thousands look upon the Egyptian hieroglyphs. They all see the same inscribed objects, but only the Egyptologist gets the thought expressed by them. So in Freemasonry. Thousands see the symbols, hear the lectures, witness the rites, but know not what they say. The thought is objectively presented, but not subjectively received. They have eyes but they see not; they have ears but they hear not; they have hearts but they understand not the things which are so skillfully concealed in the symbolism of the institution.

If Freemasonry is a religious institution in which is taught a science of morality, a system of ethics, a correct knowledge of the Great Architect of the Universe, all of which are veiled in allegory, it is evident then that the allegorical language does not, in its plain natural sense, express the real moral, ethical or religious sentiment of the institution,—the sense and sentiment intended to be conveyed; but that this is to be found in that which has or is supposed to have some resemblance in form or thought to that expressed in the allegorical language. The allegory is intended as a means to conceal and not to reveal, the real principles and sentiment. The natural or ordinary sense of the language is not therefore, the Masonic sense.

If this morality or these ethical and religious principles are illustrated by symbols, and the secrets of Freemasonry are concealed in these symbols, it is also plain that this illustration is meaningless until the symbols are understood. And if the secrets of the institution are concealed in these symbols, it is also clear that these symbols do not mean in Masonry, what they do in the stone mason's craft, but have another sense and purpose, and not until that secret sense is known, do they have any meaning and force as illustrations. These symbols instead of illustrating the sentiments of Masonry to the uninstructed simply conceal and mystify the matter. But when understood in their secret sense and place, they do most clearly and forcibly illustrate this system of morality and religion.

We take it therefore that if we would learn what Freemasonry is, and determine its true nature, essence and teachings; if we would comprehend its peculiar ideas of the divine, and its religious and ethical principles and notions, and grasp its sentiments, we must not take its language at its face value, but must look beneath these expressions, beyond these external forms, and penetrate the veils which it has thrown around itself. We must decipher the hieroglyphs which it employs in its moral instruction and study the ancient types, emblems and allegories, and their ancient usage, which it employs in its communications. These will furnish us the key that unlocks its mysteries, and explain the allegories by which it vaguely sets forth its moral and religious sentiments. We must get the "thought which its founders intended to be expressed by these rites", though dextrously concealed behind its exoteric work. We must master its glyphs, symbols, and ideographs; we must study its ritual and ceremonies in the light of their origin and ancient usage. If we do this upon correct principles we certainly can discern its nature, and discover its sentiments. The whole system then will become plain. In that key too we find the reason for its peculiar rites, symbols and paraphernalia. Its secret religion, science, morality and philosophy, all become unveiled, and stand before us in their shameless nakedness. This is however what most Masons fail to do. They take the language and symbols at their ordinary value and meaning, and get for Masonry what is not Masonry but its cloak.

Is it possible for one not a Mason, one who has never been initiated into the mysteries of the order, to discover the key to the secret doctrine of Freemasonry? Masons contend that it is not possible and assign as the reason that Masonry is a secret institution whose secrets have never been found out. But if Masons must go to the ancient mysteries of Egypt, Phrygia, Greece and India, to get the thought of modern Freemasonry, and to learn what the founders meant to convey by these peculiar rites and symbols, surely the profane can do as much. If the Mason after having been initiated, needs to search for the true secret and thought of the order, then his initiation is really of no advantage in discerning the true esoteric doctrines, and he remains on the same plane with the profane. If the secrets of the craft are as densely veiled to the Mason as to the profane then both stand on the same plane of knowledge so far as the secrets, rites and symbols are concerned, and the profane has an equal chance with the initiated to learn the secrets. Mr. Charles Sotheran concedes that Masonic teaching and ritual are no longer secret from those of the profane who have the wit to read as they run. (Letter to Mme. Blavatsky, Isis Unveiled, Vol. 2:389). All that the investigator needs is the ritual to show him the habiliments of the institution.

If the ceremonies, symbols, allusions and allegories, and such like in Masonry are religious representations, which they evidently are, then in so far as religious ideas admit of being clothed in image or word symbolism at all, they become intelligible and accessible to every well educated person.

If the secrets of the craft lie concealed in the ancient symbols of Freemasonry and we can determine and identify these ancient symbols, then we also can study them, learn their meaning and their use and purpose in the cults in which they formed a picture speech. If we can show that the modern symbols of Freemasonry are but a conventional form of these ancient symbols, having the same meaning, purpose and design, and representing the same objects, then we have the secret. Modern Masonry is, as we take it, a transposition or transference of the ancient mystery religion into and under the symbols of the work tools, figures and terms of a builder's craft. The same thought, conception of the divine, religion and God-idea expressed in those ancient cults are in the modern institution, but so concealed and disguised under the language of a builder's craft, that only the most attentive and studious discern it. Why the profane, with a Masonic ritual at hand, can not study and discover this thought as well as the "sons of light", is hard to understand. Masons sure-

11

ly are not the sole possessors of the science of symbolism, nor of the religious thought and conception of the divine as held and taught in the mysteries. That none but Freemasons can understand and apprehend the profound meaning concealed in these symbols, ancient or modern, is an impeachment of the intelligence and common sense of all men who are not Masons. Yes we believe that we can show that the profane discerns in these symbols, and that their true secret too, what not one Mason in ten thousand perceives.

CHAPTER VI.

THE SOURCES OF LIGHT.

"Before we can in any degree appreciate Freemasonry or understand the significance of its mysteries, we must consult the past, and question the founders of the order. We must stand by the sarcophagus of the murdered but restored Osiris in Egypt, enter the caverns of Phrygia, hold communion with the Cabiri, and work the mystic circle of Sidon, then we shall know precisely what they mean."— *Sickels.*

AN investigation of the remains that have come down to us from antiquity shows that there existed in the ancient world and among the ethnic races, religious institutions which were in a sense to those people what the Mosaic institutions were to Israel. In their earliest forms they were marked by extreme simplicity, and the rites were simple and direct. The religious ideas were taught not in a dogmatic manner but by the ceremonial which in its primitive simplicity and realistic form was readily understood by all who witnessed it.

In course of time this simple ceremony became more and more elaborate, while the thought or religious idea became more and more obscured under the accretions of time, the corruptions of the traditionalists and the introduction of foreign elements, so that the original meaning became either entirely lost, or perverted, and was discerned only by the more sagacious of the worshippers. The primitive ideas and the facts of nature upon which these institutions were founded, became personified and allegorized, and stories were related of these divine beings to explain what had become obscured by time or lost through indifference and inattention. Gradually the religion became corrupted, magnificent temples were erected to the worship of those personified forces in nature, elaborate ceremonies devised, and priests and priestesses installed, and that which was conceived as the divine nature and which was originally worshipped in simple but native rudeness, became corrupted in man's vain imagination, and connected in story with the licentious and incestuous acts of the gods and goddess which man had devised as its representations. The lives of these deties became the examples and models after which the worshipper conformed his life, while their licentious acts became the basis of the ceremonies that were introduced.

These institutions were the mysteries. They flourished everywhere, and while simple and direct in their earlier history, gradually became esoteric, and after their contact with Christianity, secret.

The chief mysteries with which Freemasonry claims to be in unity, harmony and affinity, are those of Egypt connected with Osiris, Typhon and Isis, those of Phrygia connected with Cybele and Sabazius, those of Eleusis and Samothracia. These we shall examine in detail in the next chapter.

It is to these mysteries of the ancient world that Freemasons direct the members of the craft if they would get the thought of Freemasonry, the secret religious doctrines which it professes, and which it aims to impart to its disciples. The lexicons and monitors written for their enlightenment and for the elucidation of its own mysteries, abound in reference to and descriptions of these mysteries, and the rites, and symbols employed in them. These are further supported by direct statements of the highest authorities in the craft. On this point we cite the testimony of several of the most eminent.

Pike says: "It is not in the books of philosophers, but in the religious symbolism of the ancients that we must look for the footprints of science, and rediscover the mysteries of knowledge. The priests of Egypt knew better than we do, the laws of movement and life." "Had the interpreters of the ancient mysteries been possessed of a universal key to symbolism or a complete philosophy of its secret doctrines, the results would not have been so confusing. Guarded by a complete philosophy, armed with a key to symbolism, and aided by these Grand Masters, the lost mysteries of antiquity may be restored and made to tell their hoary secrets for the benefit of the coming age." (See Mystic Masonry, pp. XXIV, XXVI, 207.)

Ragon, Buck, Pike, Mackey and Clavel express the opinion and the conviction that the interpretation of Masonic symbols and glyphs can be derived from the ancient mysteries, and their writings, like those of practically all the Masonic writers abound in

references to these ancient institutions and
their ceremonies, to aid the reader in catching the thought of Freemasonry. A number
of the more eminent Masons contend that
instead of being an imitation of the mysteries of antiquity, Freemasonry should
become their restoration and perpetuation
through the coming centuries. On this point
Ragon the learned Belgian Mason says:
"The Franc Mason, which is not Macon
libertie or Freemasonry, knew well when
adopting the title, that it was no question of
building a wall, but that of being initiated
into the ancient mysteries veiled under the
name Franc Maconnerie; that his work was
only to be a continuation or a renovation of
the ancient mysteries, and that he was to
become a Mason after the manner of Apol-
los or Amphion." He reproaches the
English Freemasons for having material-
ized and dishonored Freemasonry, once
based upon the ancient mysteries, by adopting the name Freemasonry, owing to a mistaken notion of the origin of the craft. He
contends that the mistake is due to those
who connect Masonry with the building of
Solomon's Temple, deriving its origin from

that event. He derides this idea. (See his Maconnerie Orthodoxe, p. 44.)

Mackey calls the mysteries "those truly Masonic institutions." (Lex., p. 35), and says that "their ceremonies were afterwards adopted by Freemasons." (Lex., p. 320). He concedes the common origin of these ceremonies of the Hindoos, Greeks, Romans and Druids, a fact now established by archaeological evidence, and that Freemasonry is indebted to them for its existence. (Rit., p. 27). He thinks the truest theory of the connection of Freemasonry with the mysteries is to be found in the natural coincidence of human thought. This is substantially the view also of Stillson and Hughan. (Hist. of Freemasonry and Concordant Orders). Sickels concedes, owns and accepts the mysteries as the Freemasonry of the ancients, and that we must go to them and to their founders, to get the thought of the modern institution and its teachings. Augustus Le-Plongeon, M. D., an ardent Mason, in his "Sacred Mysteries among the Mayas and Quiches" traces Freemasonry back to the mysteries. He says: "These symbols are precisely the same that we find in the tem-

ples of Egypt, Chaldea, India, and Central
America.   Whatever may have been the esoteric meaning given to them by the initiated
of those countries, we are bound to admit
that a link exists between these ancient mysteries and Freemasonry.   It is for us to discover by whom that link was riveted." (p.
11).

Buck says that "there is both a historical and philosophical thread uniting
Freemasonry and the mysteries of antiquity
is well known to every student of Masonry
no less than to all students of symbolism and
mysticism".   (Mystic Masonry XXXV).

John Yarker, in his "Notes on the Scientific and Religious Mysteries of Antiquity"
(p. 150), contends that he has established
the fact of the connection of Freemasonry
with the speculative rites of antiquity.
Heckethorn says that the mysteries have
come down to us and are still perpetuated in
a corrupted and aimless manner in Freemasonry (Secret Societies, etc., Vol. 1: p.
13); that it is impossible to attribute the
origin of Freemasonry to one or other specific society preceding it, but that it is a
resume of the teachings of all these societies

(Id. Vol. 2:9); that Blue Lodge Masonry answers to the lesser mysteries and all subsequent degrees answer to the greater mysteries (Id. Vol. 2:19). Oliver concedes that the mysteries date their origin from the Cabiri and Thoth, who were certainly Masons. (Antiq. p. 53). Dr. Rebold concedes the connection of Freemasonry with the mysteries. (See his History of Freemasonry, p. 62). Findel does not concede that Freemasonry is derived from the mysteries, he however admits that the ancient symbolical marks and ceremonies of the lodge bear a very striking resemblance to the mysteries.

These claims made by the most eminent Freemasons that Masonry depends upon the mysteries for its thought, philosophy, ceremonies, symbols and ritual, we concede, and are satisfied that this dependence can be demonstrated beyond a reasonable doubt. In other words modern Freemasonry in its religious aspect is a continuation of the ancient mysteries somewhat modified by modern thought and conditions. It is the mysteries veiled under the term Freemasonry, or the mysteries restored, under the mask of operative masonry.

These claims of Freemasonry both to antiquity, and to derivation from the mysteries, are generally rejected and dismissed as puerile, by the encyclopedias and anti-masonic writers. But we concede them, and in the sense in which they are made by Masons, we think they can easily be sustained. These claims, be it remembered, are made in an esoteric sense. They refer to the internal, not on the external side of the order, to the essential religious doctrine not to the form. If Freemasonry can not establish historical and organic connection with and succession from the ancient mysteries, as some writers contend, it can establish religious and psychical identity, which is after all, the true line of descent and the bond of unity.

"It is of course easy to point out vague analogies between Freemasonry and the great secret organizations having social aims, which existed in antiquity. The Pythagoreans, the Eleusinians and Essenes have all been appealed to by uncritical Masonic writers in the hope of giving their craft the doubtful antiquity and prestige of ancient descent. It is possible that Freemasonry copied an older ritual, which was again imitated by younger societies.'' (Ency. Brit. Art. Freemasonry). But in the investigation of this question of derivation we must distinguish between Freemasonry in its outward form, and its inner thought, doctrines and principles. This inner thought or religious doctrine is the real Freemasonry, while the form of organization and ceremonies, are the vehicles through which it is taught and expressed. As to its outward form it is reasonably certain that it came down from very early ages, through builders' guilds. This is the opinion of most of the authorities consulted. (See Ency. Brit. 9th ed. Also Fort: Hist. of Antiquities of Freemasonry). In a recent work Dr. Wilhelm Bergemann, who is a high Mason in Germany, shows that English Freemasonry, the progenitor of the various systems of Freemasonry existing today, was in its origin the lineal descendant of the older English lodges of operative masons. (Vorgeschichte und Anfange der Freimaurerei in England. 3 vols).

In a very remote period the more discerning men among operative masons, perceived an analogy between the building of edifices, and the reproductive processes. This analogy is expressed in the realistic language of the ancients. The analogy was so evident that the reproductive processes were symbolized and expressed under the imagery and in the terms of building operations. The implements of masonry, in the thought of that age, became associated with and symbols of the organs of reproduction. The facts and processes of reproduction became the basis of religious ideas, and of these ideas, the work tools became emblems. These religious ideas in their more elaborate form took concrete expression in the ceremonies of initiation that prevailed in these guilds of stone-masons. The implements, work-tools, grips, pass-words and ceremonies of these guilds acquired an esoteric meaning which constituted the essential secrets of these ancient guilds.

These secrets were transmitted from generation to generation, through these guilds of stone-masons. As they were the builders of the temples, palaces, and cathedrals that were erected during the successive ages they came more or less into con-

tact with the cults, philosophers, and priest-
hoods connected with these edifices, and
doubtless became acquainted with the oriental mysticism that was widely disseminated throughout the ancient and mediaeval
world.   These ideas strikingly akin to those
prevailing in these guilds, would find ready
acceptance and tend to stimulate and keep
alive the spirit of speculation among the
craft, until it took revived life in the beginning of the eighteenth century, when they
became synthetized as the esoteric doctrine
of the new organization.

Heckethorn says that "the Freemasons
undoubtedly through the Templars inherited
no small portion of their ritual from the
Manicheans." (Vol. 1: p. 91). Frost says
that it is obvious that the Masons as a body
knew nothing at the time of the middle of
the eighteenth century of the order's origin,
beyond the fact that it had been graffed at
an unknown period upon the guild of masons from which it is equally obvious it did
not derive its rites and mysteries." He concedes that the rites and mysteries of Freemasonry may be much older than the order

and yet not know how they came into possession of the Masons. (See Sec. Soc. of European Revolution, Vol. 1: p. 29). Causes existed which led to the admission of a new class of members, not operative masons, into the order. As early as 1646 Elias Ashmole (1617-1692) a noted antiquarian was "accepted" as a Mason. His entrance into the fraternity paved the way for the great Masonic revolution of 1717. Charles Sotheran, a high Mason, regards Ashmole's influence as paramount in transforming operative masonry into speculative Freemasonry. The writer in Nelson's Encyclopedia, (art Freemasonry) says: "Traces of symbolism from operative masonry are preserved in the craft, and superimposed on the work of Masonic ritualists and enthusiasts, are contributions from the Rosicrucians, the Kabbalists, the Gnostics, the Pythagoreans and from Egyptian, Greek and oriental philosophers." John Yarker in his Notes (p. 150) says: "We think we have established the fact of the connection of Freemasonry with the speculative rites of antiquity, as well as the antiquity and purity of the old English

Templar rite of seven degrees, and the spurious derivation of many of the other rites therefrom.''

A critical examination of the institution shows that during the period from 1717 to 1725, certain influences were at work which gradually transformed both the forms, ceremonies, and the religious features of Freemasonry. ''This remarkable evolution of the forms, ceremonies and symbolism of the fraternity during this period has been attributed to the new membership, to antiquarians, historians and mystics who were attached to the fraternity late in the seventeenth century, and early in the eighteenth.'' (Nelson's Ency. Art. Freemasonry).'' It was discovered in 1723, when the new constitutions were published, that Anderson and Desaguilers[1] had completely changed the theory of the institution from Christian to

---

[1] The men most directly connected with the Revival of Freemasonry in 1717, were Rev. John Theophilus Desaguilers, D. D., L.L. D., F. R. S., b. Mar. 12, 1683. He was a Frenchman, and a popularizer of science; Rev. James Anderson, D. D., b. Aug. 5, 1684, a Scotch Presbyterian minister, and an antiquarian of some note. The others were George Payne, and Anthony Sayer, a gentleman belonging to the ''speculative'' craft, and ''accepted.''

the adoption of a universal creed based on the fatherhood of God and the brotherhood of man, so as to admit men of all religions, nationalities and stations in life." (Ency. Amer. Art. Freemasonry).

It is evident from the facts here stated, that other elements than mere external reorganization entered into that event characterized as the "Revival of Freemasonry". There was inserted and incorporated as an essential part of the institution, a peculiar system of religion and ethics, which had been adumbrated in the guilds of operative masonry.

Into this first Grand Lodge, founded June 24, 1717, which furnished the body, was breathed from the east, Pike thinks by certain Hermetic philosophers, the doctrine, the spirit, the peculiar religious ideas of the ancient mysteries and cults, which gave it such an impulse of new and revived life, which was of such importance, and marked such a change in its spirit, that the event is characterized as a revolution, and as the Revival of Freemasonry, which was however only a revival of the religion of the mysteries. "Operative masonry" says

12

Mackey, "was the skeleton upon which was strung the living muscles and tendons and nerves of the speculative system."

The work of these antiquarians consisted in attaching an esoteric sense to the implements, passwords, grips, initiations and terminology of operative masonry, and veil the same in allegorical narratives which would express the mystical ideas and religious notions that had been accepted, which the discerning Mason would perceive, but which would remain meaningless, or be decidedly misleading to the profane. These ideas while fundamentally religious, are positively non-Christian. They had been symbolized under Christian emblems in a number of cathedrals erected by these guilds, which emblems were designed either as caricatures of the vices of the Church, or esoteric symbols of heretical doctrines, but which are recognized and claimed by the modern craft as purely Masonic. In imitation of these methods, the founders of speculative Freemasonry dexterously clothed these peculiar ideas in the ritual ceremonies and lectures, under a biblical veil, and so skillfully was the work performed that the earlier Masons were almost to a man misled in their belief that Freemasonry is a Christian institution. The Revival of Freemasonry consisted in a resuscitation and rehabilitation of the religion of the ancient mysteries.

The conditions in England, from a religious and ethical viewpoint, immediately preceding this period in which Freemasonry arose, were favorable and conducive to such a movement, and for the insertion of the peculiar religious ideas in the new organization. The Church was in a decadent state, and Deism was rampant. The growing spirit of the reformation gave men a freedom of speech which superseded the marks and caricatures in which the old masons exposed the vices of the clergy. These caricatures which were more or less a mask and not readily understood by the uninitiated, took a deeper and more subtly disguised form in speculative Freemasonry. A new current of ideas was inaugurated by the Arabian Mysticism of Paracelsus and Rosenkreutz on the Continent, and was preached in England by Robert Fludd (1574-1637), whose central principle was that man is a representative in miniture of the universe, and he endeavored to trace an analogy between what he called the microcosm and the macrocosm. De Quincy regards Fludd as the immediate father of Freemasonry.

Besides these guilds which transmitted the religious ideas and doctrines of the ancients, there were also certain schools engaged in philosophical and religious speculation whose influence has been felt down to the present time, many of whose tenets are to be found in Freemasonry. These schools existed apart from any formal religious organization. Some of them existed as separate communities, and some simply as a society bound together by common views or elective affinity. Their teaching was predominantly esoteric, the secret doctrine of which was communicated only to select and discreet disciples. There were certain terms of admission, but no formal ceremony of initiation. To be initiated into these was to be thoroughly instructed, and that secret doctrine clearly apprehended.

The Hebrew Kabbalah is one of these ancient schools, and is pointed out by eminent Masons as one of the sources of Freemasonry and a channel through which the ideas and doctrines of the divine nature as held in the mysteries and eastern philosophies, have come down to and become incorporated in this modern institution. Buck states that "Freemasony in its purity has been derived from the Hebrew Kabbalah as a part of the great wisdom religion of remotest antiquity." (Mystic Masonry, p. 143). Garrison says that "it is in the speculations of the Kabbalah in which the traditions of the previous ages have come down to us, under the form in which we as Masons and especially in the chapter degrees are accustomed to receive them". "The points of identity are so many, so various and essential in the very structure of the order that I do not hesitate to infer, and I think every competently instructed Mason will agree with me, that at some period in their history, the association of the great builders of western Asia and which passed over later into the masonic guilds of Latin and Teutonic Europe, had made or found the mystery of the omnific word an integral element of their secret science, and that which is called the "Faculty of Abrac" under substantially the same form as the Kabbalah has preserved and still remains as an essential portion of the traditions and symbols of the Masonic order in different degrees." (Garrison, In Fort, p. 458). While Fort does not concede the connection of Freemasonry with the mysteries, he traces its descent in its outward forms from the ancient builder's guilds, but concedes the entrance into it of many heathen ideas, some of which are of a priapic character. Albert Pike drew largely from the writings of Eliphas Levi, the Abbe Constant, a great Kabbalist, and whom Buck considers as knowing more of the occult science than any one since the days of the old initiates, for illuminating and illustrating Freemasonry. A candid investigation convinces us that Freemasonry is indebted in a very large measure to the Kabbalah for its philosohpical ideas, its methods of interpreting the scriptures, its doctrines of emanations, its art speech, its cosmogonical views, and its veils and glyphs. In a certain sense it is a continuation of the Kabbalah under a different name and guise.

Another source from which Masonic ideas are derived and which also became a channel for their transmission is Gnosticism. As the Kabbalah was an attempt to harmonize the Hebrew religion with the peculiar philosophy of the east, so Gnosticism which was Jewish before it became Christian, was an attempt to harmonize the New Testament doctrines with the Platonic philosophy. This Gnostic theory of pairs, powerfully influenced the early church, and traces of it can be found in every period of her history. Heckethorn says that "Gnosticism permeates every vein of Freemasonry". The point we here wish to make is that the Kabbalah was the phallicized Judaism and Gnosticism was an attempt to phallicize Christianity so as to give it at least external harmony with the doctrines of the mysteries.

The Essenes is another one of the orders to which Freemasons look as a source of their doctrines and practices. In the ritual in our possession there is an account of the order from which we take the following. They devoted themselves to a life of contemplation and studying the mysteries of nature and revelation, they were ruled by a Rabban, they rose early in the morning and offered a prayer for the return of the light of day, they partook of a common frugal meal, had special lustrations and studied and expounded the holy scriptures. Their doctrines were completely esoteric and the most mysterious were taught only in their place of secret meeting. They were divided into three grades or ranks, and candidates were admitted only after their characters had been severely scrutinized. They were bound to the order by a solemn oath. According to this ritual, Freemasonry is a revival of this order, and its principles are adopted by this modern institution. (See Rit., pp. 5-12).

In addition to those mentioned above, the Pythagoreans, the professed followers of Pythagoras whom Freemasons regard as one of the prophets of Masonry, and various sects of the Mithraic philosophers, are sources from which Freemasonry has derived many of its ideas, and the media through which the ancient doctrines were transmitted to modern times. The channels through which these mystic ideas and religious notions passed into England are numerous, and in 1717 many of them became synthetized in Grand Lodge Freemasonry.

If Masons must go to these ancient cults in order to learn the secrets of the institution, to learn its philosophy, and the secret knowledge concealed in its ceremonies and symbols, surely the "profane" also can do so and learn what was in the minds of their founders, and get the thought the ancients intended to express by them. These mysteries we can study. We can learn their moral and religious ideas. We can trace their ceremonies and symbols back until we find in what "necessities of human nature they originated". We can ascertain what ideas concerning the divine nature pervaded these services, and what was venerated and worshiped as the Creator. All this we can do quite as well as the Mason. Sectarian bias need not affect the conclusions reached. The monumental evidence, the documentary material, and archaeological science is ample to permit a candid investigation and ascertainment of the facts.

CHAPTER VII.

THE MYSTERIES.

THE mysteries were religious institutions and may be regarded as the church of the ancient gentile nations. Their existence dates back to the remotest periods of antiquity, and their origin is shrouded in obscurity. They had so many elements in common, that it is believed they were derived either from one common original, or grew out of the common facts of nature upon which they were based. In them all there is found a peculiar though common conception of the divine nature, which constitutes their common bond of unity.

These institutions were widely distributed. They flourished in Chaldea, India, China, Japan, Egypt, Canaan, Africa, Phrygia, Greece, Rome, Mexico, and in the isles of the sea. They were not exactly uniform in their various rites, but subsantially the same religious idea is found in each of

(186)

them, so that a certain unity of thought pervaded them.

As to their mode of religious instruction they were esoteric. In them was taught not in a dogmatic way but by rite and symbol a religious conception more exalted than that held by the rank and file of the populace. These exalted doctrines were communicated to the truly initiated only. They were known and transmitted by the priests. The sages and philosophers taught in these institutions what they hardly dared teach in public, and the disciples were bound to secrecy concerning the things heard and learned. It was contended by some of the priests that if the secrets therein taught were divulged, the universe would fall.

The religious ideas of the mysteries and the rites expressing them, were based upon the facts of life, and in their primitive thought and simple expression would need no apology and no explanation. "The features of the mysteries that needs and is incapable of apology is that as known to us in later times they are not simple and direct. They are elaborate and artificial products of a diseased religion. They stand before us as a culmination of a long development, and the development has been a depravation, not an elevation of a ritual which had at first been naive and direct in its simple rudeness." (W. M. Ramsay, Hast. Bib. Dict. Extra Vol., p. 126).

These religious ideas and the ceremonies and symbols expressing them in these ancient institutions are now quite well ascertained and understood. Research, study and investigation of the remnants that have come down to our day, have removed the veil of obscurity in which they have been so long shrouded.

Freemasons, if they ever were, are no longer the sole possessors of the secrets, rites, ideas and doctrine of the mysteries. The nature, esoteric methods and doctrine of these institutions are now quite well known to scholars. The accounts given of them by the church fathers are corroborated by recent research and monumental evidence. "These accounts, hideous as they are, and concentrating attention only on the evils, must be accepted as correctly stating the facts; it would have ruined their effect if they had not been recognized as true statements of facts. Moreeover, they are corroborated in various details by pagan authorities, and as a whole they bear unmistakably the stamp of truth, but not the whole truth.'' (W. M. Ramsay, Hast. Bib. Dict., Vol. V, p. 123).

We shall now take up the mysteries in detail, and give what Mr. W. M. Ramsay ''one of the strongest, most useful, most comprehensive workers on the New Testament, and one who deals with questions of fact'' and other eminent scholars, have to say concerning them. Ramsay says: ''But with all their ugliness the Phrygian mysteries must always remain one of the most instructive and strange attempts of the human mind in an early stage of development, to form a religion, containing many gems of a high conception expressed in the rudest and grossest symbolism, deifying the natural processes of life in their primitive nakedness, and treating all that veiled, or modified, or restrained, or directed these processes, as inpertinent outrages of man on the divine simplicity''. (Cities and Bishoprics of Phrygia, Vol. 1: p. 89).

The two chief deities of the Phrygian

religion, which was of a melancholy and mystic tone, were Cybele, the Mother, the reproductive and nourishing power of Earth, and Sabazius, the Greek Dionysus, the Son, the life of nature, dying and reviving every year. The mimic rites of the worshippers enacted the story of his birth, and life, and death; the Earth, the Mother, is fertilized only by an act of violence by her own child; the representative of the god was probably slain each year by a cruel death, just as the god himeslf died. The rites were characterized by a frenzy of devotion, unrestrained enthusiasm, wild orgiastic dances, and wanderings in the forests, accompanied by music of the flute, cymbal and tambourine. The story of the life of these divine personages, formed the ritual of the Phrygian religion and was acted before the worshipper by the officials who played the parts of the various characters in the divine drama. Clement describes them correctly. (See Cities and Bishoprics of Phrygia, Vol. 1: p. 87).

The ritual of the Anatolian religion, so far as known, is founded entirely upon the idea that the divine nature that is the inclination born with the gods and expressed in their acts is the model according to which human life is to be arranged. What man has to do is to imitate the divine life and the acts of the divine beings and practice the divinely revealed methods. The ritual is the whole body of the divine teaching, and is the repetition before successive generations of mankind, of the original life of the divine beings. The successive priests in the cults were each of them representatives for the time being of the god; each wore the dress and insignia of his office, and even bore the name of his god. The primitive ritual was retained, though modified and corrupted by later additions in the mysteries, in which the primitive Anatolian religion became crystallized. Here the idea of the recurring death and birth of the divine nature was combined with the fact of the sequences of generation in human life. The drama of the divine life was set before the worshipper in the mysteries. The stream of human life goes on continuously changing yet permanent. Human life is regarded as permanent and everlasting as the divine life of nature, and the individuals made their lives right by performing their actions after the divine plan. (Based on Ramsay. Art. Religion of Greece in Hast. Bib. Dict.).

The symbols employed in the Phrygian mysteries to convey the ideas intended to be set forth, were realistic, seldom conventional images of the generative organs. Symbolism instead of dogmatic instruction was employed to impress the initiated with the facts and duties of life.

The Phrygian religion exercised a very strong influence upon Greece and the worship of Demeter at Eleusis was modified by influences from Asia Minor. Much similarity existed between the Eleusinian and Phrygian mysteries, while there were also differences. After Christ, only the Phrygian and Egyptian rites retained much hold upon the Graeco-Roman world. (See Art. Phrygia in Ency. Brit., 9th Ed.).

The Eleusinian mysteries of Greece upon which Masonic writers lay much stress and characterize as the Freemasonry of that day, are generally conceded as the most noble of them all. But the testimony of Clement of Alexandria, and others, is that they were based upon the adulterous and incestuous acts of Zeus and Demeter, and commemorated the obscenity and indecencies of these deities, which were enacted in realistic form before the neophyte.

Every act of the great Eleusinian festival even to the shameless exposure of female nakedness, reproduced the incidents of the story of Demeter. This was not improbably an old religious ceremony, as we find it also was enacted in Egypt by women at the festivities of Bubastis, the daughter of Isis. In the processions of Athene and Dionysus, there were exhibited precisely the same symbols which mark the worship of Vishnu and his sakti in India, of Isis in Egypt, and of the Teutonic Hertha.

The story upon which the Eleusinian mysteries are based is as follows: Zeus violates his mother Demeter, and as a penalty for his wantonness, pretends to mutilate himself, but instead of doing so perpetrates a fraud and deception upon the victim of his lust, by tearing away the orchites of a ram and casting them at the breast of Demeter. Demeter enraged and chagrined at her disgrace, conceals herself during the winter in a cave. In the spring her child was born

13

who, when grown to womanhood, was stolen away by Pluto. Demeter in search of her lost daughter breaks down with fatigue near Eleusis, and sits by a well overcome with grief. Here she is hospitably received by three natives who try to cheer her and induce her to drink. In order to please her, one of the natives, Baubo, indecently exposes her person to Demeter at which she appears much pleased and quaffs the proffered cup.

The one great specific feature in the Eleusinian rite was the shockingly indecent and dramatic symbolism which described or symbolized the revivification of the earth after the death of winter. "The impregnation of the mother goddess forms a part of the sacred ritual enacted in the mysteries, but everywhere it was represented as an act of violence, stealth and deception." (W. M. Ramsay, Contem. Review Oct. 1893, p. 571). This symbolism assumed forms which would explain their meaning to the initiated. There was no dogmatic teaching in the mysteries. The thought was left to be determined by the wit of the candidate. But the revival of nature would be inseparably associated with the thought of the life into which the human soul passes through the gateway of death; and in a festival were everything was dramatic, the one truth or fact would be expressed by signs no less than the other. In the great Dionysiac festival at Athens, the phallus was solemnly carried in procession. The mystic chest or box answers to the yoni as the phallus to the linga of the Hindoos. (See Ency. Brit., Vol. 8, p. 120, 9th Ed.).

The password or token of recognition of those initiated into the Eleusinian mysteries was "I have fasted, I have drunk the cup, I have received from the box, having done, I put it into the basket and out of the basket into the chest". (Clement, Exhor. to the Heathen, Chap. 2). That these were phallic symbols is certain from Clement's description of the contents of the "box". So obtuse became the public sense of decency, that in Attica the phallus and other obscene emblems were carried abroad in processions both by men and women. "In the mysteries of the Athenians the members paid shameless worship to a boy torn to pieces, and a woman in distress, and to parts of the body that in truth can not be mentioned for shame." (Clement Id.).

The secret of the Eleusinian mysteries probably consisted simply in certain ritual acts which appeared mysterious to the worshipper, because their original meaning had been forgotten and which were chiefly impressive because the worshipper believed that through them he reached closer union with the divine nature, and received the hope of eternal life. (Jevon's Introduction to the Study of Religion, p. 362).

The myth of Osiris upon which the Egyptian mysteries were founded, is given by Lange as follows: (Ency. Brit., Vol. XVII, p. 158) "Osiris introduced civilization into Egypt, and then wandered over the earth making men acquainted with agriculture and the arts. On his return Typhon had a plot for him. He had a beautifully carved chest made which exactly fitted Osiris, and at an entertainment offered to give it to any one who could lie down in it. As soon as Osiris tried, Typhon had the box nailed up and threw it into the Tanaite branch of the Nile. Isis wandered mourning in search of the body. At length she found the chest, which in her absence was again discoverd by Typhon. He mangled the body of Osiris and tossed the fragments about. Whenever Isis found a portion of Osiris, she buried it. The phallus alone she did not find, but she consecrated a model thereof, and thus phallus worship arose in Egypt''. This myth of Osiris is viewed as a picture of the daily life of the sun, combatting darkness yet at last succumbing to it, to appear again in renewed splendor, as the young Horus, his son. It is also viewed as a picture of human life, its perpetual conflict and final seeming destruction, to be restored in the new youth of brighter existence. Isis is the same as Demeter, earth mother or nature. Osiris is the sun, the fertilizer of earth, and generator of earthly life.

The Egyptian rite was a dramatic representation of these events and its purpose is sufficiently obvious.

Clement pronounced a sentence of severest condemnation on the mysteries, of which to all appearance he had accurate knowledge. These as he represents them, had sown far and wide the seeds of wickedness and corruption in the life of man. They were institutes full of deceit and imposture in which a mangled boy, Zagreus, a wailing woman, Demeter, and members which modesty refuses to name, were adored. Tertullian, Arnobius, Eusebius, and Firmicus make precisely the same statements. Gregory of Nazianzen as he mentions the scandalous things which the Demeter of the mysteries did and submitted to, says, ''I take shame to myself for drawing the mystery of darkness into the light. Eleusis knows it, and the epoptai (initiated) who conceal these things which indeed deserve concealment.'' We learn from the heathen's own mouth how often the Greek mysteries and their purport was exposed by the initiated who had become converted to Christianity, in the very assemblies of the Christians. (See Doellinger, Gentile and Jew, Vol. 1: p. 144). These charges made against the mysteries by the early Christian writers are sustained by the facts ascertained by thorough investigation.

The mysteries of the Cabiri, celebrated in the island of Samothracia, were second only in importance and renown to the Eleusinians. Their exact nature is not positively known, but it is certain that the secret worship was dedicated not only to Rhea or Cybele, but also to Demeter and Kora. These rites, judging from objects found where they were celebrated, were orgiastic in character. The Cabiri were the great and mighty gods, the supreme powers of nature who were adored at first, without specific names. Their worship was doubtless of Phoenician origin. Axieros, the mother goddess, the Creatrix, who occupied the chief place in Samothracia, was afterward identified with Demeter, Rhea or Cybele. This Cabiric religion was introduced into Thebes by the Cadmeans, where it flourished until the time of Cambysses. Those who know anything about the Samothracian mysteries will also remember that the generic name of the Cabiri was the Holy Fires. These holy fires are the two principles, male and female, essential to the kindling of human life. Heckethorn says that there were four gods, Cashmala the last of the four was slain by his three brothers, who carried away with them the reproductive organs; and that this allegorical murder was celebrated in the secret rites. Cashmala is the same as Osiris, Adonis, Attis, and Hiram, and whose murder symbolizes the loss of the generative power. (Sec. Soc., Vol. 1:58).

The Sidonian mysteries to which Mr. Sickels directs us if we would get the "thought" of Freemasonry, were one of the several variants of the Baal cult that prevailed in the Canaanite lands. This Baal worship was the Canaanite type of sun worship and was decidedly phallic. The Baal was the male principle of life and reproduction, and was viewed as abiding in the sun as his heavenly abode, and in the phallus as his earthly abode. The solar disk was the symbol of the former, and a slender stone placed upon or near the altar, was the symbol of the latter His consort was the earth, the nourishing principle. The symbol of this was the ashera or poles, and a small cone-shaped stone, placed on or near the altar, representing the female breast. In this cult there was a close connection in thought and rite between the sun as a generative deity, and the earth as a nourishing deity, and the phallus as a generative organ, and the breast as a nourishing organ. The rites consisted in men and women exchanging garments, and in exposing to Baal that part of the body which decent people take the utmost precautions to conceal. These rites were accompanied by immoral and licentious indulgences at his shrine, for Baal was the patron of the grossest sensuality and of systematic prostitution. The relation of the Baal and his mate the Ashera, was set forth as the example and the motive for unbridled sensuality. It encouraged and made lawful and right, sexual uncleanness. This cult was introduced into Israel by Jezebel, the wife of Ahab, who was an ardent devotee. It aroused the vigorous opposition of Elijah and Elisha, and culminated in the overthrow and captivity of Israel.

The Mithraic mysteries were the institutions in which the worship of the sun in its Persian aspect, became concrete. The worship of this god can be traced back to a very early period, when it presents itself as a pure monotheism. It came in contact with other faiths and by assimilation of other elements degenerated into a sensual and debasing nature worship. It became very popular, and employed a very elaborate ritual and expressed its ideas of the divine nature in an extensive symbolism. The worship was very probably conducted according to elaborate ritualistic prescriptions.

The rites of Mithras were celebrated in a cave. Mithras proper was the generative principle in the sun, and always conceived of as distinct from the sun, but clothed in the light of the sun. The god was conceived as always performing the mystic sacrifices through which the good will finally triumph. The human soul was viewed as separated from the divine nature, to which it can only re-ascend through a series of probationary degrees of penance, scourgings and fastings. The first of these was the lowest and admitted those who passed it as soldiers fighting for Mithras. The second and third degrees were that of the Bull and the Lion. Other grades could be passed which if accomplished the soul became pure fire, and re-united with the divine nature. This cult spread over the Roman world during the second and third centuries after Christ, and its influence was felt for a long period throughout Europe.

CHAPTER VIII.

THE RELIGION OF THE MYSTERIES.

THE rites practiced in the mysteries were intended to express in concrete form the religious ideas that prevailed in these institutions. They consisted of words and acts which supplemented one another and formed an intelligible whole. They were based upon the acts of the divine beings and became the models to which the initiated conformed his own life and acts.

In these mysteries the multitude of deities was conceived as the forms of the ultimate single divine life dividing itself into male and female to become the origin of life on the earth. This was the theory of the Orphic theology and many facts show that it moulded the Eleusinian ritual. The religion of the mysteries placed man face to face with the actual facts of life, the facts of generation, birth, life and death. The goddess or the female was conceived of as the nourishing or productive power in nature, whose fertilization is always represented by an act of violence, stealth and disguise, because of which the victim is enraged, humiliated and conceals herself. The forms vary, but the idea remains essentially the same, for the ancient world as a whole, saw something supernatural, something demoniacal in the act of generation.

The god represents the generative power in nature, the masculine principle, essential to the fertilization of the nourishing power. In an examination of the rites of all the mysteries, Asiatic, Hellenic and Egyptian, we find one feature common and essential to all, and upon which they are founded, namely a god of nature violently deprived of his power of generation. This deprivation is either through mutilation or death; but the god reappears again either in the form or person of a son as his substitute, or in a new and resurrected form. A mutilated god is the basis of all the myths that are told to explain the ritual.

The mysteries celebrated in Egypt were all attached to the legend of Osiris, Isis and Typhon. Osiris was the sun, the generator of all mundane life. He was slain by

Typhon, the destroying power in nature, and thus deprived of his generative power. But Osiris reappeared in his son, Horus, in renewed power and glory. Isis was the feminine nature power longing for the masculine impregnating principle, seeking it in her wanderings and mourning in its absence. From Osiris whose prostrate form she raised, Isis took his essence, conceived and brought forth a son, whom she suckled in secret, and who became the substitute for Osiris. Osiris is the masculine generative principle personified and deified. When slain by Typhon his generative power was lost, but it is recovered in a "future generation", namely his son Horus.

In the myth of Zeus and Demeter the same ideas appear, but somwhat modified by local conditions. Demeter, the earth mother, the feminine or nourishing power, in an act of stealth and violence, is violated by her son the god Zeus. As a penalty for his wantonness he pretends to mutilate himself, but perpetrates a fraud. The offspring of this incestuous act is a daughter, Kora, whom the father Zeus also violates, and a son, Dionysus, the life of nature is the offspring. Here Zeus, the generative principle, the divine father reappears in the son, Dionysus, while the feminine principle, represented by Demeter, reappears in the daughter Kora. Thus the divine life divides itself and reappears in the life of man on earth, and perpetually reproduces itself through the male and female forms, the "necessities of human nature" upon which the mysteries are based, and out of which they have arisen. In the myth of Zeus and Demeter, the masculine principle is viewed as the dominant one.

In the Phrygian mysteries we find essentially the same ideas only that the universe is viewed as contained in the female principle. Here the earth mother is Cybele. She is the mother of Zeus. By her he has a son Sabazius. Sabazius violently violates the mother Cybele whom she in her indignation slays. Sabazius is the life of nature annually dying and reviving, while the female principle continues. Here the son is slain and revived again. The life of Zeus, the divine father reappears in Sabazius the life of nature, while Cybele continues as its nourishing principle.

Eliminating from the mysteries all the accretions of time and variations introduced because of locality, and the admixture of foreign elements, we find that in their earlier and purer form, they were based upon the facts involved in the generation of life. Sexual passion was regarded as the expression of the divine force, and hence the facts and acts of generation were made the basis and the model of the religious rites, for in these acts, or in the imitation of these sexual acts it was belived that the worshiper came into mystic communion with the divine nature. By partaking of these rites a man was believed to part with his former sins, to form a special union with the deity, and made to partake of the divine nature, and started in a career in which he could not fail to grow morally better. This divine nature was conceived of as the deity and enthusiastically worshiped. The life of nature was conceived of as the divine life, and the acts of generation the means by which the divine nature perpetuated the divine life. In the masculine and feminine principles were perceived the two elements into which the divine nature had divided itself for the per-

petuation of the divine life, and hence their
union essential to the generation of life was
regarded simply as the act of the divine
nature. These sexual acts were regarded as
divine acts modeled after the acts and
examples of the gods and goddesses, and in
the mysteries were expressed in allegorical,
ceremonial, or mimic forms. "The ground
upon which the teachings of the mysteries
were based was the knowledge of the whole
state, the rise, the workings and the processes of all nature, together with the unity
that pervades heaven and earth." (Heckethorn).

In the speculations of the philosophers
and priests, this perpetual generation of the
divine life by the divine nature and its
nourishment, was intimately associated with
the generative processes and the generative
organs. That the ceremonies might express
the facts and processes of life true to nature,
the phallus became an essential factor in the
rites of the mysteries, expressing the generator of life; the yoni, the breasts, ears of
corn and other objects were employed to
express the life nourishing ideas. The
myths and legends were related to explain
14

their place and meaning.   These myths
were usually the story of an outraged goddess, and of a god who was deprived of his
generative power either by self-mutilation
or perishing as the victim of the wrath of
the outraged goddess. This story may have
been originally an allusion to the sun which
was deprived of its vivifying power by the
three months of winter, but it also betrays a
close association in the religious thought of
the mysteries, of the generative power of the
sun, or of the god, with the generative power
of the phallus.   The divine nature, the
divine life, human nature,human life, and
the sexual functions were all most intimately associated in the religious ideas set
forth in the mysteries.

We find then in these institutions not
only a common fact in nature as their foundation, a common legend as the explanation
for their rites, but also a common religious
conception pervading them all and binding
them into an essential unity.

This peculiar religious conception common to all the mysteries is termed Phallicism. It took organic and ritualistic form

in the mysteries, and can be discerned in varied and modified forms in the different religions and cults from the earliest ages down to the present. The 'wickedness' of the Antediluvians, the Nimrodic apostacy, the apostate worship fostered by King Solomon, the Baal Peor of the Moabites and apostate Jews, the 'iniquity' of the Amorites and Canaanitcs, the Osiris, Isis, Aten and Apis worship of Egypt, the ancient religions of Japan and of China, the Cybele worship of the Phrygians, the Demeter worship and its various modifications among the Greeks, the religion of the Romans, of the Druids, of the Aztecs, Quiches, all were phallic. In all of them homage was paid either to the phallus as an object of adoration and worship, or as the symbol of the creative principle, or to the sun as the generative principle. In this phallicism we find their common bond, their essential unity, although very diverse in the outward ceremonies. "If there is one point more certain than another, it is that wherever tree and serpent worship has been found, the cultus of phallus and ship, of the linga and yoni in connection with the worship of the sun has been found also." (Coxe, Aryan Myths, p. 362).

Phallicism, fundamentally, is the deification, adoration and worship of the procreative or self propagating power of the life of nature, that secret mysterious energy, endowment or power which animates all vegetable and animal creatures, and which perpetually dying, renews itself in new, similar yet different forms. Phallicists view this mysterious energy as the divine nature, and usually in the conception of the divine triad, the creator, the preserver and the destroyer of life, and worship and adore it as the deity. Phallicists recognize no author of life separate and apart from this energy in nature, but adore it as a great self-originating, self-preserving, self-destroying, self-reproducing, unifying and united divine power, pervading the universe.

One of the most ancient as well as the most widespread forms of phallicism was sun worship, heliolatry, or light worship, Mithraism. It is evident that the most wise and learned of the heliolaters viewed the sun as the life giver to all terrestrial creatures, and the source of all terrestrial life, and therefore divine. Light, in which the fructifying power of the sun was borne to earth, was viewed not only as a symbol of life, but also as a bearer of it. Heliolatry was a natural outgrowth of the mystery involved in the generative and fructifying power of the sun. The vulgar doubtless worshiped the sun as such, or light as such, without conceiving this relationship of the sun to earthly life, but it is plain that the priests who conducted the worship, adored the mysterious generative power in the sun as a divine living potency, which they regarded as deity and to which they gave a mystic name. Light worship and sun worship are forms of phallicism and were very widely diffused among the ancient nations. The sun and light were the symbols under which the generative energy or principle was worshiped, and his mystic name designated the life essence the sun was supposed to possess.

Another very ancient form of phallicism was the worship of the generative power in man. The generation of life, doubtless, was one of the first mysteries that attracted man's attention. The reproduction of his own life in another, similar but different form, begetting offspring in his own image, was to him a profound mystery. This holy function, like many others, became perverted, and instead of adoring and worshiping the Author and Giver of life, man deified his own generative power, adored and worshiped it under realistic and conventional symbols of the generative organs. Phallicism in one of its specific forms is the deification, adoration and worship of the generative power of man, and of the organs involved in the procreation of life under realistic or conventional symbols, and under veiled phallic language and ceremonies.

Still another form was animal and plant worship. It was not the animal or the plant itself that was worshiped, but the generative or reproductive power inhering in it. This reproductive power was conceived of as the divine nature and regarded as the deity. The life was viewed as the manifestation of this divine nature resident in the animal or plant. The deity was regarded as dwelling in the animal or plant, and re-manifesting himself in the offspring. The reproductive organs naturally became venerated as the local habitation of the deity, his mystic shrine, and therefore sacred. Animal worship, plant worship, beetle worship, reptile worship, all were in their deeper meaning modified or varied forms of phallicism. In these cults flowers were sacred because in them were the organs essential to the reproduction of the plant life. The evergreen tree was sacred, because in it the life continued, over against deciduous trees which annually seemed to die, and revive. Animals, especially those in which the sexual powers were strongly marked, were sacred, in that they exhibited in an unusual degree the divine nature. In view of the conception of the unity of the life of nature, animals and plants became viewed as brothers or fathers, and totemism resulted.

In a number of cases, owing to certain environments and to the tendency to syncretize these religions, cults arose in which the several forms of phallicism became combined. In the Baal cult tree, man and sun worship were united. The solar disk was the visible symbol of Baal. The ashera or trees were symbols of the tree life. The slender and cone-shaped stone images were the symbols of the man and the woman. In the calf worship introduced by Jeroboam there was an effort to clothe the Jehovah worship in the garb of the phallic apis worship of Egypt. In the Eleusinian mysteries the reproductive power in nature and in man were worshiped. The former under the mystic symbols of the ear of wheat, the vine and the cakes, and the latter under the conventional or realistic symbols of the human generative organs.

"The essence of the Anatolian religion, which took organic form in the Phrygian mysteries, was the adoration of the life of nature, that life subject apparently to death, yet ever dying but reproducing itself in new forms, different and yet the same. This perpetual self-identity under varying forms, this annihilation of death through the power of self-reproduction was the object of an enthusiastic worship, characterized by remarkable self-abandonment and immersion in the divine, by a mixture of obscene symbolism, and sublime truths, by negation of the moral distinctions and family ties that exist in more developed society; but do not exist in the free life of nature. The mystery of self-reproduction, of eternal amid temporary diversity, is the key to explain all the repulsive legends and ceremonies that cluster around that worship and all the manifold manifestations or diverse embodiments of the ultimate single divine life that are carved on the rocks of Asia Minor, especially at Pteria." (W. M. Ramsay, Cities and Bish. of Phrygia, Vol. 1:87).

In the Phrygian religion the mother and the maiden are the divine prototypes of earthly life; the divine nature is as complex as humanity and contains within itself all the elements which appear in our earthly life. But how does Kora, the daughter originate? There must be in the ultimate divine nature, the male element as well as the female. From the union of the two originates the daughter goddess. But even this is not sufficient; the son also is needed, and he is the offspring of the daughter goddess, and her father.

The essence of the ancient religion of Phrygia was a deification of the perpetual self-identity of the life generating and life nourishing principle, and the formal worship thereof consisted in the imitation of the natural processes of life, and of the adoration of the organs incident to those functions, in their realistic form.

The conceptions of this divine nature were almost as varied and complex as was the divine nature itself. The divine nature in the Phrygian cult, was conceived as female, as the great mother, the nourishing power of nature. The masculine principle was the life of nature. This was essential to fertilize the nourishing power and incite it into activity. In the nourishing power of the mother the life of nature was perpetuated. But the mother combined within herself the male and female element, which would divide itself in the male and female offspring. The process of the divine life evolves itself in the reciprocal action of the divine pair, and in the offspring in which are reproduced the same nourishing and fecundating powers. The god-father, the goddess-mother, the divine son and the goddess daughter are all assumed as essential to the drama of the divine life in the numerous cults and myths.

The secret doctrine or the essence of the

religious teachings in the Eleusinian cult was the idea of the divine in the creative energy, the worship of nature in her mysterious creative and nourishing powers and activities. This was the underlying thought of the rites, and that which they were intended to set forth. The symbols by which these facts were expressed were the phallus and the chest or basket, the symbol of the womb. The belief was that when a man died, he became a god and his deification was regarded as the result of his initiation, and his grave was regarded as a temple. (See Ramsay, Hastings Bib. Dict., Extra Vol., p. 125). As his conception by his mother became the gateway to his manhood, so his initiation in the mysteries, became the gateway to his deification.

This phallic idea was the essence of the religion of the mysteries. In Egypt Osiris represented the masculine, and Isis the feminine principle whose union were essential to the begetment of life. In India each of the three gods in the triad were regarded as masculine, and each one had his sakti or female consort. The rites based upon these god-ideas, and intended to express the divine activities in the reproductive processes of life, were practically identical throughout the mysteries, and the identity of rites which was the worship of the generative power, under the symbol of the phallus proves the identity of the doctrine. (See Cox, Aryan Myths).

The phallus was an essential part in the rites and symbolism of the mysteries. Its office was to convey to the initiated a profound and sacred meaning. It was a common object of worship and of ornament. Originally it had no other meaning than that union of male and female upon which depended the procreation of life. As an ornament it was worn by women especially upon festive occasions, and as a religious emblem it symbolized the procreating power of nature whose worship extended through all natural religions from their rudest beginnings until the decay of heathenism. (Winzschel). In Greece, phallic processions were general, the images ranging from three inches to thirty feet in height. In the feasts of Dionysus-Osiris they were especially prominent, and designed to attract attention. (See Grimm's Deutsche Mythologie, II, p. 1209; Schliemann's Ilios, p. 277). The entire symbolism of the mysteries, even to the processions attending them were phallic. Whatever may have been the primitive thought or the religious notions of the mysteries, whether the remnant of primitive revelation, or the harmless veneration of the generative power upon which the mysteries were based, they were the artificial product of a diseased religion.

The ancient Semitic mysteries or cults gave a prominent place to the adoration of those powers in nature which either fertilize or produce, and upon these the religions were based and to them the rites were conformed.

The gods were male and female, and the worship of the sexual was prominent in these cults. The religious ideas were based upon the sexual facts, and grew out of a profound veneration for the generative principle. Ritual prostitution which was possibly a decadence, was a recognized and wide spread institution, and grew out of a purely religious point of view. At the shrine of Baal and Astarte in Phoenicia and similar sanctuaries elsewhere, sexual intercourse was a part of the rite. In the times of Abraham, Isaac, Jacob and Joseph they swore by the sexual organs, which seems to have been the legal oath. The Arabs to this day swear by the phallus of Allah Phallicism with all its horrible and abominable accompaniments was the religion of the non-Israelitish Semites, and it was a herculean task for the prophets of Jehovah to prevent it from becoming the religion of Israel. While there are evidences that phallicism existed among the Israelites, they do not prove that all Israel were phallicists. (See Jewish Ency., Art., Chastity; McAllister, Bible Side Lights from the Hill of Gezer; Jeremias, The O. T. in the Light of the East, Vol. 1, p. 123).

The Kabbalah is a system of theosophy or Jewish mysticism whose cardinal points embrace the doctrine of the deity, the divine emanations, and other questions such as cosmogony and anthropology. On its philosophical side it is an attempt to explain the existence of the universe without admitting any direct contact between God and Creation. On its religious side it is a system of the mystical interpretation of the Old Testament, so as to harmonize these sacred writings with universal reason and with the several cults of the eastern nations with which Judaism more or less came in contact. These cults were esoteric, and phallic, and the Kabbalah naturally partook of the same character, for the pagan conception of the mystery of sex, passed in a refined form through the Talmud into this Jewish speculation. So also the Gnostic idea of pairs, was adopted by the Talmud and was later developed into a system by the Kabbalah. The doctrines of the Kabbalah were communicated to the few only.

The origin of the Kabbalah like that of the mysteries, is shrouded in obscurity. The principles upon which it is based, are very ancient. The Jews claim for it a great antiquity, that it came down as a revelation from the remote past, to elect saints, and preserved only to a privileged few, as a key to the correct understanding of the scriptures. The term seems to point out not only its descent, by oral tradition, but also its ascent to ancient sources. While its highest development seems to have been reached about the eleventh century, A. D., eminent scholars concede that it derived its origin from the eastern religions with which Judaism came into contact during the Babylonian captivity. The Hindoo philosophy exercised more influence upon the Zohar, the official book of the Kabbalah, than any other.

The Kabbalah remained an absolute secret cult until in the thirteenth century when a quarrel arose between some of its adherents. Owing to this quarrel, and to the conversion of certain Kabbalists to the Christian religion, the system was made public, and its secrets divulged. Its principles were widely diffused and accepted, and it had many adherents from that time until in the eighteenth century. Among these adherents were many of the most prominent and learned men in public life and in the professions. For a long time the Kabbalah was regarded by many Christian scholars as a correct method for interpreting the scriptures. This opinion is no longer held by any Christian scholars of note.

We here give a summary of the teachings of the Kabbalah in those features in which we find a striking similarity to the ancient Hindoo theosophy, to the Greek divine genealogies, to the Phrygian conceptions of the divine nature and the origin of earthly life, and to the fundamental conceptions of the operations of the Great Architect of the Universe in Freemasonry.

The Unknowable, the concealed of all concealed, was designated as the En Soph, or Ain Soph. When he assumed a form, he produced everything in the form of male and female, as things could not continue in any other form. The first emanation from this En Soph was the Crown, or the Holy Aged. This was an androgyn, a male and female potency. It contained within itself the two principles essential to life, the male and the female. The first differentiation or expansion, was the division of the Holy Aged into Wisdom the father, and Intelligence the mother, the source of all subsequent emanations. Here is the first triad, Wisdom, the Crown, and Intelligence. These two potencies Wisdom and Intelligence, united by the Crown, the first potency, produce the first pair of offspring, the masculine Love, and the feminine Justice. From the androgynous Crown emanates the sixth potency, Beauty, also an androgyn. Love

15

and Justice, united by Beauty, form the second triad, from whom emanate Firmness, masculine, and Splendor, feminine. From Beauty emanates Foundation, and from Foundation, Kingdom, which embraces all the other emanations or potencies. Foundation is the genital of the archetypal man. This organ is the basis and source of all things, "all marrow, all sap, and all power are congregated in this spot. Hence all powers which exist originated through genital organs". (C. D. Ginsberg). "Foundation" in the Kabbalah is the reproductive principle, the root of all existence. "Foundation" is the medium of the union of sexes, and the means by and through which these emanations are continued throughout time and in the animate world.

This "foundation" in the Kabbalah, is the third successive direct emanation from the androgynous Crown, and retains its androgynous nature. It is unlike the other emanations which are distinctly masculine or feminine. This foundation contains within itself like the ultimate divine nature, the male and female principles which through the reciprocal action of the male and female element in union, engenders the offspring. It contains within itself as a totality in a latent state all the powers, intelligences, faculties and principles that manifest themselves in the offspring. It is a recurrence or reappearance of the divine nature contained in the first emanation, the Crown. It is therefore the goal of the emanations, growing out of the Crown, and the Crown, Source and Foundation of all subsequent life and beings begotten by it. It may therefore be viewed as the local habitation of the deity. In the Kabbalah the "foundation" was viewed as the Living God, and with this deity Freemasonry identifies its Great Architect of the Universe. The "foundation" is simply the self-identity of the Crown reappearing in each successive generation, the generative power found, which was lost in the generative act of the Holy Aged when it divided into Wisdom and Intelligence.

This system of speculation, as is obvious to every attentive reader, has a phallic basis, and attempts to explain the world of created intelligence, as originally coming into being not through the creative fiat of God, but by emanations through sex principles, and as primarily proceeding from the unknowable En Soph, and his substance. It is an effort to explain in the abstract what is attempted in the concrete in the ancient myths, in the genealogy of the gods and goddesses, the origin of earthly, especially human life. The Holy Aged or Crown in the Kabbalah is essentially the same and identical with the divine nature of the Phrygian mystery cults, containing within itself all the elements found in human nature. As the divine nature divided itself into the male and female principles in order that the life of nature might continue, so human nature divides itself into the male and female perpetually, so that human life may continue. The essence of human nature is in the "foundation" where it is androgynous, but in the generation of a new entity, it divides itself into male and female through reciprocal action of the parents, and thus the constant alternations of sex takes place. The persistence of this sexual differentiation and the mutual affinity for the opposite in the sex principles is in the emanation termed Kingdom. It embraces all the other emanations.

These emanations taken as a whole constitute the Archetypal Man, the Heavenly Man, the Adam Kadmon, the Tree of Life, the pattern after which all human beings are built by this invisible architect which inheres within the living entities.

These emanations are generally arranged in three columns or groups. Those constituting the right side of the Adam Kadmon are masculine, those constituting the left of the Adam Kadmon, are the feminine, and the androgynous emanations form the middle pillar. These three groups of emanations constitute the pillars of the universe, and are designated the Wisdom (masculine), the Beauty (androgynous), and Strength (feminine) pillars, and in Freemasonry are represented respectively by the Doric, the Corinthian, and the Ionic columns or orders of architecture.

CHAPTER IX.

THE MASONIC MYSTERIES.

THE mysteries of Freemasonry in their last analysis are based upon the facts and processes involved in the mysterious and secret forces connected with the generation, preservation and cessation of life; the mysteries involved in the origin, nature and destiny of the human soul, and of its relation to deity. These are the fundamental secrets concealed among Masons which have never been found out. But these secrets of nature upon which the institution is based, are spoken of under the legends of "The Temple", of "The building of Solomon's Temple", of "Hiram Abiff, the chief architect of Solomon's Temple," of "Solomon King of Israel," and of "Hiram King of Tyre". The various things in the Masonic ritual ascribed to these personages, and related concerning the temple and its workmen are about as well authenticated as are the myths of Zeus and Demeter, Cybele and Sabazius, Osiris and Isis in the cults in which they respectively figure. Beyond the few statements in the Old Testament concerning Hiram Abiff, there is absolutely nothing known of him. Outside of Freemasonry history is silent concerning him. Very little also is known concerning Hiram King of Tyre.

Rabbinic and Masonic tradition however relates much concerning these two Hirams and King Solomon, which can not be vouched for by the records of history. According to the former and some other sources Hiram King of Tyre lived to a great age, surviving King Solomon many years. In his advanced age he deified himself. He became haughty because he had furnished cedars for the Temple at Jerusalem, and for this self-deification God permitted the temple to be destroyed in order that he might punish him. The punishment consisted in a piece of flesh being cut off his body every day and which he was compelled to eat until he died a miserable death.

The rabbinic legend of Hiram Abiff is to the effect that while all the workmen were killed so that they should not build another temple devoted to idolatry, Hiram himself was raised to heaven like Enoch. It is to this legend that the traditions of Hiram in Freemasonry may be traced. Heckethorn says that Hiram is remembered nowhere except in Freemasonry. In this institution his death concerning which there is a mystery involved, is sincerely mourned.

Other traditions which are related concerning Hiram are as follows. He had the workmen under perfect control, and would frequently assemble them by describing in the air the mystic tau, T. This so impressed the queen of Sheba, that she fell in love with Hiram, and repudiated her engagement with King Solomon. The latter was so incensed at this that he resolved to humble Hiram, and in doing so, became *particeps criminis* in his death.

Hiram also before his death, threw the golden triangle which he wore suspended from his neck and on which was engraved the master's word, into a deep well. The triangle was subsequently found and Solomon caused it to be placed upon a triangular altar erected in a secret vault, built under a most retired part of the temple. This triangle was further concealed by a cubical

stone, on which the sacred law was inscribed. The vault was then walled up. This
triangle was afterwards found in excavating for the second temple, and forms a part
of the legend upon which Royal Arch Masonry is based. Solomon also knew that the
temple would be destroyed and therefore he
had an underground receptacle built in
which the ark of the covenant was concealed
when the destruction was impending.

These traditions based upon Heckethorn
the Jewish Encyclopedia, and some other
sources are here given, as they all figure
quite prominently in Freemasonry. Much
of this language evidently is esoteric and
conveys a meaning which is intelligible only
in a phallic sense, the sense in which we
think it is intended to be understood.

The story of Hiram Abiff is related as
follows by Anderson. At the building of
King Solomon's Temple Hiram was super-
intending architect. Three craftsmen having determined to secure the master's word
from him at all hazards, placed themselves
at the three principal entrances of the edifice in order to waylay the illustrious architect. His fidelity caused him to be assass-

inated with a mallet. A search was made
for his remains by a party traveling towards
each of the cardinal points, who discovered
Hiram's tomb. It is then added that the
artizan was brought from his grave as all
other Masons when they receive the master's word.—(Anderson, Lect. on third degree). With this the esoteric lecture of the
Grand Orient of France, prepared in 1801,
agrees entirely. The whole incident with
some flourishes, is enacted in the ceremony
of the third degree.

In the ceremonial of the third degree this
myth of Hiram figures quite prominently,
and these things are related to explain the
rites. The story of Hiram's career is enacted, in which the candidate plays the role
of Hiram Abiff, the master of the lodge the
part of King Solomon, and fifteen of the
lodge members the part of the craftsmen,
three of whom are the ruffians. But as to
the real secrets and principles of Freemasonry in the higher degrees, Pike says, Blue
Lodge Masonry is dumb. "Never were any
pretenses to the possession of mysterious
knowledge so baseless and so absurd as those
of the Blue and Royal Chapters." This

pretense to the possession of mysterious knowledge is designed to divert the candidate's attention from the real Masonic doctrine. We transcribe in a condensed form the details of this tragedy as it is given in the ritual. (P. 155 seq).

It was the usual custom of that great and good man at high twelve, when the craft were called from labor to refreshment, to enter into the Sanctum Sanctorum or Holy of Holies to offer up his adorations to deity and draw his designs upon his trestleboard. He then passed out of the south gate to the workmen as you will now do. The candidate is then taken by the left hand by the senior deacon and is conducted a short distance and is met by a brother representing Jubela, who accosts him: "Grand Master Hiram Abiff, I am glad to meet you thus alone. I have long sought this opportunity. You promised us, that when the temple is completed we should receive the secrets of a Master Mason whereby we can travel in foreign countries and receive wages as such. Behold the temple is almost completed and we have not received what we served for. At first I did not doubt your veracity but now I do. I demand of you the secrets of Masonry." After some parleying between them, the person representing Jubela strikes Hiram with the twenty-four inch gauge across the throat, and the candidate is hurried by the senior deacon to the west where he is assaulted by a brother representing Jubelo, who demands the secrets also. To him Hiram replies that they can not be given except in the presence of Solomon, King of Israel, Hiram, King of Tyre and himself. Jubelo replies that his life is in danger, the avenues of the temple are closely guarded, and escape is impossible, and therefore demands the secrets of a Master Mason. After some parleying here, Jubelo strikes him a blow with a square across the breast. The candidate is then violently hurried away to the east where he is accosted by another brother, representing Jubelum, who also demands the secret, and upon its refusal strikes him a blow with something representing the setting maul on the forehead from the effect of which he falls to the floor. The body is then carried by the three ruffians to a retired corner and buried in the rubbish of the temple. The ruffians then retire until low twelve, when they return, carry the body in a due westerly course from the temple to a brow of a hill where Jube-lum had dug a grave six feet due east and west and six feet perpendicular, where they bury the 'slain' candidate. They remove the candidate to the west of the altar, with his feet to the east, and place a sprig of acac-ia at the head of the grave. They then en-deavor to make their escape out of the coun-try by way of Joppa, but are refused passage in the boat because they have not passes from King Solomon, who strictly forbade workmen on the temple leaving the country without a permit from him. When Hiram is missed, there is con-fusion and excitement. Search is made. The craftsmen are assembled, the ruffians are found, ordered executed, the grave of Hiram is discovered, the body is identified by a jewel upon his breast, and after due preparation and solemn ceremony, is resur-rected by the strong grip of the lion's paw. When his body is found there is much la-mentation. When he is resurrected, the "word" which was lost in his death, is not recovered, but a substitute is given.

These details will give the reader some idea of the salient features of this myth of Hiram as it is portrayed in word and action in the ceremonial of the third degree.

Whence came this myth of Hiram? Masonic authorities are not at all agreed, at least not in their exoteric accounts and explanations. Fort traces this myth to that of Baldur, citing a number of parallel features. Heckethorn gives it a cosmological and an astronomical interpretation and derivation, which furnishes a clue to its real meaning. This myth of Hiram is only a Jewish mask for the same ideas we find in the myths of Osiris, Typhon and Horus, of Zeus and Dionysus, of Cybele and Sabazius. Sickels says: "This myth of Osiris is the antitype of the temple legend. Osiris and the Tyrian artist are one and the same, not a mortal individual, but an idea, an immortal principle." Here then we find the solution. The idea and the symbolism are practically the same. Only the language and setting differ. There is a change of name, a change of scene, but not a change of idea. It is a translation of the Egyptian religion into the imagery of the building of the temple at Jerusalem, the Egyptian cult clothed in a Hebrew garb. It is a Jewish mask for the Egyptian phallicism.

Note the parallels. In the Egyptian myth, Osiris is slain by Typhon, the three winter months, his body cast into the Nile, subsequently found by him and again concealed. In the myth of Hiram, the architect is slain by three craftsmen, his body concealed, afterwards recovered and buried. The body of Osiris afterwards is found in the roots of the living oak, Hiram's by the sprig of acacia. In the Egyptian myth Osiris is caught in a box, Hiram is caught in the Holy of Holies. In the Egyption rite, Isis seeks Osiris, and mourns his death. In the Masonic the lodge seeks Hiram and mourns his death. In the Egyptian when Osiris is found, the phallus is lost. In the Masonic when Hiram is found, the 'word' is lost. Isis furnishes a substitute for the phallus, the master furnishes a substitute word. "Isis raises the prostrate form of him who was slain, she takes from him his essence, she conceives and brings forth a son." In the Masonic rite the master raises the prostrate form of him who was slain, whispers in his ear the mystic word, and a son, a Mason, is born into the lodge. In the Egyptian rite Osiris lived again in his son Horus, in the Masonic the slain Hiram lives again in the newly made Master Mason, who is frequently termed the widow's son.

The myth of Osiris formed the basis of the initiation of the three degrees in the Egyptian mysteries. There are Osiridian elements in the initiation of the three degrees of Freemasonry, but the third degree is the most dominantly Osiridian.

Heckethorn says that Hiram is a cosmological and astronomical symbol or allegory. He is cosmological in his representation of the dual powers on which all oriental initiations were founded. The dramatic portion of the mysteries of antiquity is always sustained by a deity or man who perishes as the victim of the evil power and rises again in a more glorious existence. This approaches the correct solution but does not in our judgment reach it. Baldur, Hiram, Osiris, Zeus, Baal, and a host of other gods are but variants of one primitive story or fact, which is the germ of them all. They are personifications of the generative principle in nature.

In a comparative study of the mysteries, it is hard to determine which are the older. They evidently are derived from a common original, and they may be developments or perversions of that one original, along different lines modified by local influences and conditions. There are common elements in them all; but which was the borrower and which the lender, it is now, with the present knowledge of the facts, impossible to decide with any degree of certainty. In Freemasonry we find these common elements and these aid in identifying and establishing the unity of this modern form with the ancient.

In the Phrygian mysteries the representative of the god was probably slain each year by a cruel death, just as the god himself died. In Freemasonry the candidate who represents the god, the architect of the temple, Hiram, is theoretically slain by the three ruffians. In the former the mother, representing nature, is fertilized by an act of violence by her own child. In the lodge which represents the microcosm, there is also vio-

lence and commotion, by which a son is born
into Masonry. In the ceremony in the
Phrygian mysteries, the priest assumed the
name of the god, in Freemasonry the master
plays the role of King Solomon, which is
a veil for the sun, the great Osiris.

Many of the features of the ceremonial
of the Eleusinian mysteries are reproduced
in Freemasonry, either in direct parallels,
imitations, or in disguised forms. To get
the force of the conventional forms, the reader is referred to the interpretation of the
Masonic symbols as given in a subsequent
chapter. In the myth of Eleusis, Zeus substitutes the orchites of a ram for his own.
In Freemasonry there is a substitute for the
lost word of Hiram. In the former Baubo's
nakedness was exposed in realistic form, in
the latter it is exposed in a conventional
form in the apron, and in the compass. In
the former generative acts and ideas were
set forth before the initiated by use of realistic phallic images, in the latter the same
ideas are set forth by means of conventional
phallic symbols. In the former Demeter
wanders in search of her lost daughter Kora,
the candidate in Masonry wanders in search

of 'light'. In the Eleusinian rite, Demeter hides herself in a cave, in the Masonic rite, the candidate is hidden in the rubbish of the temple and in the grave. In the one the daughter Kora is snatched away by Pluto, in the other the candidate is snatched away by the ruffians. Demeter in search for her daughter breaks down with fatigue. In Masonry one of the craftsmen is overcome by fatigue, and sits down to rest by Hiram's grave and discovers it. In the Eleusinian rites processions go forth to celebrate the revivification of nature, in Masonry the lodge goes forth in procession to resurrect Hiram Abiff. The underlying ideas are the same in the two institutions.

The Masonic mysteries are a composite of these ancient mysteries, intermingled in a bewildering manner. The stories of the life of the divine personages, Zeus, Kora and Demeter, Osiris, Isis and Typhon, Cybele and Sabazius, and their various modifications as these stories passed on from age to age, constitute the basis of the Masonic ceremonial. All the elements are present along with others borrowed here and there, the more completely to hide its real self. The

Masonic ritual doubtless is old in its essential elements, and its original meaning is either lost or purposely obscured under the terminology of operative masonry. The myths of Hiram, of King Solomon, of the Word, the Temple etc., are told to explain the ritual, and to give it an Old Testament color.

However these myths and the rites explained by them, may have originated, there can be no doubt that they are based upon the generative facts of life. These facts being universal and constant, ever recurring in each generation, furnish a common basis for interpretation, and for religious ceremony. In these facts and functions of sex we find the basis for all the legends, beautiful and repulsive, of the gods and goddesses found everywhere on the earth, and found also in the institution of Freemasonry.

The Masonic mysteries are these ancient mysteries clothed in biblical terms and imagery. In the first degree the scene of the lodge's activities professes to be on the pavement of Solomon's temple; the second degree is acted in the middle chamber of the temple; while the third degree purports to take place in the Holy of Holies. But this is simply a veil under which the Phrygian, Hellenic and Egyptian types of nature worship are concealed. In the first degree the idea of the generating power of nature is the dominant one. In the second degree, the nourishing power is the dominant idea, and in the third the maturing, perfecting, destroying and renewing power prevail. All these ideas are allegorized under the narrative of the building of Solomon's temple. The mysteries of Freemasonry are the ancient mysteries translated into scripture imagery and story, and so colored, veiled and transposed as to prevent detection of the trick.

In the second degree this mystery idea is still further veiled under the terms of geometry. The emanation ideas are prominent here, and hence the geometric figures, the letter G, the points, circles, superfices, solids, columns, spheres and such like. Here the fundamental religious ideas of Freemasonry are hidden under a double veil, biblical and geometrical, or architectural.

The Hiram Abiff in Freemasonry is identical in every important aspect with Osiris, Zeus, Baldur, and other masculine deities that figured in the mysteries of antiquity. Hiram Abiff as the architect of the temple is the counterpart of the Great Architect of the Universe, the great temple of nature. He is the generative and constructive principle in man, the temple of humanity, as the Great Architect is the generative and constructive principle in nature. In the third degree the master assumes the role of King Solomon, the sun, the generator and builder of the temple of nature, and resurrects the slain Hiram, that the temple may be completed, the generative principle recovered and that human life may go perpetually on, that is, that the life principle ever dies to be renewed and to reappear in the new generation.

The Great Architect in Freemasonry is essentially identical with the Holy Aged or the Crown in the speculations of the Kabbalah. This Holy Aged exhausted his generative power in the series of successive emanations in and through which his substance flowed forth in producing the universe. His own generative power (word) is lost, until it is found again in a future generation, that is in future emanations, which in the Kabbalah, is the 'Foundation'. There that generative 'word' or power is found again and the circle of life is completed and going on continually. The wheel of life eternally revolves. The Holy Aged then is also a deity who has been deprived of his power of generation. He is the generator of the microcosm and macrocosm. Over against him appears this Hiram Abiff, the generator in the microcosm, of which the lodge is a symbol, and as the macrocosmic generative power reappears in the universe of all things, so this microcosmic generative principle reappears in the new generation which is the substitute for the old. Hiram is the earthly generator as the sun is the heavenly. He is to the microcosmic universe what the sun is to the macrocosmic.

Thus it is seen that the mysteries of Freemasonry parallel so perfectly with the mysteries of antiquity and the phallic cults, that the conclusion is irresistible and the demonstration complete, that Freemasonry is not an imitation but a restoration of the mysteries of antiquity, in rite, symbol, and in its essential religious ideas and doctrines.

CHAPTER X.

THE ESSENCE AND NATURE OF THE MASONIC RELIGION.

"Our rites will be of little value to us if we accepting the symbol have lost the sense."—*Sickels.*

HAVING taken for our guidance the statements of eminent Freemasons that if we would get the thought of Freemasonry and the hidden meaning of its rites, we must go to the ancient mysteries of Phryia, Greece, Egypt, Samothracia, Sidon, and other nations of antiquity and study those institutions and discover their ideas of the divine, we now feel prepared to take up this modern institution and ascertain what its essential religious notions and doctrines are. As we have learned by study and research in what 'necessities of human nature' those ancient institutions arose, and what ideas of the divine their founders intended should be shadowed forth in them, so also do we believe we can discover the real doctrines of this modern in-

(248)

stitution. If Freemasonry is the mysteries restored, the task need not be difficult nor fruitless.

It is with this religion set forth in the mysteries that Freemasons claim for their institution a unity, harmony and identity. They claim and profess to set forth the same religious ideas, worship the same deity, and employ in their religious and moral instruction the same hieroglyphic methods and art speech, that prevailed in those cults. While the forms and rites have undergone a change they contend that the ideas conveyed by them are identical. The religion is constant, the rites and symbols have become modified, so as to conceal the identity of thought. They speak of these mysteries as the ancient Freemasonry, and while the modern institution does not retain the particular ceremonies of the mysteries, it has retained the spirit of them by other forms not less expressive and instructive. (See Sickels' Ah. R., 154). Upon their own confession and declarations Freemasonry and the mysteries are in essential unity and harmony in every important point. This unity is religious and psychical. It involves the doctrines of the divine, of the origin, nature and destiny of the human soul.

In the foregoing chapters we have shown from trustworthy sources the nature and essence of the religion of the mysteries, their notions and conceptions of the divine nature and the divine acts, as they obtained in them and for which they as institutions stood. We have found that the religious acts consisted in paying homage to the generative principle or the reproductive power in its several aspects in nature and in man, and that this worship was aided and emphasized by the use of realistic images of the generative organs. The individual's life was made right in being guided and modeled by the ideas thus expressed and by the acts of the divine nature exhibited in the lives of the gods and goddesses. The devotee learned how to subdue his passions not only by contemplating the objects of passion, but by gratifying them after the manner of the gods.

From this examination of the mysteries we learn that the 'necessities of human nature' in which these institutions as well as Freemasonry arose, are the physiological differences of sex upon which the propagation of the human race depends. The divine nature was viewed as having divided itself into male and female for this purpose. The mysteries involved in the generation of life are the facts upon which the mysteries as religious institutions were founded, and to the processes involved in the former, the rites of the latter were conformed. If then there is a unity in the religious ideas and conceptions of the divine nature in the mysteries and Freemasonry, upon Masons' own confessions and declarations, the proof is conclusive that Freemasonry is a sex-cult, in which the generative powers are adored and worshiped under disguised phallic rites and symbols. Phallicism is the essence of the religion of the mysteries, and phallicism is the essence of the religion of Freemasonry. This we believe we can demonstrate beyond a reasonable doubt.

Remnants and disguises of the several forms and types of phallicism are present and discernible in the Masonic institution. In the emphasis laid upon 'light' in the lodge and the candidates search for it, we have a remnant of Mithraism. In the position of the three officials who are representatives of "the sun in the east," "the sun in the south," and "the sun in the west," and in their respective duties as set forth in the ritual, we have a form of sun worship. In the relative position of the altar and lights, the colmuns or pillars, and in the symbolism of the apron, and of the 'furniture' on the altar of the lodge, we have a remnant of the Baal cult. In the ceremonial of the third degree we have the Osiris type of sun and phallus worship. Tree worship is discerned in the sprig of acacia. Combinations of these in their divers forms as found in the several ancient cults, constitute the almost endless and bewildering rites of the institution. The symbols, emblems, jewels, ornaments, chests, arks, coffins, and other articles are the visible objects by which the phallic religious ideas are expressed. In all these things the phallic character of Freemasonry is made obvious.

This unity of Freemasonry with the ancient cults is not to be sought in the externals of the institution, not in exact identity of ceremony and symbol, but in the religious ideas, in the object of its adoration, in its conception and definition of the deity. The unity is religious, psychical and ethical, rather than formal. Freemasonry is the religion of the mysteries translated into a new and more modern ceremonial, and expressed by a new system of glyphs and ideographs. It is couched in terms of operative masonry, and explained by legendary narratives of King Solomon and his architect. But the religion is the same. That has remained unchanged. The form and manner of expressing it have changed.

The mysteries were esoteric organizations, and became more exclusive and secret when they came in contact with Christianity. Tertullian declares that it is in the secrecy of the Eleusinian mysteries that is their disgrace; that all their divinity lies in their secret recesses, (evidently the generative organism) and that the entire mystery of the secret tongue, that is the reason for their silence is in the symbol of virility; that the real sacrilege is concealed under an arbitrary symbol, and that falsehood is obviated by images; that the Valentinians have formed their customs after the Eleusinians, and that by the use of sacred names and titles and arguments, they have fabricated the vainest and foulest figments for men's pliant likings (See Ad. Valent., Chap. 1). Of this heretical sect Freemasons appear to be brilliant disciples, for their divinity also is concealed in their secret recesses, and their sacred objects are arbitrary symbols of the virile organ, and falsehood is obviated by images of builder's tools, and in the use of art speech.

It evidently is in the ceremonies, symbols and allusions that the so-called secrets of Masonry lie concealed, and to these we must look for the evidence that identifies the thought, the principles, the teachings, and the religion, yea the very essence of Freemasonry with the ancient mysteries and religions.

"The real secrets of Masonry lie concealed in its symbols." (Buck 257). Pike claims that the real secrets of Masonry are the philosophy concealed in its symbols. Philosophy seeks to know the reason of things, the why of things. The philosophy of Masonry or of its rites and symbols is the why of those rites and symbols, why they have that particular form, why they are used in a patricular way, why such and not other ceremonies. For these there is a reason, and the answer which correctly states or explains this reason, necessarily reveals the secret of Freemasonry. That answer and reason is to be found in its religion, phallicism. The reason why it is secret, is possibly because of the sense of shame, but more probably because the objects worshiped are the secret parts.

Philosophy as mere science or knowledge, would require that the thought or doctrine intended to be expressed by these symbols and rites, be understood by the Mason. The science which Masonry teaches and professes to know, is creative or generative science, the science of the origin, nature and transmission of life, and the moral duties arising from it; or an intelligent apprehension of the relation of the male and female principles essential to life; the functions essential to the generation of life. In either case, as a religious principle, or basis of religious life, it is none the less phallic.

We also know that to read or interpret symbols and rites retroactively without reference to their derivation and uses in different ages and among different people, is to violate every principle of science. We can understand them only in the light of known facts and usage. Masonry as the science of symbolism is the knowledge and art of making certain conventional objects set forth ancient religious ideas, and yet concealing those ideas from the profane; the science and art of originating religious ceremonies, which seem to exhibit Christian truth and facts but which in design set forth the ancient phallic religion. It is the science of making symbols and allegories most to teach what they least do show.

"The secret doctrine is the complete philosophy of Masonic symbolism. So long as this philosophy is unknown to the Mason, his symbols are to a great extent dead letters, the work of the lodge a dumb show beyond its moral precepts, and the genius of Masonry for the members of the craft is largely the spirit of self interest, mutual support and physical enjoyment and revelry. In retracing the steps by which these ancient symbols and their profound philosophy have come down to our time, more and more obscured with every passing century, students have gathered a large number of facts, a great mass of traditions and general information which have been variously interpreted by Masonic writers. All agree that these symbols come from the far east and go back to the remotest antiquity." (Buck, 257).

Pike says "that the real secret of Masonry, the philosophy concealed in its symbols, are far older than the Vedas, and are at least 10,000 years old, and that the art speech, which symbolism is, was designed by real princes of the royal secret, to preserve and convey this ancient Wisdom to the latest generation of men."

The identity of the Masonic symbols, and of their meaning, purpose and use in the lodge with those ancient phallic symbols in the mysteries and ethnic religions is not only conceded but claimed by the highest Masonic authorities. Buck admits that these traditions and symbols of Masonry do not derive their real value from historical data, but from the universal and eternal truth which they embody. "These great truths, obscured and lost in one age by misrepresentation or persecution, rise Phoenix

17

like, rejuvenated in the next. They are immortal ideas, knowing neither decay nor death." (Mystic Masonry, XXX). "The whole ceremony, traditions and glyphs of Freemasonry is shown to be a symbol of a deeper mystery, a concealed potency." He concedes that the antiquity of these symbols is far more easily established, than their meaning. But their meaning is readily determined from their prominence, place and use in these cults, and from the testimony of contemporary writers and monumental remains. And that testimony is conclusive and overwhelming, that these symbols are phallic. Garrison says: "I think there can be no doubt, at least to any thoughtful Mason, that the keynote to much of our symbolism, and the true spirit of it all are to be found in the traditions and meditations of the old searchers after the lost word." (Fort's Hist. of F. M., p. 466).

Monumental, historical, and philological evidence shows that phallus worship is among the oldest, if not the oldest form of idolatry. Reverence for the phallus or for phallic emblems shows itself in the earliest historic remains of Babylonia, Assyria,

India, China, Japan, Persia, Phrygia, Scandinavia, France, Spain, Great Britain, North and South America, Africa, and in the islands of the sea.   Phallicism is the bond that unites all forms of idolatry into one great system.   It is the essential principle that pervades them.   It is the basis of tree worship, animal worship, serpent worship, sun worship, and man worship.   It was the basis of the mysteries of Phrygia, Egypt, Greece and Rome.   It is the basis of all the mythology of the past ages, for as Weiss says "Freemasonry (Phallicism ?) may be traced in all the mythology to the remotest part of the globe".   (Obelisk and Freemasonry, p. 40).   It is the specific form of idolatry against which the revelation of God is a continual and an emphatic protest.

Phallus worship doubtless arose from the perversion of an earlier and purer idea which is the basis of the highest religious conception ever held by man. Dr. Hilprecht says: "There is no doubt in my mind that all these different rites, phallus, tree and serpent worship, however independent of each other they may appear to be in later times, are but different outgrowths of the same original root and later perversions of original uplifting thought, search for unity between man and God."

In view of the divine command "Be fruitful and multiply", the generation of human life became a most solemn and responsible privilege, a pure and holy function. The mystery of it must have impressed most profoundly the first human pair, and doubtless the first religious act on the part of this first human pair was an appeal to the Source and Author of life for the power to procreate it.

In course of time this Author and Source of life became associated with the organs and factors of its reproduction, and then supplanted by them as an object of veneration and worship. The rite mysterious of connubial love became perverted. The imagination of man's senseless heart became corrupt. The power of procreating life became deified and worshiped under phallic emblems, which in turn became the deities. The perversion continued until it culminated in many places and in divers ages, in sacred prostitution. The phallic emblems became objects of adoration. The passion and power of procreation became a god, and was worshiped with degrading, impure and shocking accompaniments. There is much in the ancient ritual of the Attis-Cybele worship, in the Isis ritual and others, that shows the prevalence of the belief that communion with the deity could be obtained through semblance of sexual intercourse. This evidently is the idea upon which the ceremonies in these cults were based. (See Farnell, Cults of the Ancient Greeks).

We hold it as demonstrably true that Freemasonry is a sex cult that has survived to this day; that it is a perversion of an original up-lifting thought; that it venerates, adores and worships the generative principle as its god, under the name The Great Architect of the Universe, and symbolizes this deity and his operations by conventional phallic symbols and rites. The Supreme Council of the Ancient and Accept Rite of Lusanne, has declared as follows: "Freemasonry proclaims as it has ever proclaimed from its origin, the existence of a Creative Principle, under the name of the Great Architect of the Universe." Concerning this declaration, Gen. Albert Pike declared: "It is but an old term revived. Our adversaries numerous and formidable as they are, will say and will have the right to say that our Creative Principle is identical with the Generative Principle of the Indian and Egyptian, and may fitly be symbolized as it was symbolized anciently by the linga. To accept this in lieu of a personal God is to abandon Christianity and the worship of Jehovah, and to return to wallow in the styes of Paganism." (Quoted in Isis Unveiled, Vol. 2, p. 377)[1]. From what we have learned in our study of Masonry, it is this creative or generative principle that it worships as its specific god, and if this be true, then according to the testimony of Mr. Pike, the greatest of Masons, Masonry has abandoned the worship of Jehovah, and is simply wallowing in the styes of Paganism.

A number of other Masonic authorities agree with Pike and concede that the symbolism of the institution in its original and proper meaning refers above all to the solar and phallic worship of the ancient mysteries. He contends that it is in the antique

---

[1] This action and protest are found in Proceedings of Supreme Council of Sovereign Grand Inspectors-General, of the 33d and last degree. N. Y. City, Aug. 15, 1876. p.p. 54, 55.

symbols and their occult meaning that the true secrets of Freemasonry exist, and that these reveal its nature and its true purpose. (Inner Sanctuary, 397). This phallic interpretation of the religion of Freemasonry is therefore warranted by the statements and concessions of the most eminent Masons of America and Europe.

It may be contended that there is an exception to this phallic character of the Masonic religion in the Knights Templar degree. But this exception is only apparent. Templarism when interpreted consistently with the fundamental principles and the hieroglyphical methods of ancient craft Masonry from which it has been evolved, proves to be a disguised phallicism and in perfect harmony with genuine Freemasonry.

Templarism is a side degree in American or York Rite Masonry, and is characterized as a "Christian" degree, and as Freemasonry "Christianized." This "Christianization" applies only to the symbolism or to the exoteric aspect of Templarism, and not to its essential doctrines. The religion of Templarism is of one piece with the religion of Blue Lodge Masonry, for "evolution in

York Rite Masonry has reached its climax in the Knight Templar degree, and the fundamental principles are identical with the ancient craft."

The basis for this claim that Templarism is Christian is the symbolism employed, which is apparently Christian, together with the theological terms that occur in the ritualistic work and the socalled "test of faith" as the condition for admission, namely belief in Jesus Christ as the Son of God. But these symbols, terms and test are no more proof of the Christian character of Templarism, than is the cross carved upon the Aztec ruins, evidence that the Aztec religion was Christian. It is not the exoteric but the esoteric sense which these things have in Templarism that determines the essence and the nature of the religion of this degree. We must determine this religion not from the ecclesiastical use and meaning of these symbols, terms and the phrase "belief in Jesus Christ as the Son of God," but by the Templar use and meaning. The question then arises: Are these symbols employed in the Christian or in their prechristian sense? Determine this, and it will solve

the question whether Templarism is Christian or phallic.

Without entering into details concerning the derivation, origin and history of
Knight Templarism, it may be stated that
some Masonic writers attempt to trace it to
that religio-military organization bearing
the same name, which arose at Jerusalem
about A. D. 1113, during the crusades. Others deny this connection, and this denial is
sustained by the best modern authorities,
both Masonic and non-masonic. While "it
is within the range of possibility that a connection exists between the chivalric order of
the Knight Templars and the fraternity of
speculative Freemasonry of mediaeval
times," there is insufficient evidence to establish conclusively any historical or organic
connection of the modern Templars with
those of the middle ages. But while not a
direct, organic and lineal continuation, there
is evidence for regarding the modern order
as a resuscitation and restoration of the
former, with some modifications, but possessing the same essential principles, ceremonies and symbols. That these fundamental
ideas are Christian in either the mediaeval

or modern institution is therefore a matter to be inquired into, for in this degree as in all others Masonic language and symbols least do mean what they most do say and show. Knight Templarism is esoteric and misleading interpretations are given to lead conceited interpreters and over-confiding Christians astray.

The old Order of the Temple was an esoteric fraternity and was the last European organization which as a body had in its possession some of the mysteries of the east. The Templars during and in consequence of their sojourn in the east attached themselves to the doctrines of the Gnostics and Manicheans, as is sufficiently attested by Gnostic and Kabbalistic symbols discovered in the tombs of the Templars, and by the peculiar architectual features in their chapels and temples. They were scions of those heretical sects, and like them masked Gnostic and Kabbalistic ideas under Christian names and rites. While their profession was to protect Christian pilgrims to Jerusalem, their aim was to restore the secret worship which its founders, Hugh de Payens and eight companions obtained from one Theoclitus in Palestine. When they were suppressed in 1313, some of the charges against them were that their religious teachings were anti-christian, and some of the Templars who were tried, confessed to these charges under torture, but subsequently repudiated their confession. Their guilt or innocence on the charges made against them is one of the most difficult problems of history. The historians who have throughly investigated the matter, examining carefully all the available material, are about equally divided in their opinions. But this much is generally conceded, that Gnostic ideas permeated the order, that anti-christian sentiments were expressed, that indecent kissing was practiced in the initiations, and that many knights were licentious. It was also shown that an image Baphomet, was worshiped, which had a veiled meaning, and that the vow of chastity towards women had been turned into a sanction for more horrible offences. A number of scholars who have given this matter much attention are of the opinion that their religion was not the orthodox faith, but a secret religion of a dualistic nature, embracing Islamic,

Gnostic and other heretical principles which was masked under Christian names symbols, and rites. This opinion is sustained in the pratices of the Templars who performed their religious ceremonies in the strictest secrecy, while the ecclesiastical worship was publicly performed in the chapels of the order. They rejected the Christ of the New Testament and of the Church, but accepted the man Jesus as a brother, thus accepting his humanity, but denying his eternal Godhead and divinity.

Findel says that during the eighteenth century when Freemasonry erroneously believed itself to be derived from the Templars, great pains were taken to show the order innocent of the heinous crimes laid to their charge. For this purpose not only legends and unrecorded events were fabricated but pains also taken to repress the truth. (Hist. Freemasonry, Appendix). If the old Templars are the spiritual, ethical and religious forebears of the modern order, then the latter have inherited much that is repugnant to Christianity.

The modern Templars whose origin is somewhat obscure, after several futile efforts had been made to resuscitate the mediaeval order, emerged under the magic hand and skill of Jesuits who were or had been Freemasons, one of whom was Dr. Fahre-Palaprat, who assumed the name Benard Raymond, and also became the first Grand Master. The two elements, Jesuitism and Freemasonry are cunningly interwoven in the order and readily perceived by the discerning student, but so concealed as to evade suspicion. At first only Roman Catholics could be admitted, but Fahre gave the order an opposite tendency. Charles Sotheran declares that the order is the fruit of Jesuit intrigue whose center was the Jesuit College of Clermont, Paris. Other Masons contend that the aim of these founders was that the Jesuits might secure control of the Masonic institution. Templarism is looked upon by a number if not all the Jewish Masons as Jesuitism, and is held in great disfavor by many others of the craft, because it is viewed as a contamination of Freemasonry and as an attempt to Christianize and sectarianize it.

While the modern order can not lay valid claim to being a continuation of the mediaeval organization, it has however much of the form, religion, and spirit of that society. The Gnostic and Manichean religious ideas with which the old Templars were imbued are unmistakably in the modern order. The mingled and corrupted Freemasonry which the old society adopted and expressed in its initiations, are also present in the modern order. In the fundamental religious ideas there is no essential difference between Templarism and genuine Freemasonry. The sole difference exists in the symbols. In Templarism these ideas are veiled under symbols and emblems which are generally considered positively and exclusively Christian, while in the ancient craft Masonry they are veiled under the tools of operative masonry. The Christianization consists solely in the symbolism, in putting on a Christian mask to conceal the phallic features. We are persuaded that many Templars honestly believe that Templarism is Christian, and do not in their guilelessness suspect any deception, but we are also persuaded that in this they are most shamefully and cruelly deceived by those who are high up in the Masonic institution.

We offer the following in support of the position taken:

1. *Knights Templars are Freemasons.* They have taken the obligations and passed all the Blue Lodge and Chapter degrees. This is imperative. Before any man, Christian or non-Christian can become a Knight Templar, he must first become a Mason, a phallicist, a man who, tacitly if not knowingly on his part, but in reality from the view point of the lodge, has renounced Christianity, and sworn perpetual adherence to Freemasonry. Now the essence of Freemasonry is such that it is morally and absolutely impossible to hold and to adhere to it, and to hold and to adhere to Christianity. The two are antithetical and mutually exclusive, and no juggling with or distorting of religious terms can circumvent this fact. One can no more consistently hold fast to Templarism and Christianity, than he can serve Belial and Christ.

2. *The Religious Test.* Knight Templarism requires as a condition of admission into the order, belief in Jesus Christ as the Son of God. This religious test if honestly

used and in its Christian sense, would exclude on the one hand all persons who do not believe that the unique Person, the Jesus Christ of the New Testament, is the incarnate Son of God, and the Redeemer and Savior of mankind; and on the other hand it would admit only those who do thus belive in him and accept him as their Lord and personal Savior. It is upon the assumption that this "test of faith" is used and understood in the Christian sense, that Templarism is claimed to be a Christian institution, and sets forth nothing but the Christian religion.

Few things can be more misleading. The first element of truth that names be honestly used, is here ruthlessly violated. If this name of Christ were honestly used and in its Christian sense, this conclusion might be warranted. But it is not so used in Templarism, as any discerning student can plainly see, and it is therefore that sense in which it is used in this order, that determines the kind of religion, and the character of the religious ideas that qualify for admission into the order. Not what this name means in Christianity but what it means in Templarism determines whether this test is Christian.

The faith in Christ that is demanded as a qualification for this degree is historic faith, a belief that the person presented to us in the New Testament as Jesus Christ, did actually live in the time and land therein set forth, and that he is the Son of God. This much devils believe and tremble because of it, but this belief does not make them Christians. This much we will grant that Templarism demands and believes, but it does not make Templars or their order Christian. They must in order to be Christians believe from the heart that this Jesus, God has made Lord and Christ, that he is the Messiah of Moses and the prophets, that in Him all the promises of God made to the fathers, are fulfilled and accept him as their personal and only Redeemer and Savior. They believe in Jesus as a man, as an historic personage, or even as a divine person, but no more. They do not accept him as earth's creator and man's Redeemer from sin, death and the power of Satan. This is not the faith in Christ which the Church demands, and which Christ demands. This is not

18

saving faith in the Christian sense. This is not that faith which makes men Christians, and the confession of which marks them as Christians. True faith in Christ compels its confessors to rest absolutely in Him as their sole way to God's forgiveness and eternal salvation.

This "Christ" of Templarism is not the Christ of the New Testament and of orthodox Christianity; the personal Being, Son of God and Son of Man, "the Mystery of Godliness," "God manifest in the flesh," "the Word made flesh." He is not the Christ confessed in the ecumenical creeds and by orthodox churches, the "Person in whom dwells all the fulness of the Godhead bodily," the One who is "true God begotten of the Father from eternity, and also true Man, born of the Virgin Mary." The "Christ" of Templarism is not the Christ of orthodox Christianity. The one is the product of human speculation, the other is God manifest in the flesh, the express image of his person, a record of whom we have in the Holy Bible.

This "Christ" of Templarism is the "Christ" of the Gnostics, the "Christ" of the old Templars, not a divine-human per-

son, true God and true man, but a mere idea,
an elastic glyph, a philosophical notion, an
aeon, an emanation, a spiritual and ethical
concept, one or all of these personified, but
separate and distinct from that Person Jesus Christ of Nazareth, and so flexible in his
nature and constitution as subjectively conceived of, as to satisfy the most diverse opinions, speculations and religions of men. This
"Christ" is a false christ, and if accepted is
fatal to the individual's Christian faith and
religion. The Templar's "Christ" is one of
the false christ's that has arisen, that makes
his appearance in the secret chamber and
in the desert of human speculation, and has
deceived many. This "Christ" has nothing
in common with the Christ of pure Christianity. Belief or faith in this "Christ"
of Templarism no more makes a man a
Christian, than paint on a pump gives character to the water, or painting a negro white,
makes him a Caucasian.

The qualification "the Son of God" attached to this phrase and test of Templarism, does not change the matter. The Templar view of the "Son of God" is the old
Gnostic view, the view that has passed down

through many sects which were influenced in their theology far more by the oriental and Platonic philosophies, than by the Word of God. The "Christology" of Templarism is irreconcilable and incompatible with the Christology of orthodox and New Testament Christianity.

3. *The place of Templarism in the Series of Degrees.* The order of succession in which the degrees in York Rite Masonry occur, aims to symbolize the Masonic idea of the evolution of Christianity out of Freemasonry. The Masonic assumption and contention is, that not only are all religions identical at heart and in essence, but also that they each and all have been evolved out of the one primitive religion which they contend is Freemasonry. "As Knight Templarism is an evolution of York Rite Masonry, retaining the same fundamental principles that exist in the ancient craft," so in the Masonic view Christianity is an evolution of the Freemasonry expressed in the first three degrees, and at heart identical with it. Templarism then, instead of being pure Christianity, or even essentially Christian,

is the Masonic phallicism masked under Christian names, symbols and rites.

4. *The Root, Sap and Branches.* We have shown in the foregoing portions of this Chapter, that genuine or Blue Lodge Masonry is phallic. Out of this phallic root, Templarism has been developed. If this Masonic root and sap is phallic, the institution also is phallic in its branches, whatever may be the artificial foliage in which it bedecks them. Templarism is not Christianity graffed upon the Masonic stock, but Freemasonry bedecked with Christian symbols and emblems. It is not a Christianzation of Freemasonry by the elimination of its heathen elements, and an insertion of Christian elements, but simply bedecking the Masonic bramblebush with the foliage of the figtree. The old nature is there but skillfully concealed under an attractive and guileless garb.

5. *The Christian Symbols.* Practically all the Christian symbols and emblems were originally derived from the heathen religions. As many of the words in the Greek language took on a distinctively Christian

sense in their Christian usage, so also did the symbols and emblems of the pagan religions. The cross was a phallic symbol ages before Christ was crucified, and it has retained this phallic meaning in a number of cults until the present time. The emblem the "cross and crown" was derived from the crux ansata. The red cross upon the white mantle or the white cross upon a black mantle, in the old order of Templars, had the same significance with them as with the old initiates, in the phallic cults. These symbols and emblems then, as they are employed in Templarism are therefore not to be undertsood necessarily, in a Christian sense, but rather in their prechristian sense and usage. This prechristian sense is the esoteric sense in Templarism, and determines the nature and essence of the religion of Templarism. The theory that these symbols and emblems are used in a Christian sense breaks down in the test, and proves that they are employed in the prechristian sense, and exhibits Templarism as a Christian mask for the phallic nature of the institution.

The Mystic Shrine which is characterized as "the play ground for high degre Masons," and as "the vaudeville show of the craft," is also a side degree and can be reached by way of Templarism in the York Rite, or by way of the thirty-second degree of the Scottish Rite. This is an Islamized form of Freemasonry. In its relative position to Templarism and Scottish Rite Freemasonry, it symbolizes the place of Islam as an evolution of Freemasonry. The Mystic Shrine is the Masonic phallicism veiled under Islamic religious symbols and terms.

Having now gone to the sources from which Freemasonry claims to be derived, and studied them in their several aspects and relations one to another, we find the one thing that is common and runs through them all, is phallicism. We are led therefore to the conclusion, that Freemasonry is a cult, a religion in which all religions are esoterically synthetized under the garb, imagery and terms of operative masonry, but whose real essence is phallicism; that phallicism is the essence of Freemasonry, the real secret which is symbolized by its entire ceremonial, and that this being the fact, the perpetuity of the institution depends upon keeping this secret doctrine concealed from the knowledge of all except a tested few. Phallicism as the key, interprets consistently every rite, symbol and ceremony and monitorial lecture in the institution. It unlocks this synthesis of all knowledge and of all religions.

CHAPTER XI.

THE MASONIC THEOLOGY.

"I publish without reserve what has been involved in secrecy, not ashamed to tell you what you are not ashamed to worship."—*Clement of Alexandria.*

FREEMASONRY professes to have in its possession a correct knowledge of the Great Architect of the Universe who in its view is the true God. This knowledge it professes to teach inerrantly to its disciples by means of its symbolism and ceremonies. Correctly stated it constitutes its body of divinity, its "divine truth which is the center of its system, the point from which all its radii diverge." Upon this correct knowledge of its deity and the doctrines concerning his attributes, nature and work, the institution is founded, and in this god-idea is the key that unlocks its secrets, interprets its symbols and emblems, and explains its allegories and ceremonies. Given this god-idea and the chaotic mass of objects, symbols, and philosophical remnants resolve

(281)

themselves into system and order. This peculiar god-idea, in order to conceal its true nature, the institution deeply veils and conceals beneath the garments of Christianity, "so as to lead conceited interpreters astray."

Freemasonry then, has a system of divinity, a body of doctrine concerning this Great Architect. This doctrine it holds as absolutely correct both in content and in statement. In its opinion it is the Truth of the Divine.

This Masonic doctrine concerning the divine is as may be expected, peculiar to this institution. It has nothing in common with Christian theology, except certain theological terms, which it employs not in the Christian but in the Masonic sense. Its term the Great Architect of the Universe, is not a mere Masonic name for the living and true God of Christianity, but it denotes an entity that can not be identified with Jehovah. It is not a synonym for Jehovah, as it is generally believed to be. It denotes another entity just as Baal, Molech, Brahma, etc., denote entities distinct from Jehovah.

The task we have set before us in this chapter is to remove the veil behind which this Masonic doctrine of the divine is concealed, to show what this Great Architect really is by identifying him, on the one hand, with a mysterious force in nature, and on the other differentiating him from Jehovah, with whom Masons persistently confuse him. In how far we shall be able to make this plain, we will let the reader decide.

1. *The religion of Freemasonry is a theism*—Mackey says: "The religion of Freemasonry is a pure theism upon which the different members may engraft their own peculiar opinions, but they are not permitted to introduce them into the lodge or to connect their truth or falsehood with the truth of Masonry." (Lex. 404). This language plainly implies that the theistic conceptions of Freemasonry are unique and peculiar, and that the truth or falsehood of other theistic religions are not to be connected with it. It stands alone. It has its own peculiar views which make it Masonry, and which differentiate it from Christianity, but harmonizes it with the religions of the ancient cults.

Theism is a term of wide application. It is inclusive rather than exclusive. It is a generic term for all systems of belief in the existence of the divine. Thus understood it includes pantheism, deism, polytheism, monotheism, and specific theism, and it excludes only atheism. In its narrower sense it is identified with monotheism. Theism is not necessarily Christian, for theism can be reached quite apart from Christianity.

Upon the strength of Mackey's statement given above, and his further statement that "Freemasons have always been worshipers of the one true God," and of the intense symbolism and ritualism of the institution and the devotions conducted in the lodge, it is plain that Freemasonry is not an atheistic organization. It believes in the existence of a deity, whom it worships and adores in its devotions.

In its doctrine concerning the revelation of God, the institution is deistic. It denies that the deity has made any supernatural revelation of himself, or of his will to man. It rejects the Bible as a supernatural revelation. It recognizes no revelation except that set forth in nature.

What revelation it may find in the Bible Freemasonry regards as a duplication of the natural revelation. Pike says: "The universe is the only uttered word of God, the thought of God pronounced." "The permanent one universal religion is written in visible nature, and explained by the reason, and is completed in the analogies of faith. There is but one true religion, one dogma, one legitimate belief." (M. & D., 516). Buck says: "God never manifested himself to be seen of men. Creation is his manifestation." "The whole manifestation of nature is the uttered word of divinity." (Mys. M., 276). Charles Sotheran speaks of the Bible as a pseudo-revelation. Masons deny that Freemasonry is founded upon the Bible, that if it were it would not be Freemasonry, it would be something else. Many Masonic writers ridicule the Christian doctrine that the Bible is a supernatural revelation from God. They say it is a book written for the vulgur, by the ancient priests, and that they concealed under its exoteric language, the secret doctrine, which is the true Freemasonry.

We concede that the Bible is not a revealation from the Masonic Great Architect, the god in Freemasonry, and to be as charitable as possible it may be that it is in this sense that Masons deny its supernatural origin and divine character, for the Great Architect of Freemasonry is not to be confused or identified with the Jehovah who speaks to us in the Bible. This Great Architect has not made any supernatural revelation of himself.

Freemasons who know, when speaking of God, always mean this Great Architect, but the non-masonic reader understands them to mean Jehovah the God who has revealed himself to Israel. Therefore while the peculiar theology it teaches refers to the Great Architect, yet it pretends to predicate these things of Jehovah. "God" in Freemasonry is not the divine personal entity worshiped by Christians. This explanation will aid the reader in understanding more clearly, the Masonic theology.

In its doctrines concerning the divine immanence Freemasonry is decidedly pantheistic, partaking of the various shades of that view of the divine. God (the Great Architect) is the "soul" of the universe, and the universe is the garment in which he is clothed. He lives in it, sustains it with his

powers of wisdom, strength and beauty, and
animates it as the soul does the body. The
universe is the temple in which he lives and
moves and has his being. The peculiar doctrines concerning the Great Architect, held
by Freemasonry, gives to its pantheism, a
peculiar character.

Freemasonry denies the personality of
God, (the Great Architect). He is a principle not a person, an eternal, boundless, immutable principle, in all, through all, and
over all, divinity immanent, not transcendent. The only personal God Freemasonry
accepts, is 'humanity in toto.' God (the
Great Architect) personifies himself, that is
expresses that potency of himself which personality is, through man. Humanity therefore is the only personal god that there is.
(See Mys. Masonry, 216). In the entire human race past, present and future, deity has
become and is and shall be perpetually incarnate. Mr. Leon Hyneman, a prominent
Masonic writer, declares that for thirty
years he combatted the design to erect into a
Masonic dogma, belief in a personal God.
Pike concedes that to accept the declaration
that the Creative Principle is the Great

Architect in lieu of a personal God is to abandon Christianity and the worship of Jehovah.

The statement that the religion of Freemasonry is a pure theism does not convey any very definite idea as to its specific teachings concerning the deity. These we can learn only from a study of its ceremonies, and the veiled, guarded and ambiguous language of its spokesmen. It is a theism that teaches that its deity is in the world and the world is in this deity; that the divine is in man, and man is in the divine. It is a theism which from the Masonic viewpoint, is unalterable, absolute and positive, but upon which every Mason may put his private interpretation, with the understanding however, that this private view must not be promulgated as genuine Freemasonry. A wide and essential difference may therefore exist between what an individual Mason may think and believe to be Freemasonry, and the official objective doctrines expressed in esoteric terms. The theism of Freemasonry is peculiar and every precaution is taken by the institution to preserve it uncorrupted and concealed from the knowledge of the profane, and from its own disciples until they give adequate evidence that they can be entrusted with this secret. The pure theism of Freemasonry is not Christian theism, but a theism that can be reached quite apart from Christianity. It is a purely speculative theism.

2. *Freemasonry is a monotheism*—In its teaching concerning the unity of the divine, Masonry is a monotheism. While it allows its disciples to hold their own private religious beliefs, and engage in various forms of worship outside of the lodge, in the lodge, it requires them all alike to confess faith in one specific deity. While it tacitly admits the existence of other gods in allowing its disciples to hold their private views, it does so on the theory that these god-ideas are perversions and corruptions of its own theistic conceptions and which it aims to correct. In its conceptions of the divine unity, Freemasonry is a monotheism.

Freemasonry holds its deity in high respect. It has suspended in the lodge 'in the east' an emblem of deity, which it calls the 'all seeing eye', and under it all the lodge work is performed. "The essentially relig-

19

ious character of Masonry", says Morris, "is shown under the head 'Deity'. Between the extremes of atheism on the one hand, and idolatry on the other, Freemasonry cultivates the worship of the one true and living God, omniscient and omnipresent, who answers prayers, grants his spirit of wisdom and strength to those who ask him, rewards virtue, punishes vice and reserves heaven after death for those who have faithfully served his will and pleasure in this present life." "An emblem of deity is suspended in every lodge." (Dictionary, Art., God). Mackey asserts that "Freemasons have always been worshipers of the one true God." "This," says Hutchinson, "was the first principle and cornerstone on which our originals though it expedient to place the foundation of Masonry." "While the world around them was polluted with sun worship and brute worship, and all the absurdities of polytheism, Masonry, even in its spurious forms, as the ancient mysteries have appropriately been styled, was alone occupied in raising altars to the one I AM and declaring and teaching the unity of the Godhead."

Throughout the entire Lexicon under the

proper titles Morris shows the profound veneration that Freemasonry has for the deity. Blasphemy against the deity is a punishable offence in Masonry, and in the higher degrees, it is forbidden. In brief, a strict monotheism pervades the entire fabric of Freemasonry. It is anti-masonic to require any religious test other than that the candidate should believe in God, the Creator, and Governor of the Universe. (Chase, Digest, p. 209). "The general sense of the fraternity has rejected all religious tests except a belief in God." (Mackey, Ency., 97). "The newly made entered apprentice is solemnly informed that his duty to God consists in never mentioning his name but with that reverential awe which is due from the creature to the Creator; to implore his aid in all laudable undertakings, and to esteem him as the chief good." (Rit., p. 38). "A belief in God is one of the unwritten landmarks of the order, requiring no regulation or statutory law for its confirmation. Such a belief results from the very nature of the Masonic institution and is set forth in the ritual of the order as one of the very first prerequisites to the ceremony of initiation." (Mackey,

Juris., 93). From these statements as well as others that might be adduced, it is plain that Freemasonry as to its doctrines concerning the unity of the Godhead, is a monotheism.

3. *The "One God" worshiped in Freemasonry, is the Great Architect of the Universe*—The claims of Freemasons that they worship one God only, and that the institution is monotheistic, we think too evident from Masonic authorities to be disputed. The monotheistic claim must be conceded.

But this 'one God' in Freemasonry is that entity which they term the Great Architect of the Universe. This is emphatically, pre-eminently and specifically the deity of Freemasons, and 'god' in that institution. It is this deity which is represented by the 'all seeing eye', whose creative agencies and processes are symbolized by the instruments, tools and emblems of the craft, and by the religious ceremonies engaged in. It is faith in this deity that, as a prerequisite for membership, is demanded at the door of the lodge of every candidate for Masonic honors. It is this deity in whose name the covenant is made, and who is invoked for help to keep it inviolate. It is to him that the prayers in

the lodge are addressed, (Sickels, Ah. R., 22 ;
Mackey's Rit., 276 ;Rit., p. 26),whose praises
are sung in Masonic odes and whose divinity
is extolled.   It is to him that Masonic altars
are   built,   priests   consecrated,   sacrifices
made, temples erected and solemnly dedicated.   This Great Architect of the Universe
is the 'one God' in Freemasonry and beside
him there is no other in that institution.
Freemasonry as such knows no deity save the
Great Architect of the Universe.

Speaking of deity Mackey says: "This Divine Being, the creator of heaven and earth,
is particularly viewed in Masonry in his
character as the great master builder of the
worlds, and hence Masonically addressed as
the Great Architect of the Universe."   (Juris., p. 93).   In the initiatory ceremony the
candidate's "God" in whom he confesses
faith, is qualified and identified as "that God
whom we as Masons reverence and serve"
(Rit., p. 30), namely the Great Architect of
the Universe.   Sickels in his Ahiman Rezon,
frequently uses the term God, but so qualifies
it as to refer to the Great Architect.   The
Book of the Law is regarded as dictated by
this Great Architect.   (Sickels' A. R., 81).

Throughout the entire writings of Masons, official and unofficial which we have examined, the appellations of God are so qualified as to denote the Great Architect of the Universe, and him alone. Even the language of Jesus Christ when quoted, is ascribed to the Great Architect of the Universe. Thus in its prayers, ceremonies, addresses and public utterances the monotheism of Freemasonry is shown to be a recognition and worship of the Great Architect of the Universe as the one true and only God. It is therefore to this entity that all theistic terms in Freemasonry are to be referred. Masons who know what Freemasonry is always mean this particular entity when they speak of God.

4. *Who or what is this Great Architect of the Universe?*—We shall now endeavor to show who or what this Great Architect in Freemasonry is. Can we identify him and prove from Masonic authorities what particular force, or principle, or energy, or creature is denoted by this name. We think we can.

We take the following official declaration as the key for the correct answer to this inquiry. "Freemasonry proclaims as it ever

has proclaimed, the existence of a Creative
Principle which it terms the Great Architect
of the Universe." (Supreme Council A. &
A. Rite, Lusanne, 1868). Here we have an
official declaration as to who and what this
Masonic deity is. Against this declaration
there were some protests by Masons who supposed that in worshiping this Great Architect, they were worshiping Jehovah under
a different appellation. But Masons who
really know the true theological position of
the institution, when speaking of deity,
mean this creative principle. Pike declares
that this is but an old term revived, and
identifies this creative principle with the
generative principle of the Egyptian and
Indian religions, and distinguishes it from
the Jehovah of Christianity. Buck defines
God as an omnipotent, eternal, boundless
principle, and declares that the recognition
of this principle of principles as the Great
Architect, is the real genius of Freemasonry.
We have it therefore upon the highest Masonic authority and testimony that the Great
Architect denotes the same thing which was
deified and worshiped in the Indian cults
and in the Egyptian mysteries in the differ-

ent ages and under various names. This generative principle of the Indian and Egyptian cults is substantially identical with the "Divine soul" of Pythogoras, the "Holy Aged" of the Kabbalah and the "Demiurge" of the Gnostics. The "one god" of Freemasonry is the Great Architect, who is identical with the creative principle.

This creative or generative principle is that mysterious force or energy which renews the earth in springtime, and quickens all animated nature; that energy, force or power which perpetually dying, renews itself in new, similar yet different forms. It is the original created reality from which other like things are derived through generation and their element of subsistence. This dynamic, procreative, reproductive power or energy in nature and especially in man maintaining a perpetual self-identity, Freemasonry conceives of as the divine nature, as the deity immanent in nature, and it is this life force or energy that it deifies, venerates and worships under the name The Great Architect of the Universe. This is "God" in Freemasonry. And those, who with Spencer and other naturalist philosophers of the age call the hidden all-powerful principle working in nature, God, are acknowledged by the craft as Freemasons, whether or not they have been initiated into the institution. A Mason then is one who believes this life energy in nature, in the totality of its various qualities, is the Divine nature or the true God, though he never may have been initiated into the order. "There are many Masons who have never been initiated", say the Masonic spokesmen.

This principle is conceived of as an architect because it has inhering in it not a mere causal power, but the constructive principle which builds the new bodily form in which the generated life is to dwell, after inhering unsubstantial and invisible plans, which are a copy of the parent form. It is the generator of a new life, the assembler of its substance, and the builder of its bodily temple. And as this principle builds and upholds the individual bodily form against the active destroying forces in nature, so it is also viewed on the one hand as the artificer of the body and the source of its life, the divine architect in man, and on the other as the artificer of the universe and the source of its life. This generative principle under the term of the Great Architect is thus viewed as the soul of the universe, its divine draftsman and builder of its material form. Man is only one of its infinite number of manifestations.

This "all soul" this divine artist is conceived of as pervading all living things. The universe is its outward material manifestation, and the life of nature is its quickening manifestation. In that life it perpetually manifests itself as dying yet reappearing in new and different forms, but ever maintaining its self-identity. What the body is to the person, the universe is to this deity. This creative principle inheres in and is incarnate and operative in humanity, and hence as Buck says, "Humanity in toto is the only personal god."

Freemasons speak of this deity as a living god. This creative or generative principle is an active living energy, and if deified may well be viewed as a living god. It is conceived of as the life of nature. And as this creative principle was worshiped in the earliest ages of antiquity, Masons can very properly claim that these ancients who had this god-idea, this conception of the divine, were Freemasons, and that Masons were engaged in erecting altars to the I AM that is this ever existing life of nature, while the rest of the world, in their estimation, were addicted to the absurdities of polytheism.

In the Kabbalah this generative principle was viewed as dwelling in the 'foundation' of the archetypal man, and was termed the living God.

5. *The Great Architect of the Universe is not identical with Jehovah, the God of the Bible.*—Freemasons attempt to identify its Great Architect with Jehovah, the Father of our Lord Jesus Christ, but these attempts are simply cunning devices for misleading and deceiving both the Mason and the profane. They are examples of clever sophistry, of skillful syncretism, of cunningly devised fables and delusive fictions, which have a semblance of truth and fact, but which in reality are only veils and disguises for its refined idolatry. They are skillful professions of adherence to the first commandment while in fact they are palpable violations of it. The Masonic god is a secret deity, whose

nature, name and worship is veiled under the name and guise of Jehovah. This cunning sophistry and fiction must be seen in order to apprehend the true nature of the religion of Freemasonry. From the Christian viewpoint, the two, Jehovah and the Great Architect of the Universe, are entirely separate and different, mutually exclusive, and no syncretism can harmonize them.

We have shown that this Great Architect of Freemasonry is none other than the generative or creative principle, and that this is declared and confessed by the highest Masonic authorities. Having shown to their own satisfaction that this is the only true, living and most high God, they attempt to show that the Jehovah of the Holy scriptures is, when rightly apprehended, none other than this generative or creative principle. This identity is shown not by exalting the Great Architect to the place of Jehovah, but by degrading Jehovah to the level of the generative principle. In this attempt at their identification, they accept the speculations of the Kabbalah and of the Gnostics as of greater authority and weight than the declarations of the word of God. As the

Kabbalah identified the living God with the generative principle, and the Gnostics identified Jehovah with their Demiurge, so Freemasons identify him with their Great Architect.

Freemasons take it for granted or endeavor to make it appear that there is a secret meaning in the name JHVH, which secret meaning was lost with the loss of the correct pronunciation of that name. This secret consisted in this, namely that the root ideas composing that name are the male and female principles in their highest and most profound sense, and that in the divine entity denoted by that name the generative spirit and the productive matter, that is the female principle, are constituent elements, so that the deity denoted by JHVH is an androgyn, a male and female god whose sex principles differentiated themselves as they went forth into creative activities. (See Morals and Dogma, p. 700). That this is true they attempt to show by an analysis of the name הוה the "Jah" being masculine, and the 'Vah' feminine. Jehovah is therefore a binary. Madame Blavatsky who is held in high repute by a number of Masonic writers, argues for the same view, and contends that Adam also was an androgyn for he was created in this "image" of God. A number of Masonic authorities take the same view. This therefore established beyond controversy that the Masonic view is that the Jehovah of the Bible is the generative principle in its generative, nourishing and constructive aspect, and is identical with the Great Architect. The Mason's obligation to respect all religions *as his own* is thus made intelligible, for he is to view them as in essence a worship of the generative principle. This identification of Jehovah with the Great Architect by this analysis of the name JHVH, makes the religion of Israel phallic and harmonizes it with Freemasonry.

This assumption that Jehovah and the Great Architect are identical divine entities, or that these names denote the same divine being, is not true nor can it be proven to be true. An arbitrary interchange of names does not identify the entities which those names represent. This Masonic argument is based upon the assumption that all monotheisms are not only identical subjectively and objectively, but that they are each and

all fundamentally a deification and worship
of the generative principle, and that this
generative principle is God. This is a fallacy. The "God" of Islam is not the God
of Christianity, neither from the Moslem nor
from the Christian viewpoint, though each
of these religions is a monotheism. "The
'God' of Philo is not the God of that Israel
which was Jehovah's chosen people." (Eder-
sheim). The "God" of the Unitarian is
not the God of the Trinitarian. Allah, Ormuzd, the "Holy Aged" and the "Living
God" of the Kabbalah, neither represent entities identical with Jehovah, nor are they
different names for the divine essence Jehovah, not any more than are Ashteroth,
Zeus, Baal, Moloch or Brahma. The one
divine essence is Jehovah, and of it man
knows nothing except through the revelation of himself to man. Man can not find
this Jehovah by searching, that is by his
own powers of speculation. The world by
wisdom knows not God.

We must distinguish between the one
God of revelation Jehovah, and the "one
God" of speculation. We have knowledge
of the former only through the revelation of

Jehovah to man. The latter is the end of human speculation, the answer the human mind gives to the question why is the universe as it is. But we must not confuse these two, nor regard them as identical. The "Supreme Being," the "Causeless Cause," the "En Soph", the "Unknowable" and similar things which thinkers supply as an answer to why are things as they are, and assume to be the true God are creations or deductions of the human mind, and can not be identified with the God of Revelation. These are philosphical necessities to satisfy man's reason, but they are not He who spake by the prophets and became incarnate in the person of Jesus Christ. These "Gods" of of non-Christian monotheisms, or of philosophical thinkers are either pure assumptions or corruptions by human reason of the divine Essence known through revelation, or identifications of this Essence by the finite mind with the deep and unfathomable mysterious forces in nature, which are deified and worshiped by man in the pride of his powers and thereby congratulates himself that he has found God. Jehovah is the God revealed to us in the full light of his glory in Jesus Christ. These other "one Gods" are what man finds while groping in the darkness of a world benighted by sin. To accept this creative or generative principle as our God in lieu of Jehovah is to abandon revelation and to wallow in the styes of paganism.

This argument of Masonry does not hold good when examined on its subjective side. Jehovah alone is God to me. Neither Brahma, nor Allah, nor the Great Architect of the Universe can be God to me as identical with Jehovah. It is impossible. It is unthinkable. "Even in the case of a monotheistic religion like Mohammedanism, we make a distinction between the Christian God and Allah. Both are designations of a supreme Being, yet the conceptions of God are so different that we hold them apart in thought and give them different names." (James Orr, Problem of the O. T., 132, note)[1]. For any of these "Gods" of the non-

---

[1] Allah is the name of the supreme universal God in the Arabic religion. Sexual dualism dominated the oldest Arabic idea of the godhead. The God Allah is not identical with the God Jehovah. Mohammed simply divested him of his consort, Al Let, affirmed the unity of this deity and assumed his identity with Jehovah.

20

Christian religions or monotheistic philosophies to be God to me, is to exclude Jehovah, and contravenes the commandment which says Thou shalt have no other gods before me, and Jehovah's declaration "I am the Lord, that is my name, and besides me there is no other."

We know that the truth or falsity of the Masonic interpretation of the name JHVH, and of the nature of the entity denoted by this name, is not to be determined absolutely by a show of hands. But in this matter the opinions of the most learned, most conscientious and most devout biblical scholars, have weight. They too have been searching for the truth about this matter and are as competent to give a correct interpretation as are the highest Masons. We therefore cite the testimony of some of these as to the meaning of the name Jehovah and as to the nature of the deity denoted by this name, as it is set forth in the Hebrew Scriptures by the men who claimed to be His prophets. The Jehovah as these prophets conceived of Him, and as He revealed Himself unto them is absolutely irreconcilable with the ideas and conceptions of Jehovah as set forth by Freemasons.

"Jehovah designates God as 'He who is what He is'. God is Jehovah in as far as He has entered into an historical relation to mankind, and in particular to the chosen people of Israel. The name carries us into the sphere of the divine freedom. It expresses the absolute independence of God in his dominion as well as the idea of the absolute immutability of God, and implies the invariable faithfulness of God." (Prof. R. F. Weidner, D. D., LL. D., Theologia, p. 27). In this name are included also the ideas of an eternal God, and the living God.

"This name Jehovah is a redemptive name. It does not describe God on the side of His nature, but on that of His saving operations, His living activities among His people, and His influence upon them." (Davidson, O. T. Theology, p 47). "Jehovah refers not to what God will be in Himself; it is no predication regarding His nature, but one regarding what He will approve Himself to others, regarding what He will show Himself to be to those who covenant with Him. Jehovah is the name of God in his new relation to Israel His people.'' (Davidson, Id., 55, 57). Jehovah represents the one self-existent immutable God as entering into progressive moral relation with men, especially with the Jewish people. The name expresses a personal and moral relationship with men. The Being who not only creates man but makes a revelation of himself to him. He is not purely transcendent and unsearchable, but comes into loving, intelligible relations with humanity. The germ of the Logos is in the conception of Jehovah. (Based on Baldwin's Dict. of Philos.). Pure religion is a relation existing between persons, and the Christian religion is the moral and spiritual relation existing between a finite personal being, man, and the infinite personal being, Jehovah. The Great Architect is not a personal God. He is not self-conscious. He is a force in nature, a creature, and can not from this fact be to me what Jehovah is.

Jehovah the living God revealed himself to Israel, and to Israel alone, and through Israel to the world. He is a self-revealing

God. He has progressively unfolded his attributes, his will, his love and his purposes, towards man, by successive revelations, until in the fullness of time, He came in the person of Jesus Christ. "God who in many parts and in many ways spake of old to the fathers through the prophets, spake, at the extremity of these days unto us through His Son." (Heb. 1:1). The revelation of his power in nature, expressed in the name Elohim, has been supplemented by His revelation of grace, the redemption and salvation of man, expressed in the name Jehovah. His attributes as revealed in His works of grace, are such as can not be discerned in nature, and are such of which no philosopher, no sage, no theosophist, and no Mason ever dreamed. These attributes are the exclusive attributes of Jehovah, and constitute the unique marks of Christianity, and prove that our God is as far above the Great Architect of the Universe worshiped by Masons, as the infinite Creator is above the finite creature.

The Masonic view of the revelation of God, in the lower degrees, is deistic, but in the higher degrees it becomes pantheistic.

The writings of Garrison, Buck, Pike, and other eminent Masons show this unmistakably. It is this peculiar pantheistic conception of deity which has passed from India through the secret doctrines of the Kabbalah into modern speculative Freemasonry, as Buck intimates, that constitutes the secret doctrine of the institution. In Masonry, a God distinct from the life of nature, has no existence.

Now over against this impersonal, pantheistic God of Masonry, Jehovah, the God of Christianity is a living, personal, triune God, existing independently of the universe, who in addition to His natural revelation, has also made a supernatural revelation of Himself, of his will, and of his love; who, in his being and essence is one, and is revealed in a triune personality, Father, Son and Holy Spirit. This unfolding of the unity of the divine Being in a trinity of persons, is eternal and necessary, constituting the ground of the divine self-existence.

The Christian's God, Jehovah, is a personal God who can and does express himself in self-consciousness, and self-determination. He has been defined by Christian writers, as follows: "God is a spiritual essence, intelligent, eternal, true, just, holy, chaste, merciful, most free, of immense wisdom and power, different from the bodies of the world and all creatures. One in substance, and nevertheless three in persons. The Father eternal, who from eternity, has begotten from his own essence the Son, His image; the Son, the coeternal image of the Father, begotten of the Father from eternity; and the Holy Ghost, proceeding from the Father and the Son. And that this eternal Father with His coeternal Son and the Holy Ghost coeternal with the Father and the Son, has created and perserves heaven and earth, things visible and invisible, and all creatures." (Chemnitz). The Augsburg Confession gives the following: "One divine essence, eternal, without body, without parts, of infinite power, wisdom and goodness, the maker and preserver of all things, visible and invisible." The Westminster Larger Catechism gives the following: "God is a spirit, in and of Himself infinite, infinite in being, glory, blessedness, and perfection, all sufficient, eternal, unchangeable, incomprehensible, everywhere

present, almighty, knowing all things, most
wise, most holy, most just, most merciful,
and gracious, longsuffering and abundant in
goodness and truth." The reader can readily see the marked difference in the nature
of the Great Architect of the Universe, as
defined by Masons, and of Jehovah, as defined by Christians. The former shows what
men find when groping after the first cause
of what is, the latter taking the way in
which God is found, find Him to be not one
person, but three persons in one Being.

If we view God as life, we can not however, identify Him with the life of nature.
He is the absolute, inorganic, uncreated and
underived Life. He has life in Himself
alone. The life of God subsists in his triune
nature as its basis. But the life of nature
is created, originated, derived, transmitted
and dependent upon a material substance
and organism for its basis. Nature does not
have life in itself absolutely. Its apparent
inherent life was placed there through the
creative fiat. Hence Jehovah the self-existing ever living God, is not identical with
that power or energy which renews the face
of the earth, the creative principle which

Masonry designates and worships as the Great Architect. "God" from a Masonic viewpoint is not God from the Christian viewpoint.

The life of God is in Himself. The life of the Great Architect is in the world of living creatures, the life of nature. The life of God has for its basis the eternal trinity. The life of the Great Architect has for its basis, the male and female sex principles. Natural life or the life of the Great Architect is the perpetual reproduction of the self-consciousness in man, throughout time. When this power ceases the life of the Great Architect ceases. The life of God is the eternally reproducing self-consciousness of the divine existence.

In the Christian view, the creative principle or the reproductive power in nature through sex agencies, is a product of God's power implanted there, and not God himself, nor a part of God. It is the result, or rather it obtains throughout all time by virtue of the word of God, "Be fruitful and multiply," (Gen. 1:22), and will remain operative until He shall recall it. The perpetual self-identity in the successive generations of offspring is due to and involved in the divine fiat, "after his kind", beyond which the generative forces in animate nature can not go. That word is the expression of His will and by the perpetual causative generative power mediated through creatures and the fountain of the perpetual life generating entities. To deify this power, and adore and worship it, instead of Him who implanted it, is to worship the creature instead of the creator.

"To the Hebrew God and the world were distinct. God was not involved in the processes of nature. These processes were caused by God, but were quite distinct from God." (Davidson, Theol., O. T.).

God is a personal Spirit, not a force in nature, separate from the world, yet his spirit is the creating and moving principle of all life (Ps. 104:29 seq.), and particularly of man's life. It is this ethical and religious conception of God, and not the divine unity or monotheism, which is the distinguishing feature of the Old Testament teaching. And in the New Testament He becomes a Father to His children. The monotheism of Israel was singularly comprehensive, sublime and

practical, a faith which rested not on speculation and reasoning, but on a conviction of
God having directly revealed Himself to the
spirits of men, and ascribed to God all the
metaphysical as well as the moral perfect-
ions; a faith which in spite of its simplicity,
so apprehended the relationship of God to
nature as neither to confound them like pantheism, nor to separate them like deism, but
to assert both the immanence and the transcendence of the divine; a faith in a living
personal God, the Almighty and sole Creator, Preserver and Ruler of the world.
(Ency. Brit., Art. Theism., Prof. R. Flint,
D. D.).

What are we to think of when we speak
of God, or what are we to imagine when we
think of God? This question is difficult to
answer, from the fact that the finite mind
can at best form only a very inadequate
conception of an infinite Being   But we can
know God relatively not what He is to Himself, but what He is to us. We can know
something of God from the names by which
he has made Himself known and from the
attributes that are predicated of him. We
can know something of Him from the work

He has wrought, both in nature and in grace and from all these taken together, we can obtain a very clear though limited conception of Him. And this Being, the objective entity of our subjective conception is the God of whom we speak, in whom we trust, whom we reverently fear and love. We know Him because He has revealed Himself to us in the Word, and in Christ Jesus. In this revelation we are taught how God who is, is known, and known to be what He is. We know Him as God in Israel and God in the Church, and beside Him there is no other.

Jehovah can not be identified with this so-called Great Architect of Freemasonry because of the different objective conceptions of these entities. We identify Him with the God who revealed Himself to Abraham, Isaac and Jacob, the Father Almighty, Maker of Heaven and Earth, but differentiate him from the Great Architect of the Universe, from Allah, Ormuzd, Brahma, and all other so-called gods. He is the Being who says: "I am the Lord thy God, thou shalt have no other gods before me." We identify Him with the Being who appeared to Moses in the burning bush, who gave the law on Sinai, who spake by the prophets, and who in the fullness of time manifested Himself incarnate in the person of Jesus Christ.

This is the Being I as a Christian conceive of when I speak of God, when I worship Jehovah.

In this matter, Christians aim to be as specific as possible. Our theologians endeavor so to qualify the terms that they can apply to this Being only. This is done in order that men may know who is meant when the name of God is used. The design is to be clear and unmistakable in their meaning. Such definitions and qualifications of terms, eliminate all other deities, and preclude the possibility of confusing the mind of the disciple.

The Great Architect, the god of Masonry, is not this Jehovah of the scriptures. The two are by no means alike or identical. Masons positively refuse to define their God in, by and with these terms. Their pitiful excuse is, it would sectarianize their God.

Masons as such positively refuse to accept the following Christian teachings as to God: "The Father made of none; neither created nor begotten; the Son, of the Father alone, not made nor created but begotten; the Holy Ghost, of the Father, and of the Son, neither made, nor created, nor begotten but proceeding; one Father, not three Fathers; one Son, not three Sons; one Holy Ghost, not three Holy Ghosts; in which Trinity none is before or after the other; none greater or less than another; but the whole three persons coeternal together and coequal so that in all things the Unity in Trinity and the Trinity in Unity is to be worshiped." (Athanasian Creed).

This is the Christian definition of God, based upon the revelation he has made of Himself, so far as language can define Him. The divine Being therein set forth, the Trinity in Unity and the Unity in Trinity, is our God and to be worshiped thus. If one does not accept this truth, he is not a Christian in the true historical sense of the term. He may be a Deist, a Theist, a Theosophist, a Mason, but not a Christian.

And more, this God who is He that speaks in the first commandment can have no other gods before Him. There is but one divine

Essence in fact. There may be others existing in the imaginations of men, such as the Ensoph of the Kabbalah, the Aum of the Indian theosophy, the Unknowable of the scientists, or as the "End" of their speculations, but they are in fact idols, creatures of the mind, philosophical necessities, etc. Over against them all only the one divine Being or Essence has any objective real personal existence, and this is the Jehovah, the God of the Church. The Christian can not, he dare not recognize other deities, or assent to their worship. This God is of necessity jealous of his honor, and he can not give his glory unto another.

Jehovah is the Supreme Being, self-revealed, not the "Supreme Being" of non-Christian thinkers. He is God to me, for He is the object of my affection, service, worship, the supreme Good to me. He has redeemed me, saves me from sin, and will graciously own and receive me unto Himself.

The "Supreme Being" in Masonry and other non-Christian religions, is the limit and product of human speculation. The mind goes back in its endeavors to account for the things that are. It reaches its limits, and as it must have a cause for what is, it satisfies itself by saying that there is a great first cause. But in none of these speculations or cults is the "Supreme Being" or the "Great First Cause," identical with Jehovah. They are the conclusion, the end of human speculation. But Jehovah is the beginning of revelation, the self-revealing God. The others are man-assigned causes, or the human answer to the question, Why is the universe as it is.

It is plain then, that Freemasonry, like a pirate ship floats a friendly banner inscribed with Jehovah's name that the unsuspecting may become an easy prey.

CHAPTER XII.

THE MASONIC DOCTRINE OF THE UNITY OF GOD.

W E have shown in the preceding chapter that the Masonic religion is a monotheism, that it teaches that there exists only one "God" whom it worships under the conception and name of the Great Architect of the Universe. We have also shown that this Great Architect as conceived by Freemasons is not identical with the Jehovah of Christianity, but that he is another and distinct entity.

As Freemasonry is a monotheism, and as its spokesmen have much to say concerning the 'unity of God', 'the divine unity', and 'the unity of the divine', phrases expressing the several aspects of the Masonic view, there remains yet to be considered this doctrine. Freemasons speak freely on this point, and assert that Freemasonry is the search after divine truth, and that that truth is the unity of God, and in such language as to produce the impression that it is

21 (321)

in perfect doctrinal accord with Christianity. But here also it least does mean what it most does say, and we purpose therefore in this chapter to show that the Masonic teachings on this subject when correctly interpreted and understood are absolutely irreconcilable with the biblical teachings. We purpose to show that its doctrine of the unity of God, and of the essential and fundamental unity of all religions is a pure assumption veiled under sophistries and false analogies, for it is upon its peculiar doctrines of the unity of God, that it predicates its doctrine of the unity of all religions.

Freemasons in their religious discussions, and in their endeavors to show the identity and harmony of Freemasonry with Christianity relative to its teachings concerning the unity of God, employ the same terms that the church uses, but give to them a distinct Masonic meaning. They therefore by this use of words which have a double meaning, confuse the Mason and the non-Mason, and debase the conception of Jehovah. It is not the language but the thought intended to be conveyed that determines the identity of the expressions. So

Masons employ the terms 'God', 'Jehovah', and the 'Unity of God', but not in the Christian sense. This Masonic meaning must therefore be determined in order to understand the Masonic doctrines and sentiments.

In the Christian and biblical usage the term the unity of God denotes not only that He is one over against many gods, but also his absolute oneness, that he is absolutely single; that the essence of God, that which makes him God, God in himself and God to the universe, is absolutely indivisible, so that God is incapable of any division of himself.

In the Masonic usage the term does not denote this absolute oneness of the deity, but this, namely that the 'one God' in the several monotheistic religions, by whatever name he may be designated in them, is the identical objective entity as that designated by the Great Architect. It is a unity based upon the assumption that all monotheisms are subjectively and objectively identical, because monotheisms.

The Masonic argument on this point when summarized, is as follows: There exists but one God. Masons, Moslems, Brahmins, Parsees, Jews and Christians all respectively worship "one" God, therefore all these different religionists worship the same God only under different appellations. To them this argument is convincing and conclusive.

In this argument there is a fallacy, a sophism. The fallacy lies in the use of the word 'one' in a double sense. It is as logical as the following: Nothing is heavier than gold. Feathers are heavier than nothing therefore feathers are heavier than gold. The oneness or unity of Jehovah denotes not only his singleness over against many, but also the absolute indivisibility of his essence and his absolutely supreme separatedness from all other entities. The 'one' in other monotheistic religions denotes numerical unity but not unity of essence. The essence of Brahma, if we can speak of him as having essence, is not that essence which constitutes Jehovah God, God in himself and God to the universe. Brahma and other 'one Gods' are not identical with Jehovah.

It is true that in the biblical view there exists but one God; that this God is from the human standpoint, unsearchable and beyond the sphere of human discovery by speculation; that He is known to man only through the act of revealing himself to man as God in Israel, and God in the Church and through these to the world; as God entering into the history of man as a factor in it. Revelation as a record, teaches how God who is, is known, and is known to be what He is. Revelation as an act, is God manifesting himself to man. Creation as a product is a record of God's material works, and from which He can in part be discerned, yet the knowledge of Him derived from creation is inadequate and imperfect. He can not be known from nature as God except through his supernatural revelation in the work of redemption. It is only and solely in the biblical revelation of Him that the God of nature in the sense of its creator and originator is identified as and identical with the Jehovah of Israel. This identification of the Creator of the Universe and Jehovah the Covenant God of Israel, is a matter of revelation. That identification in the biblical view, lies beyond the sphere of speculation and philosophy. The Jehovah of Israel reveals himself and identifies himself as the Elohim of creation.

From God's material workmanship which is nature, and the attributes it necessarily presupposes and expresses, the human mind may reason back to a first cause, and construct out of these attributes a subjectively conceived being, or principle, or substance, whom it may term God, or Brahma, or the Great Architect, or something else, and whom it may honestly believe to be God, and worship as God. The annals of speculation abound with these intellectually created gods from the fetich of the pagan, to the "Substance" of Spinoza and the Great Architect of Freemasonry. They all agree in kind, but differ in degree of perfection and skill of construction as the skill of their philosophical creators differs. But the human mind can not by searching find Jehovah. Nor can it with certainty identify the 'First Cause', 'The Unknowable', 'The Substance', 'The En Soph,' 'The Demiurge', or 'The Great Architect', or any 'philosophical necessity' with Jehovah, or prove their identity with Him, who spake by the prophets, and became incarnate in Jesus Christ.

These philosophical necessities and intellectually constructed gods fashioned after their makers, have been variously named, and identified with certain mysterious forces and energies in nature, and worshiped as the diety, or as the divine nature. When these cults, schools and philosophies came into contact with the revelation of Jehovah in the scriptures, they endeavored to identify and harmonize these 'beings' and 'divinities' with Him, to show their essential unity. But all such attempts are failures. The thinking mind instinctively perceives the fallacy thereof. Jehovah is unique. There is no unity or identity between these gods and Him. Their essence is not His essence. There is a chasm between Jehovah and these philosophical necessities which no human philosophy or human speculation, and no human wisdom has been or ever will be able to bridge.

And so with speculative Freemasonry. It may make a very plausible showing by its peculiar analogy of faith, by the syncretism of the divine names of the respective gods and by the co-ordination and interchange of the divinities, that all monotheisms are identical and each monotheistic deity identical

with every other monotheistic deity, and
therefore enjoins the Mason 'to regard every
religion as his own;' but this syncretism and
co-ordination of names and deities does not
make identical the entities denoted by these
names. There is a difference between the
name and the thing designated by the name.
The transposition of names does not carry
with it the transposition of the things; but
the transposition of the things carries with
it the transposition of the names.

It is conclusively established by archeo-
logical research that the primitive religion
was a monotheism, and that man's earliest
ideas of the deity were not the poorest; that
polytheism, fetichism, totemism, and animism are degenerations of monotheism. The
evidence points conclusively to monotheism
as the primitive religion of Egypt, India,
Chaldea, China and Persia, while a monotheistic strain permeated the religions of
Greece and Rome.

Now while it is true that the primitive
religions of these nations were monotheisms,
it does not necessarily follow that the 'one
God' worshiped in them respectively is the
sole divine essence, Jehovah. Monotheisms

are not necessarily identical nor Jehovistic.
To prove them identical it must be shown
that the objective entity worshiped as the
divine is identically the same in each and
that the subjective god-ideas of the monotheists are substantially alike. And in order
to prove that these monotheisms are in substantial unity with the biblical monotheism,
it must be shown that the so-called First
Cause, or Principle, or the Divine Nature
therein worshiped, is identical with that objective divine essence, Jehovah.

Conceding that Freemasonry is a monotheism, it is not Jehovistic monotheism, although we concede its essential unity, harmony and identity with some of the other
monotheisms that exist or have existed.
Freemasons endeavor to prove it in harmony
with biblical monotheism. This is important in order to commend the institution to
the favorable consideration of Christians.
But we must make, and the thinking mind
does make a distinction between the Great
Architect and Jehovah, because they are different entities. There is a very essential
difference between the Great Architect as
subjectively conceived of and objectively

presented to us by Freemasons, and Jehovah as conceived of by Christian theologians, and objectively presented to us in the Bible. These subjective conceptions and objective presentations of the Great Architect and of Jehovah, respectively, are so diverse that the thinking mind instinctively holds them as different and mutually exclusive, so that the monotheism of Freemasonry is not Jehovistic monotheism.

The Masonic argument assumes that the name Jehovah is only one of many co-ordinate divine names, and is identical in meaning and application with the names of the supreme god in the several monotheisms; that the names Jehovah, Brahma, Ra, Allah, Baal, Zeus, etc., are coordinate and essentially synonymous; that they each and all designate the identical principle denoted by the Great Architect of the Universe; it assumes that Jehovah is not a revelation to Israel, but that the Hebrew prophets discerned this generative principle and named it Jehovah, as the Hindoos discerned and named it Brahma, and the Egyptians as Ra. This assumption is unwarranted and untenable, and so also are the conclusions. If it be true that these ancient people were monotheists and monolators, yet no one who has any grasp of spiritual entities will contend neither from the biblical nor from the philosophical viewpoint, that all these several worships were therefore offered to the true and living God, Jehovah. There is but one God who is one and indivisible in his essence, one numerically and one essentially, and the real question is, which of these several divinities is that sole and absolutely single intelligent divine being, God, God in himself and God to the universe. Is it Brahma, Allah, Zeus, the Great Architect, whom men have discovered or have assumed as necessarily existing, or Jehovah who has revealed himself to Israel? In the biblical conception Jehovah alone is that one true divine, intelligent, self-conscious, indivisible Essence which in itself constitutes and makes Him God to himself, to the universe and God to me. There can not be from the biblical viewpoint any other monotheism in the sense and nature of biblical monotheism. Jehovistic monotheism like Jehovah himself, stands absolutely distinct and alone.

The biblical writers do not attempt to

prove the existence of God, nor do they speculate upon this question. They know God because He revealed Himself to them. They were conscious of His presence and of His words. They teach how God who is, is known, and is known to be what He is. The biblical position is that men do not and can not know God by speculation, but only by the revelation of himself to man. Revelation as an act, is God manifesting himself to man's consciousness. Speculation is man groping in the darkness to find God, and is satisfied that he has found Him when he has hit upon that which is mysterious and beyond which he is powerless to go. But speculation and revelation can never meet. They move in opposite directions. The deity discovered by speculation is not and can not be the God who discloses himself in revelation.

The Bible does not sustain this Masonic doctrine of the unity of God. The Hebrew prophets never admitted, conceded or believed that Molech, Baal, or any of the 'one Gods' worshiped by the adjacent nations were merely different names of the divine essence Jehovah, whom Israel worshiped.

Among the Hebrews the name Jehovah was never a mere sign whereby their God could be distinguished from other divinities, who were equals or co-ordinates. Jehovah is the essential name of God and as the Hebrew prophets understood it, never denoted a mere tribal god for the Hebrews; but as the adjacent nations understood it, it doubtless did, for they judged the God of Israel by their own god-ideas. Among some of the Israelitish kings this confusion and corruption of the god-idea of Jehovah became evident, for they made repeated and desperate attempts to conform the worship of Jehovah to the pagan cults, or to apply these cults to His worship, on the assumption that the deities were identical. In the history of Israel before the captivity nothing comes out more clearly than that the mass of the people found the greatest difficulty in keeping their national religion distinct from that of the surrounding nations. Those who had no grasp of spiritual principles and knew the religion of Jehovah only as a matter of inherited usage, or looked upon Him as a tribal god for Israel as Baal was of the Canaanities, were not conscious of any great difference between themselves and their heathen neighbors, and fell into Canaanite and other foreign practices with the greatest facility.

The Israelites spake of Jehovah as Baal, and this double use of the term Baal for the generative principle and for Jehovah, tended to produce confusion between them, and by this syncretism the conception of Jehovah was debased by elements borrowed from nature worship. The introduction of these noxious elements not only degraded Jehovah, but they enthroned in His place the symbols of reproduction, and ministered to licentiousness which this syncretism encouraged and legalized. The relation of Baal and his mate, the Ashera, was set forth as the example and the motive for unbridled sensuality, and the climax was reached when Jehovah himself became regarded as one of the Baals, and the chief of them. Thus through this doctrine of the unity and identity of Jehovah and Baal, the name and the honor of Jehovah was degraded to a sensual deity whose most acceptable worship was the indulgence of lust. Elijah forced on the popular mind the conviction that

Jehovah and Baal were not only distinct, but mutually exclusive.

And so Masons in speaking of Jehovah as the Great Architect of the Universe, and of the Great Architect as Jehovah, produce by this double use of these names, and by their interchange as equivalents, confusion in the minds of the members of the craft, and in the minds of those who are not Masons, and debase the conception of Jehovah by elements borrowed from this modern nature worship, but disguised in terms of a builder's craft. There are many, both among Masons and non-Masons, who have little or no grasp of spiritual principles and who are not conscious of any great difference between Freemasonry and Christianity, and hence fall into this modern nature worship and its attendant practices with the greatest facility, and see no inconsistency in doing so. By this syncretism of names, Freemasonry keeps the hoodwink on the eyes of its disciples so that they fail to perceive this sophism concerning the deity.

Freemasons take it for granted and as proved that the mystical interpretation of the scriptures according to Kabbalistic principles and methods, is the correct one. The eminent Masons all contend that there is a veil upon the scriptures, which when removed, leaves them clearly in accord with Masonic teachings and in essential harmony with other sacred books. To sustain this view they cite many authorities, and even the scriptures themselves. They assume that the doctrine of emanation, and not that of creation, is the correct one. They reduce Jehovah to an identity with the Holy Aged of the Kabbalah, with the self-created and self-existing Brahma of the Indian, with the Demiurge of the Gnostics, and with the Great Architect. They seem to have no doubt about this identity, and hence speak of the Great Architect as only another name for the objective divine entity, Jehovah. They assume the essential identity of the Great Architect with the I AM of the Bible, and regard all those patriarchs who worshiped the I AM as Freemasons. This is the 'unity of God' that Freemasonry teaches. It reduces all monotheistic deities to one and the same thing as its Great Architect, and all the great religions as identical with itself. This is one phase of the Masonic doctrine of the 'unity of God.' It is a unity which syncretizes the names of the deity in the several monotheistic religions of the world, and assumes that this syncretism neccessarily identifies these respective deities with the generative principle, the Great Architect.

This peculiar Masonic doctrine of the unity of God is also expressed in its combination of the names of the several deities in the ancient religions for the formation of certain of its glyphs. In the ceremonial of the third degree, the master of the lodge plays the role of King Solomon. He represents the sun and especially the life generating principle in the sun, which was worshiped in the Egyptian mysteries, whose peculiar god-ideas dominate this degree.

Now in Freemasonry this name Solomon is not the name of the Israelitish king. It is the same in form, but different in its meaning. It is a substitute which is 'externally' like the royal name. This name is a composite, Sol-om-on, the names of the sun in Latin, Indian and Egyptian, and is designed to show the unity of the several

22

god-ideas in the ancient religions, as well as with those of Freemasonry. It is a glyph which indicates the unity of the god-ideas of these various cults, a co-ordination of their deities, and expresses the Masonic idea of the "unity of God" as it was conceived of in these religions.

In the Royal Arch degree the word is Jabulun. This is the word, they say, that was lost through the death of Hiram Abiff. In this degree, it is pretended, this word is found. It is inscribed upon the golden triangle discovered in excavating for the foundations of the second temple. This word according to high Masonic authorities, is a composite of the names of the sun-god in three religions, the Hebrew, Assyrian and the Egyptian, Jah-Bel-On. The Masonic assumption here is, that the Hebrews worshiped the sun as Jehovah, or that Jehovah is the sun or the generative principle in the sun and that the Israelitish religion was a sun worship. In this compound name an attempt is made to show by a co-ordination of divine names in forming a Masonic glyph the unity, identity and harmony of the Hebrew, Assyrian and Egyptian god-ideas, and the harmony of the Royal Arch religion with these ancient religions.

This Masonic 'unity of God' is peculiar. It is the doctrine that the different names of gods as Brahma, Jehovah, Baal, Bel, Om, On, etc., all denote the generative principle, and that all religions are essentially the same in their ideas of the divine. It is in this sense that the injunction to every Mason 'to regard every religion as his own' is to be understood. "To make this obligation reasonable", says Buck, "the Mason is shown through the Kabbalah or secret doctrine that at the heart of every great religion lie the same eternal truths. Forms and observances only differ." (Mystic Masonry, 150). These 'eternal truths' in the Masonic view, are that all religions are based upon the worship of the generative principle, and that this principle is the true God.

Pike calls attention to the names of the three ruffians, Jubela, Jubelo, and Jubelum, and says that the final letters form the A. O. M. or Aum of the Indian religion, and asks whether this is a mere coincidence. It may be, and it may be one of those veils in Freemasonry behind which

the pagan religious ideas are concealed and
expressed.   The mystic Aum of the Indian
was the generating, preserving and destroying energies combined, by which the world
was kept in poise.   And in the ruffians of
the third degree this idea obtains, for if Hiram Abiff were not perpetually slain he
could not be perpetually raised and regenerated, and labor on the temple would cease.

Over against this syncretic monotheism
of Freemasonry the Bible teaches that its religion and doctrines are true, while all others are false, that it alone has within it the
true knowledge of the true God, that its
knowledge is positive and absolute, a revelation and not a speculation.   It does not sustain the claim that Freemasons were the first
to erect altars to the I AM, that is, that
Abraham, Isaac, and Jacob, Adam, Abel and
Enoch, who worshiped the I AM in so doing
worshiped what Freemasons do under the
name the Great Architect.   Nor does it sustain the Masonic claim that the sages Zoro-
aster, Pythagoras and Buddha, were dictated to by the Lord under the particular aspect of the Great Architect, as the Old Testament prophets were by Jehovah.   Nor does

it sustain the assumption that Jehovah and the Great Architect are identical, or that Jehovah is the male and female principle in the generative power. The only conceivable manner in which the Bible can be made to sustain these Masonic claims is to read the Masonic value and meaning into the words and terms employed in the scriptures. It is therefore by putting the Great Architect as identical with the I AM that Freemasons arrogate to themselves the honor of being the first to erect altars to him, and to worship Him, while the rest of the world was involved in the absurdities and pollutions of polytheism. This attempt on the part of Freemasons to harmonize the biblical doctrine of the unity of God with their ideas of the identity of deities is derived from the Kabbalah, the essence of which is not Jewish but evidently derived from more remote eastern people. By means of this oriental philosophy the Rabbis were enabled to read wonderful things into their scriptures which in a measure harmonized their theology, cosmogony and anthropology with that of the oriental religions. And it is by this Kabbalistic principle that Freemasonry is enabled to find in the scriptures an apparent warrant for its peculiar views of the divine.

"The prophets of Israel denounced the worship of the false gods. The philosophers of Egypt found accommodation for them as manifestations of the one real existence. The belief that the one reality is equally real in all its forms, and that all its forms are equally unreal, is not a creed which leads to the breaking of idols, the destruction of groves and high places, or the denunciation of all worship save at the altar of the Lord. Pantheism is the philosophical complement of a Pantheon, but the spirit which produced the monotheism of the Jews must have been something very different." "Amongst the Jews, alone of the Semites, did monotheism follow a line other than its natural development." (Jevons' Introd. to the Study of Religions p. 390). "The one thing not proved is that Jehovah ever denoted in Israel a merely tribal God." (Orr, Prob. of O. T. p. 498). And a thing that Freemasons have not proved is that the Great Architect of the Universe is identical with Jehovah.

"Although the Old Testament faith in

God, as contrasted with the heathen polytheism is a strict monotheism, yet it can not, like the religion of Mohammed, be termed an abstract monotheism. The Old Testament points to a distinction between God in his immanence, and in his transcendence." (Tholuck, Com. on St. John, p. 58, Krauth's translation).

"Jehovah is to Israel, not a God among other gods, neither is Jehovah God simply. He is God in Israel, God saying I will be God in the act of unveiling his face more and more, in the act of communicating the riches of himself more and more, in the act of pouring out all his contents into the life of Israel, or God the constant one, the same yesterday, today and forever." (A. B. Davidson, Theol. O. T. p. 58).

Biblical monotheism is an absolute monotheism, a solity of God and demands a worship of Him and Him only and in His name only. It demands that there be neither belief in the existence, neither the recognition, nor the worship of other gods. It denies that God can be known from speculation, but only by the revelation of Himself, in His Word. Biblical monotheism is incompatible with the idea that the entities or principles represented by Brahma, Allah, the Great Architect of the Universe, are identical with Jehovah. God in the Christian conception is a monad, a unity; so distributed as it were within itself, as to admit a perfect interchange of reciprocity of those affections which can exist only as between persons. A monad triune in his nature but one in essence. The monotheism of Christianity is as distinct and different from that of Freemasonry as Christ is from the worshipful master.

"And who is this Jehovah? The Creator and Sustainer of the world, immanent in all its forces, cause in all its causes, law in all laws, yet Himself not identified with the world, but above it, ruling all things in personal freedom for the attainment of wise and holy ends." (Orr. Virgin Birth, p. 13).

Christianity knowing itself to be the only true religion, and possessing the true knowledge of the only true and living God, denounces all false gods and false religions and false philosophies. It refuses to recognize them as helpful to itself, much less as on an equality with itself. What truth is to be

found in them, it recognizes, but it claims
for itself the possession of a saving truth, a
saving knowledge that is not to be found in
any other. The truth found in other religions, is the exact conformity in statement
to the facts and processes of nature. The
truth which is unique in Christianity, and
which it alone possesses, is the perfect fulfillment in Jesus Christ of the promises of
Jehovah made to Israel, a steadfast fulfillment of the divine intention or promise.

If the Bible is a supernatural revelation
from God, the biblical doctrine of the unity
of God, the biblical monotheism, is also a
revelation and can not for that reason be
identical with a doctrine based upon natural
revelation, or a doctrine derived from pure
speculation. As biblical theism is not identical with philosophical theism, so the biblical doctrine of the unity of God is not the
Masonic doctrine.

But Freemasonry rejects the Bible as a
supernatural revelation from God. It rejects the God of the Bible. And in its rejection of the Bible as a supernatural revelation, it also rejects the biblical doctrine of
the unity of God. This is conclusive proof

that Masonic monotheism is not biblical monotheism, and that the Masonic doctrine of the unity of God, is not the biblical doctrine.

Another phase of the Masonic idea of the unity of God growing out of its peculiar god-idea, is its teachings on the unity of the divine. On this point it is in harmony with the theological ideas that prevailed in the mysteries.

The chief esoteric doctrine taught in the mysteries was the unity of the divine. This doctrine was known by the priests alone, and communicated to such only as were shown worthy of confidence by severe tests, and qualified to keep it concealed.

The divine in the mysteries was the life of nature. In the totality of all its complex elements it was viewed as the divine nature, that mysterious energy, force or power which annually dying renews itself in new, similar yet different forms, ever preserving its self-identity; that mysterious endowment which enabled all living creatures to reproduce their life in offspring; that nature which perpetually dividing into male and female, perpetuated itself through the union of these. This diversified mysterious energy was conceived as a single, unified, living divine power, a unity in multiplicity and a multiplicity in unity, permeating all animated nature, but manifesting itself in an infinite variety of forms. This unity of the life of nature was symbolized by the Sphynx and other monstrosities, in the ancient religions. It was this divine nature that was viewed as the deity, and enthusiastically worshiped in the mysteries.

This divine nature was viewed as containing in itself all the elements that appear in the early life. In it as in a totality were the generating, nourishing, constructing and destroying principles. That the divine nature may continue in the earthly, or in the form of human life, it divided itself into the male and female principles, or into the god and goddess. Through the union of these principles the life of nature or the earthly originated. The masculine fecundating principle fertilizing the passive feminine principle, generated a new life, containing within it the power to nourish itself, and build for itself out of the maternal substance a tabernacle in which its earthly life is to be spent, and endowed with the power to propagate its life in another as it had been propagated by its parents. Thus through these processes, the life of nature was continually to go on. The earthly life is but a continuation of the divine life, and the earthly nature a reproduction of the divine nature. The origin for this earthly life and nature is accounted for in the legends of Zeus and Demeter, Kora and Dionysus. Thus is explained the unity of the divine as conceived of in the mysteries.

The Masonic doctrine of the divine nature and of the divine unity, or the unity of the divine is not only akin to this view as held in the mysteries, but in substantial unity with it. Its god broadly speaking is the life of nature in all its mysterious complexity, constituting the divine nature with all its attributes, the life of nature in the divine nature, and the divine nature in the life of nature. But specifically the Masonic deity is the constructive principle in this divine nature, that principle which fashions out of the maternal substance the bodily temple in which the life is to dwell and live and fulfil its mission. As this constructive principle is an element in every form of life it is viewed as one unified intelligent energy pervading all animated creatures, and inhering in the divine nature as its divine artist, the architect of its temple, and the divine draughtsman whose plans are perpetually drawn upon the trestleboard of nature. This architect is viewed as the chief and essential element in the divine nature, for unless there be a temple for the life to dwell in, the life will perish, and although the old temple is continually falling into decay through the destroying principle, the new is ever building though never finished by this divine architect. Thus it is that 'God,' the generative principle, 'is in Freemasonry viewed in the aspect of the master builder.'

The Masonic unity of the divine is further expressed in the view that this life of nature is the soul of nature. God is the All-soul, and every human soul is an emanation or scintillation of this All-soul. This All-soul is incarnate in humanity in toto, and constitutes humanity as the only 'personal God' that Freemasonry recognizes. The immortality of man rests first in the ever dying and the ever regenerating, in a carnal sense, of human life, from generation to generation, and secondly in the notion that every human soul is an inextinguishable spark from the All-soul.

This All-soul is the All-life, the sum total or the totality of all intelligences in the universe. Souls are not begotten, or created, but detached from the deity, and transmigrated until they are again attracted and absorbed in the eternal All-soul. (See Buck.) Masons become partakers of the divine nature and come into communion with the divine, when they become generators of human life. In the procreative acts they become gods, and enter into co-operation with the divine nature.

"The Christian view affirms the unity of God but requires us to conceive of His unity, not as an abstract or indeterminate self-identity; not as a sterile monotonous simplicity; but as a unity of an infinite fulness of life and love, the unity of a Godhead in which there are Father, Son, and Holy Spirit, a trinity of persons, a diversity of properties, a variety of offices, a multiplicity of operations, yet sameness of nature, equality of power and glory, oneness in purpose and affection, harmony of will and work." (Prof. R. Flint, D. D.).

PART III.

———

The Masonic Hieroglyphs.

(353)

CHAPTER XIII.

THE MASONIC SYMBOLS AND THEIR MEANING.

"The symbolism is the very soul of Freemasonry."—*Pike*.

WE have shown in Part II that the Masonic religion is a veiled phallicism. We purpose to show in this part, that the symbolism of the institution interpreted in its historic usage, and in accordance with Masonic declarations, sustains this phallic character. We shall show that Freemasonry is disclosed to us in all the ugliness, nakedness, and obsceneness of the ancient mysteries and of the sakti cults of India, when the geometrical, architectural and biblical imagery in which its ideas are expressed, is understood, and the veils thrown around it, are removed. Phallicism is its essence, and furnishes the key that unlocks its secrets, and solves its mysterious rites and ceremonies. It is the cord that binds Freemasonry into unity with the ancient mysteries and with the oriental sex-cults of the present.

Phallic worship is characterized by imitating in its rites, the acts and processes of the generation of life. It emphasizes its ideas of the divine, and aids the mind in their comprehension, by the use of realistic or conventional symbols of the generative organs, and by ceremonies illustrating the generative acts and processes. In phallicism these organs and their representatives are regarded as sacred, and are adored, because of their connection with the mysteries of the generation of life. Phallicism is most strongly expressed by the deification, adoration, reverence or worship of the generative organs and of their functions, whether in plants, animals, or man.

Phallic religions and cults are almost invariably secret, due doubtless to the adoration of the secret parts, as the agencies of the secret processes of life, and the secret operations of the generative principle. "As the fathers of Freemasonry discovered that all life and beauty were elaborated in night and mystery, they made the institution in this respect conform to the divine order in nature." "The great life force which vivifies, moves and beautifies the whole world is the profoundest of all mysteries." (Sickel's Ah. R. 62).

The distinctive peculiarity of Freemasonry is its theistic conception. Its Great Architect of the Universe is the creative or generative principle involving the male and female elements which inhere in all forms of life, and the procreative, reproductive, nourishing energy in this life force. This generative principle involving all the functions of the life force, Freemasonry conceives of as the divine nature, as the deity, and as an architect because it is regarded as the artificer of the body as well as its source of life. The known facts of this principle constitute the science, and the actions based upon them, the morality of Masonry, the 'two mighty pillars' upon which Freemasonry is founded. The processes involved in the operations of this creative principle, and the known laws governing them, are the bases for the rites and ceremonies of Freemasonry. The organs through which as agencies or media, this principle propagates the life in which it inheres, are the sacred vessels, the sacred objects, and the real work tools of Freemasonry, and are the things represented by the symbols, employed as visible aids to the Masonic worship. The mysteries involved in the procreative energy and in the origin of each individual life are the real 'secrets which have never been found out,' and of which the conventional secrets are symbols or types. The institution itself is secret because it deifies, venerates and adores the secret parts of animate organisms, and the secret mysteries in which are involved the origin of life, and especially of the human soul. Masonry views, receives, believes and lives these principles as a solemn duty and sacred privilege. It gives concrete form to these ideas in ceremonies and rites, worships this deity by means of these, speaks of these sex agencies and processes in allegory, and represents the generative organs and functions in symbols and ideographs which have some supposed or real resemblance to them, but which speak something else. The Masonic religion is the practice of these functions as a solemn duty and sacred privilege, and the Masonic worship consists in bestowing divine honors under intensely emphatic symbolism upon this procreative power or energy, which it views and adores as the Great Architect of the Universe, but under forms which least do mean what they most express.

"The real secrets of Masonry lie concealed in its symbols, and these constituting as they do a picture language, or art speech, are made to carry a complete philosophy of the existence and relation of deity, nature and man. The average Mason, taking the symbols for the things symbolized, and knowing nothing of the profound philosophy upon which they rest, is incredulous that it ever existed." (Mystic Masonry). "The secret doctrine is the complete philosophy of Masonic symbolism. So long as this philosophy is unknown to the Mason, his symbols are to a great extent dead letters, the work of the lodge a dumb show beyond its moral precepts, and the genius of Masonry for the members of the craft, is largely the spirit of self interest, the latest embodiment of which is the 'Mystic Shrine.' There are some among the members who believe that Masonry means far more than this, and who have already discerned in its symbols, and traditions, something of their real meaning." (Mystic Masonry, 256).

"In the investigation of the true meaning of the Masonic symbol we must be governed by the simple principle that the whole design of Freemasonry as a speculative science is the investigation of divine truth." (Sickels' Ah. R. 159). "The real truths of Masonry are hidden under the symbols and enigmatical forms, which without a key, appear as absurd and debasing rites and ceremonies." (Heckethorn, Vol. 2:9). "All these symbols, such as triangles, circles, etc." says Garrison, "are only different forms of the one old conception which we have been tracing down as the mystery of the omnific word, through the long track of more than forty centuries, and which we have found everywhere, throughout that long stretch of ages, employing essentially the same symbolism and setting forth essentially the same truths." (See Fort, p. 465). "Added to this science of symbolism there is an archaic art speech, by the use of which a double meaning is given to language so that the most ordinary form of speech may be used to convey a deep scientific or philosophical meaning." (Mystic Masonry, p. 241). "Freemasonry is a science which is engaged in the search after divine truth and which employs symbolism as its method of instruction." (Mackey, Ency. p. 210). "The symbolism of Masonry, which is its peculiar mode of instruction, inculcates all the duties we owe to God as being his children and to men as being their brethren." (Id. Nat. Freemason. Apr. 1872). "Masonry teaches by symbols, allegories, symbolic forms and ceremonies. Every ceremony, every badge of office, every ornament of the lodge, every article of Masonic clothing and furniture, in fact everything upon which the eye rests and every sound which reaches the ear in the working of the lodge, are intended to teach or to impress upon the mind of the initiate a precept or principle of Masonry while to the profane they are meaningless." (Universal Cyclo. Art. Freemasonry). These symbols reveal or illustrate a complete philosophy of the creation, of the universe and of man. They are designed to symbolize the unfolding of all essences and powers and potencies in their mutual relations and correlations, and secondly they aim to unfold the processes of initiation as synonymous with the evolution of man. These symbols then when understood, set forth the facts of nature, of the generation of life, and of man's sacred duties relative to them, as they are conceived by Freemasons. Interpret these symbols and we have this secret doctrine. Solve its enigmatical forms, and we have its meaning.

The symbols or images which were used as conventional forms of the phallus and yoni in the several ethnic religions and mysteries and which were calculated to set forth their ideas of the creative principle, were numerous and varied. Widely extended in space and time as was the worship of the phallus as the symbol of masculine potency, is the recognition of the tree of life, as the symbol of feminine nature and fruit bearing capacity. A single tree, groves, lotus, flower, fig, pomegranates, all appear as symbols over against the phallus in its realistic or conventional form, as a representative of life. Pillar and tree erected in front of altars of worship became conventional symbols of male and female elements. (See The Threshold Covenant, p. 234-237).

In the ancient mysteries the ideas concerning the deity seem to have originated either in the knowledge of sex, or in the sex principles, male and female, which animate nature, or in the procreative instinct. There can be no doubt that in the earlier stages of human existence, the reproductive power throughout nature, but especially in animals and man, was worshiped as the creator.

"Freemasonry," says Buck, "is modeled on the plan of the ancient mysteries with their glyphs and allegories, and this is no coincidence, the parallels are too closely drawn." "The real secrets of Freemasonry lie in its symbols, and the meaning of its symbols reveals a profound philosophy and a universal science, that have never been transcended by man." "Masonry's prerogative is to teach the philosophy of nature, and of life." "In their emblematical relations, these figures unfolded to the brethren a more profound wisdom, to the master an immutable clue and to the fellows and apprentices, a fingerboard in the ever lengthening routes of knowledge." (Buck). This sentiment, namely that there is a concealed thought, or veiled meaning in the Masonic symbols is expressed by other Masonic authorities. That but comparatively few

Masons get this meaning, is the conviction of a number of Masonic writers.

According to the declarations of these high Masons, the symbols and emblems of the craft are the glyphs and ideographs which express the secret science, philosophy and religion of the institution; the rites are the allegorical actions by which these religious notions are illustrated. And in order to discover the key by which these may be interpreted, we must go to the ancient mysteries.

And what we want in order to form conclusions concerning these religious ideas of Freemasonry, are not theories, but facts. What are the facts that lie concealed under its ceremonies and symbols? Are they the processes of nature, the functions of life, or are they the acts of operative stone masons? Determine this and we have a working basis.

The symbols used in the mysteries as aids to the worship, were phallic, generally realistic, seldom conventional. We also learn from trustworthy authority that those mysteries which survived the contact with Christianity became secret, that is, they veiled and disguised their phallic religion under the terms of the Christian religion, so as to deceive more effectually the church fathers. Those *mystai* did not change their religion or religious ideas, but the garment in which these ideas were clothed. It is therefore to be expected that the symbols would become disguised. We purpose to show that the Masonic symbols, glyphs and ceremonies are disguised phallic symbols and rites, and mean in this craft exactly what the realistic symbols meant in the mysteries.

According to Buck, the Masonic symbols constitute a picture language or art speech, and are made to carry a complete philosophy of the existence and relations of deity, nature and man. The secret doctrine of Masonry is the complete philosophy of this symbolism. If then we can interpret this "picture language" and understand this "art speech," we get this secret doctrine. And reading these symbols in their proper place in the institution, and in their place and usage in the mysteries, and in the light of their derivation, we get this secret doctrine.

Many Masonic authorities, Clavel, Ragon, Pike, Mackey, and others declare that Masonic symbolism in its original and proper meaning refers above all to the solar and phallic worship of the ancient mysteries, especially those of Egypt. This Masonic opinion furnishes a basis for a rational and consistent interpretation of the symbols, and furnishes hints for the secrets that are concealed in the antique symbols of the order. A phallic interpretation is therefore in perfect consonance with the opinions of the most eminent and best informed Masons.

If these symbols constitute a picture language or art speech, and are made to carry a complete philosophy of the existence and relations of deity, nature and man, then they can be broadly classified as symbols referring to deity, symbols referring to nature, and as symbols referring to man. These relations are set forth in emblems which express ideas more complex than do simple symbols. The ceremonies are symbolic actions, setting forth in allegorical or mimic forms, the activities, the processes, and the modes of the operation of these life forces. The lectures are intended to explain, but in veiled form, these symbols, emblems and ceremonies, and their offices. It is beyond our purpose to trace in detail every idea that is expressed in this medley of combinations. The attentive reader can do that with the key herein given.

1. *Simple Symbols Referring to Deity.*

The letter G.—The ritual says concerning this symbol that it is the initial of Geometry, that "by virtue of it the candidate is admitted into the middle chamber of King Solomon's temple," that "it is universally displayed over the master's chair," and "that it alludes to the sacred name of deity before whom all Masons, from the youngest apprentice in the north east corner to the worshipful master who presides in the east, with reverence most humbly bow." (pp. 112, 128). It is characterized by Masonic writers as "that hieroglyphic bright which none but craftsmen see." While it is the initial of Geometry, of God, and of G. A. O. U., the sacred and mystic name of the Masonic deity, it symbolizes the generative principle, and the initial of the work of emanation, or generation.

The Hebrew yod, ' according to some high Masonic authorities, means the same

thing as the letter G and should, they say,
be displayed in its stead over the Master's
chair. This is the first letter in the Hebrew
name JHVH, which Masons identify with
the generative principle. This letter in the
Kabbalah denoted this principle, especially
in its masculine aspect. When it occurs in
Masonic emblems it denotes the same thing
as the letter G, the masculine generative or
fecundating principle.

The point or dot.—The point or dot .
figures prominently in Masonic symbolism.
While it like the two mystic letters G and '
also denotes the generative principle, it primarily indicates where that principle inheres, or where its activities are especially
manifest, or whence it emanates. The mystic letters denote that principle as the deity,
in its divine aspect, while the dot denotes
the place where it especially is active, or inhering, or in its first going forth into activity.

The All Seeing Eye. —This is a
symbol of the Masonic deity, and
expresses the universal presence of the generative principle in nature, especially as
the male and the female principles combin-

ed. The Masonic deity is viewed as a sexual binary, that is that the male and female principles are inherent in him. His nature is as complex as is human nature, save that the male and female elements are, or were originally in him, and are differentiated only as they go forth from him in created entities. It is this aspect of the deity that the all seeing eye symbolizes.

The Sun. —This symbol denotes the generat ive principle, but more particularly as inherent in that luminary, and as the source of all terrestrial life, and as ever going forth in creating, preserving and destroying aspects.

The straight lines, symbolizing rays of light, radiating from these symbols, or as they appear as elements in the numerous emblems, denote the generative principle in activity, or going forth into creative action, as in the state or process of generating life or in creating a temple in which that life is to dwell. These irradiations in Freemasonry do not symbolize the glory of God as they do in Christian symbolism, but the generative and creative activities of the Masonic god, the Great Architect of the Universe.

24

'Light' is not only a symbol in Freemasonry, and a veil, a word upon which there are many plays, but it is also viewed as a bearer of the life generating energy, and the garment in which it is clothed. The 'light' which the candidate so frequently demands is a symbol for the key to the veiled doctrines of the institution.

The horizontal line is a symbol of the female ray, and the perpendicular line of the male ray. In every irradiation these two rays appear and indicate the bisexual generative activity. These rays are sometimes elongated.

Geometry.—The Pythagorean art speech under a mathematical disguise is employed in Masonry. Under the garb of geometry it veils its peculiar ideas of the emanations of the generative principle. The term is much dwelt upon especially in the fellowcraft degree. There are lectures upon the "moral advantages of geometry," and moral ideas and precepts are expressed in geometric figures and terms. The ritual says that, "Masonry and geometry were originally synonymous terms; that geometry is the basis on which the superstructure of Freemasonry is erected; and that by geometry we may curiously trace nature through her various windings etc." To get the idea that these Masonic writers express and conceal under this geometric veil, we must go back to the old mathematician.

Pythagoras, who was a great philosopher, a mathematician, and in religion a phallicist, is frequently spoken of by Masons as one of the "prophets" of Freemasonry. This statement is based on the fact that he expressed his ideas of the emanations of the deity in geometric terms, and the nature of all things, in numbers, that is under mathematical conceptions, and in this way made Masonry, that is phallicism and geometry synonymous terms. The numerals and geometric figures in his system were "hieroglyphic symbols by means of which he expressed all ideas concerning the nature of things." (Porphyry, De Vita Pythag.). He founded an esoteric system in which the elements and conceptions of the divine in the phallicism of his time, were veiled under geometric terms. He had been initiated into the Orphic mysteries, had traveled and studied the mysteries in Egypt, and subsequently founded his school.

Under the teachings of these cults, he conceived of the divine nature as operating in harmony with mathematical principles; that the emanations went forth as the mathematician conceives of the generation of space, namely that a point is simply position, but when conceived as moving it generates a line, or extension; that the line conceived as moving generates a surface or plane, and the surface conceived as moving, generates a solid, or space, there being length, breadth and thickness. All solids can be considered as generations or emanations from a point. (See Rit. Lect. p. 108). So the divine nature is viewed as going forth into its generative activity from a point, and the successive emanations as eventually constituting space, in which the universe is located, and which it occupies. Thus deity and space, the En Soph and emanations, the celestial and terrestrial spheres were continually associated in the minds of these philosophers, and regarded as inseparable. And as geometry is the science of magnitude, and space, the science which treats of powers and properties of magnitude (Rit. p. 108), God and geometry were perpetually revolving in the minds of these prophets of Freemasonry, as Masons say. These ideas of the divine emanations are well expressed in these primary elements of geometry, and hence it is and was frequently termed the divine science, and by Masons the 'noblest of sciences.'

It is in this way and in this sense that "geometry and Masonry were originally synonymous terms," and that "by geometry we can trace nature through her various windings, and most concealed recesses; that it is enriched with the most useful knowledge, proves the wonderful properties of nature, and demonstrates the more important truths of morality." (Rit. p. 115.) The Great Architect of the Universe being the generative principle, his activities are viewed as emanations and not as creative acts. 'Geometry' is a veil for this phallic religion, and its peculiar ethical ideas, and it is in this veiled sense that it is the basis upon which the superstructure of speculative Freemasonry is erected as operative masonry is upon the science of geometry, but few Masons suspect this to be the case.

The Holy Scriptures.—"The importance of the holy scriptures in Freemasonry can not be overestimated," but this importance does not rest upon any intrinsic or doctrinal value that scripture possesses, but solely upon its symbolic offices and its effectual use as a veil for the religion of Freemasonry. In Christian countries the Bible constitutes the holy book in Freemasonry, evidently to commend the institution to the Christian's favorable consideration and acceptance. But any book that purports to be an exemplar of the divine will, is recognized in Freemasonry as holy scripture, so that the term and its usual synonyms for the Old and New Testament scriptures are not honestly employed in Masonry, but always as a symbol.

The Masonic evidence is abundant and conclusive that these terms in Freemasonry are veils, and glyphs intended the more completely to conceal the deceivableness of the institution. Freemasonry is an esoteric institution and its language is not to be taken at its ordinary value. This is the landmark out of whose sight we must not allow ourselves to drift while exploring this perplexing sea of mysteries and substitutes. The Bible is the most effective veil behind which Freemasonry can conceal its phallic religion. It hesitates not to employ that holy book in order to conceal its own falsehoods and idolatries and to deceive and mislead its over confiding disciples relative to the truth as it is set forth in the Word of God.

Mackey tells us that in Freemasonry "the Bible is a symbol of the will of God however it may be expressed." As geometry is a veil for the Masonic ideas of emanation or creation, so the Bible is a veil for the Masonic ideas of revelation, but not these ideas alone. The 'holy book' appears in different aspects in the lodge, as 'furniture,' as 'trestleboard' and as the 'great light.' In each of these aspects it is symbolic. In conjunction with the square and compass on the altar, it is 'furniture,' and symbolizes the seminal principle with which the microcosm is 'furnished' in order that it may perpetually reproduce itself. As 'trestleboard' it is a symbol of the natural revelation, the great book of nature in or upon which the Great Architect has drawn his designs. As the 'great light' Buck says it symbolizes the spiritual nature of man, and distinguishes him from the beasts that perish. In whatever aspect the Bible figures in the lodge room, it is a symbol and nothing more. It has no authority over a Mason's conscience. In its symbolization it always has some reference to the operations of the generative principle, by which man may learn his duties. We can profitably bear in mind the statement of Mackey that Masonry is not founded upon the Bible; if it were it would not be Masonry; it would be something else.

II. *Symbols Relating to Man or Human Nature.*

The Square.—In the phallic cults the rectangular square ⬜ has been for ages the symbol of the masculine, or generative principle. In the Kabbalah it is the symbol of the Adam Kadmon, the archetypal man, the type of humanity as a collective totality within the creative deity. In the system of Pythagoras, it is the quarternary, a representation of the number four, which referred to deity, whose mystic name was the sacred tetractys, "the fountain and root of ever living nature," the generative principle especially in its masculine aspect.

The Masonic square is a conventional form or a substitute for this phallic square, and symbolizes in Freemasonry exactly what the rectangular square did in these ancient cults in which they figure, namely the masculine principle, and specifically the organ in which that principle was viewed as residing. It sustains the same relation to the universe of man, that the sun does to the material universe, the source and originator of life, and in the Masonic ceremonies frequently figures over against the sun. As a builder's tool it is a very suggestive and appropriate symbol. The square is dedicated to the master of the lodge, and to master Masons. As the phallus in the Baal cult stood over against the sun's disk, symbolizing the generative principle, so the square the symbol of the phallus in the Masonic cult stands over against the worshipful master in the east, the representative of the sun, and the creator of Masons. As one of the work tools of Freemasonry it is essential "to building the temple of humanity."

The Cross.—The cross is prominent in Christian symbolism, but it has none of its Christian significance in Freemasonry. In this cult it retains its ancient esoteric meaning which is phallic. "The cross is to all of us Masons an emblem of nature and of eternal life" (Pike), i. e. of perpetual life generation. It has many forms in Freemasonry. It has the same meaning as the square namely the *man,* the masculine generative principle. It is employed so as to hide more completely the phallic nature of Freemasonry under common Christian symbols. But changing the garment does not change the essence.

The Keystone.—"The Keystone," says Blavatsky, "has an esoteric meaning which ought to be, if it is not, well appreciated by high Masons." It is a symbol in Royal Arch Masonry. Dermot says that he believes "it to be the root, heart and marrow of Masonry," and in this he is correct. The Keystone is a symbol of the phallus, that masculine principle which prevents the great arch of humanity which spans the ages, from falling into ruin and decay. It supports the arch in the temple of humanity.

After delivering his lecture to the candidate in Holy Arch Masonry in the ceremony of "passing the veils" in symbolic language the lecturer says: "But these are all symbolical definitions of the symbol, which is simply solved into an emblem of science in the human mind, and is the most ancient symbol of that kind, the prototype of the cross, and the first object in every religion or human system of worship. This is the grand secret of Masonry which passes by symbols from superstition to science." (See Heckethorn Vol. 2: p. 33). This 'first object in every religion or human system of worship,' was the phallus which is 'the prototype of the cross,' of which the Keystone is an emblem. This 'symbolical definition of the symbol,' is only a circumlocution for saying that the keystone is a symbol of the phallus.

The Ashler.—The Ashler, rough or perfect is a cube or a rectangular solid, having six sides. It too, is the symbol of the man —the rough ashler representing the entered apprentice; the perfect ashler representing the Master Mason. This solid unfolded forms the cross ⊞ the symbol of the masculine principle ⊞ in the Mason. (See Buck's Mystic Masonry for illustrations of the symbolism).

The Circle.—The circle, also called a compass, is a very prominent and essential symbol in Masonry. Sickels has a long extract (Ah. R. p. 87-92), from some unnamed writer, in which its meaning and use among the ancients is given. According to this author, it was originally the conservator of a genuine moral precept, founded upon a fundamental religious truth; that its use is coeval with the first created man; that the Garden of Eden was a circular form with the tree of life in its center; that to this august circle the two forbidden trees were the accompanying perpendicular lines, pointing out God's equal justice and mercy; that the circle with its center distinctly marked became a most sacred emblem with every nation of idolators; that the Samothracians had a great veneration for the circle, which they considered as consecrated by the universal presence of deity; and hence rings were distributed to the initiated as amulets possessed of the power of averting danger; that the

Chinese used a symbol similar to the Masonic circle with parallel lines, only it was
bounded by serpents. We will not dispute
these statements concerning the prominence
of the circle in the religious symbolism of
the ancients, for there evidently is a veiled
phallic allusion in this dissertation on the
circle by this writer. The whole truth is
not given. The fact is that the circle in the
ancient religions and in the mysteries, as
now established by monumental and archaeological evidence, was a phallic symbol and
a sacred emblem among early religionists.
It is the symbol of the female principle, of
the yoni. (See Brinton, Relig. Sentiment, p.
209; Inman's Ancient Faiths; Trumbell's
Threshold Covenant). The phallic altars
were a round circular base with an upright
column or shaft. The rings or circular
cakes distributed in the mysteries, or kept
in the sacred chests, were phallic symbols.
(Clement of Alexandria). The Masonic
circle with its point in the center, is a remnant of this phallic symbolism, and means
in its esoteric sense, the same thing. The
evidence is overwhelming and conclusive
that among the Egyptians, Greeks, Assyr-

ians, Phrygians, and the ancients generally, the circle was the symbol of the female principle in nature. "In primitive symbolism, as shown in Babylon, Egypt and India, the circle or ring represents woman." (Threshold Covenant, 255).

The Compass.—In Masonry the compass is the conventional substitute for the circle, and symbolizes the feminine principle in nature and in humanity, as the square does the masculine. The statement in the ritual that "the compass is given to circumscribe our desires and to keep our passions in due bounds with all mankind, especially with the brethren," and similar expressions, are veiled. "The compass is dedicated to the craft," is also a veiled expression. Unveiled it simply means that Masonry as an institution dedicates womankind to its members to keep their passions within due bounds. The Covenant of Chastity existing between Master Masons, simply defines which class of females are excluded in this wholesale dedication.[1] It is a rem-

---

[1] The Covenant of Chastity reads as follows: "I further promise and swear that I will not violate the chastity of a Master Mason's wife, mother, sister or daughter, knowing them to be such." Rit. p. 149.

nant of the heathen idea that all women belonged as chattel to the state, and of the custom prevailing in the ancient phallic cults, that every woman must at least once in her life, yield her person to a stranger.

The Triangle.— In Christian symbolism the triangle is a symbol of the Holy Trinity. This is what is generally supposed to be its meaning in Freemasonry. But this supposition is far from the truth. The triangle occupied a prominent place in the religious symbolism of every great nation of antiquity. It was a religious symbol ages before the Christian era. In some of these ancient cults it represented spirit, the male active principle or force, and matter, the passive female element, and the dual or correlative principle which partakes of both and binds them together in one new entity. This evidently is its meaning in the Kabbalah. In other cults it was a symbol of the yoni, the female principle in nature. It is this phallic symbolization that still obtains in Freemasonry.

In the ancient cults of India, Egypt and Babylonia, in the Kabbalah, and in the Jewish symbolism, the triangle figures quite prominently and almost invariably as a phallic symbol. Placed with its base downward it represents the phallic triad, Brahma, Vishnu and Siva, of the Hindoo cults. These coalesce and form the mystic Om. "Aum or Om represents the creating, preserving and destroying power of the deity, personified by Brahma, Vishnu and Siva, the symbol of which is the equilateral triangle." (Heckethorn, Vol. 1:39). "Back of this trilaterai glyph, A. U. M., lies the philosophy of the secret doctrine, the synthesis of all knowledge." (Buck, Myst. Masonry, 262). Each deity in this triad was regarded as masculine, and as having his sakti or female consort which was represented by the triangle with its base upward, and is the symbol of the door through which every human being comes into the world, that "delta which is the vehicle of the invisible deity."

In the Babylonian cults the triangle with its base upward represented the "door of life." In the Egyptian cults the equilateral triangle was the symbol of Isis, or nature in the aspect of being embraced in the female element.

The right angled triangle the forty-seventh problem of Euclid.--In the Egyptian cults this was the symbol of universal nature. The base symbolized Osiris, the masculine principle, the perpendicular Isis, the feminine principle, and the hypotenuse, Horus, their offspring. The mathematical relation of these three sides of this triangle was known to the Egyptians, and it is under its mathematical aspect as a veil, that Freemasonry expresses this phallic feature of its secret meaning. Pythagoras learned this mathematical proportion from the Egyptians, and employed it to express his idea of the nature of things by numbers, and upon its successful demonstration exclaimed "Eureka," that is "I have found it." (See Rit., p. 192; Mackey's Ency., p. 830).

Thus under a mathematical veil, Freemasonry expresses the generative facts that obtain in nature, and upon which its religion and ethics are based, and communicates them to the candidate, who is presumed to catch the meaning and also cry out Eureka.

25

The Chest, ark, ship, coffin or box had an essential and prominent place in the initiatory ceremonies and processions of the mysteries. These were symbols of the womb and contained phallic images which were taken out, handled, and replaced by the candidate. The thought thus expressed was obvious.

In the mystic chests which figured so prominently in the mysteries of Greece, were sacred things, Clement says, "not fit for speech." "Are they not sesame cakes, and pyramidal cakes, and globular cakes, and flat cakes, embossed all over, and lumps of salt, and a serpent the symbol of Dionysus Bassareus? And besides these are there not pomegranates and branches and rods, and ivy leaves, and besides round cakes and poppy seeds? And further there are the unmentionable symbols of Themis, marjoram, a lamp, a sword, and a woman's comb, which is a euphemism and mystic expression for the *muliebria.*" (Clement). These were phallic emblems. The round and oval cakes were emblems of the yoni, the female principle. The pyramidal cakes were symbols of the breast, the nourishing power. Sickels concedes that this symbol, the circle, "became the dreadful depository of obscenity and lust." (Ah. R., 87). It was in the mysteries, and in the phallicism of the ancients, the symbol of fertility, when conjoined with the linga the symbol of virile power.

A chest or ark also forms part of the Masonic furniture. "It represents the ark that was carried in the processions of ancient Egypt, and contained seeds of various plants, a winnowing fan, and *Osiridis Pudendum.*" (Heckethorn, Vol. 2:17). The ritual says "The ark is an emblem of that divine ark which safely wafts us over the tempestuous sea of troubles." Few candidates understand this veiled language. This 'divine ark' in Masonry is not the ark of Noah, nor the ark of the Covenant, under which figures it is frequently represented, but the womb, in which human life is carried across the sea of time from one generation to another. The anchor is a symbol of the phallus which safely moors life in the divine ark. The ark of the covenant at the bottom of Jacob's well, in Royal Arch Masonry, is the womb.

CHAPTER XIV.

THE MASONIC EMBLEMS AND THEIR MEANING.

A symbol is a simple or complex thought clothed in a sensuous form." "An emblem comprises a larger series of thought than a symbol." The combination of simple symbols into groups form emblems which become ideographs. The meaning of the symbols composing the emblem, determines the larger series of thought expressed by it. Given the meaning of the symbols, the emblem is readily interpreted. "The moderns who have not been initiated into the ancient mysteries, and only know the emblems considered sacred, have need of anatomical knowledge and physiological lore ere they can see the meaning of many a sign." (Inman, Ancient Faiths, Vol. 1:308). We purpose in this chapter to show the meaning of the emblems employed by this institution, interpreting them according to the principle that has governed us in this work, and in consonance with the hints given above by Dr. Inman.

The Square and Compass. — In the ancient phallic cults, the union of the sex principles essential to the generation of life or of the life so generated, was expressed by a combination of the two sex symbols. In India by the linga and yoni. In Egypt by the circle and tau, in Babylonia by the triangle and arrow, in Phoenicia by the altar and ashera, and in other lands by the tree and serpent, phallus and ark, man and woman, etc. In some Egyptian temples the idea was expressed by a black and white stone. Eliphas Levi, an expounder of the Kabbalah, represents these male and female principles by a white man standing erect, and before him a black woman upside down, her legs passing under his extended arms and protruding behind his shoulders, while their hands join at right angles on either side. (See The Great Symbole Kabbalistique). The thought intended to be conveyed by these ideographs in these different cults, is the same. It is the "language in which Masons of all nations can converse."

In the Masonic cult the square and compass express the same idea, namely that

union of the masculine and feminine principles essential to the generation of life. It
is identical in meaning with the "linga and
yoni" and the "circle and tau."

The relative positions of the square and
compass in the first three degrees, namely
that of the entered apprentice, the
fellow craft and the Mas ter
Mason, signify the grad-
ual as cendency of the spirit,
t h e masculine principle, over matter, the feminine principle; that is of the
masculine principle building out of the material substance of woman a Mason, a temple fit for the indwelling of an immortal
spirit. The Masonic writers tell us it signifies the gradual mastery by the Mason, of his
passions, in learning how to subdue them.
Buck says: "The first declaration made by
the neophyte in Masonry is that he comes to
the lodge to learn to subdue his passions and
improve himself in Masonry, that is to engage in the building of a fit temple for an
indwelling soul." (Mystic Masonry, 215).
This 'fit temple for an indwelling soul', is
the human body, and the square and compass symbolize by what means that temple

can be built, or has been built. It is not himself that the neophyte proposes to erect into a fit temple for an indwelling soul, but to build (to generate) another temple for an indwelling soul.

The Square and Compass with irradiated Initial —This emblem appears with some variations. In Christian lands the initial G is usually inscribed and irradiated. But the Hebrew yod ' is also met with, and according to some authorities, should always appear instead of the letter G. In other cases a mystic name, aum, or יהוה appear, but the idea expressed is essentially the same. The variations are made simply to conform the symbolism to the different faiths or sectarian bias of the Mason, or to veil more completely the phallic nature.

This inscribed letter or mystic name stands for the generative principle, the god in Freemasonry in the various aspects of this god-idea. The rays of light symbolize activity, or the glory of this god, the sum total of all his attributes. The square and the compass symbolize the masculine generative and the feminine nourishing principles. The emblem then expresses this idea, namely that this deity is active through the sex principles or that it is by the union of these sex principles that the Great Architect builds a Mason, that is a temple as a fit dwelling place both for an immortal soul and for himself; or it symbolizes by what tools the temple of humanity is being built, or the temple thus built, and in which this deity ever dwells and which he upholds.

In the teachings of the mysteries it was believed that communion with the deity was had in the sexual act, or in its imitation. This idea is also expressed in this emblem, namely communion with the divine nature through the union of the sexes.

The Emblem of Emblems —This is the jewel of Royal Arch Masonry. It is the triangle with the inscribed irradiated triple tau. It means "with a depth that reaches to the creation of the world, and all that is therein." (Heckethorn, Vol. 2:32). It refers to the double quality everywhere observed in nature, the male and the female. The tau is the symbol of the masculine principle and represents it in its threefold aspect as generator, preserver and destroyer, everywhere operating with or through the feminine principle, represented by the triangle, from the creation until now, or the creator, preserver and destroyer of the temple of humanity from the creation until the present. It is the phallic triad, the mystic aum, especially in its masculine aspect, if the triangle be viewed as masculine instead of feminine, its base being down. Concerning the triple tau Seymour says: "Today these are used as a mystic symbol among secret societies who ape the form and conceal the soul that animated the ancient cults." (The Cross in Trad. Hist. and Art, p. 11). So also the fylfot cross and the swastika were phallic symbols, the latter symbolizing the wheel of life, the perpetual recurrence of life through union of sex principles. The swastika has a solemn meaning among Brahmins and Buddhists. It is a symbol of the sacred fire whose mother is the productive power of nature.

The Knights Templar Emblem Here we have the cross formed by four triangles, joined at their apices. The cross and the quarternary both symbolize the masculine principle, and the triangles

the feminine principle, or the male quarternary, the female trinary, and the cross, the
phallus, combined, or a type of humanity as
the collective totality within the generative
principle. It is the phallic idea concealed
under a common Christian symbol, for the
Knights Templar degree is an effort to
Christianize Freemasonry, that is to express
the phallic religion of Freemasonry under
Christian symbolism.

Emblem of the Mystic Shrine —In
this emblem we have the sword or scimiter, the symbol of the destroying principle. The crescent also called the Tiger's
claws is the symbol of the female principle.
The keystone on the crescent, the male and
female principles united. The five pointed
star is the symbol of creation, and its relative position to the keystone and the crescent symbolizes the manner in which creation is perpetuated. The emblem indicates
the destroying and creative powers in constant opposition. A new life comes forth
from the old which is perpetually dying to be
born again. These processes go on in the
generative region which constitutes the mystic shrine of its devotees.

This emblem also is designed, doubtless, to show the essential unity of the Islamic religion with Freemasonry in its fundamental principles. The strength of Islam lies in its protection and devotion of the female principle to its support in its legalization of polygamy. This emblem signifies that the religion of Islam is regarded by the Shriner as his own. It is an exhibition of the phallicism of Freemasonry under the symbols of Islam.

The Five Pointed Star —The five pointed star is a symbol of creation. Irradiated it is the "blazing star," the symbol of the "foundation" in whom all powers are concealed, synthetized and unmanifested. The center of the star is the pentagon, the keystone, the stone which the builders rejected. "This stone that was rejected and became lost in the rubbish not only bears an emblem and contains a mark but is itself a symbol. It is the center of a five pointed star, the Kabbalistic sign of a man." (Mystic Masonry, p. XL). (See also Hartman, Magic, White and Black).

This five pointed star is also Solomon's

seal, in which were locked up all the secret powers which were ascribed by the Rabbis to Solomon.

As the symbol of the "foundation" of the Kabbalah, this star with its pentagon or keystone representing the masculine principle, and the triangles the feminine principle, very suggestively symbolizes the source of all existence and the means by which the successive emanations were derived, and the foundation of all that exists. It symbolizes creation not as a result of a divine fiat, but as a continuous act and perpetual going forth of emanations.

The Double Triangle, or Six Pointed Star. —The two triangles united or interlaced form the six pointed star and symbolize the masculine and the feminine principles united as essential to the generation and continuation of life. Buck says: "This six pointed star is only another form of the square and compass, each now having a base line from which to form a triangle." These stars, the five pointed and the six pointed, are spoken of by Masons as the star of Bethlehem of Christian story and Christian symbolism, but they are derived from the oriental phallic cults, and form the mystic symbol in female Masonry known as "The Order of the Eastern Star."

In the phallic cults the female organs were revered as symbols of the generative powers of nature or matter, and the male organ as the symbol of the generative power of God, but they were usually represented emblematically. (See R. P. Knight, on The Worship of Priapus, p. 28). Buck in explaining this six pointed star says that it represents spirit and matter in equilibrium. Spirit in the phallic cults is the masculine generative principle, while matter is the passive female principle. These are in equilibrium during gestation when the mystic Aum or Om the generative principle in the totality of all his powers, builds out of woman's substance a temple for the soul, without sound of ax or hammer. This double triangle in the Indian cults is essentially identical in its meaning with the linga and yoni, with the circle and tau of the Egyptian cults, and with the square and compass of Freemasonry. We therefore contend that Freemasonry in its religious conceptions, and in the principles of its symbolism, is in harmony, identity, and unity with the phallic cults of the Egyptians and the Hindoos. In India the creative power or the mystic Om is still almost universally worshiped under the name of Siva and his sakti, the female energy or mother of the world. Temples to hold his symbol, the linga and yoni, which symbolize the male and female principles united in generation, are probably the most numerous in India. "Everything vital whether in symbolical representation, rites, or passwords, as used in modern Freemasonry is known in the eastern cults." (Isis Unveiled, Vol. 2 p. 367).

"In the ancestral records are contained all there is of allegory, symbolism, mysticism and ethics of modern Freemasonry. Even our Blue Lodge ritual of today is but a modern English adaptation of the ancient ceremonial of initiation into the temple of the sacred mysteries." (Life and Action. Vol. 2: No. 2, p. 96).

The double triangle represents among other things the descent of spirit into matter and the ascension of matter into spirit which is continually taking place in the circle of eternity. The six points appear and the seventh is a point in the center (See Hartman, Magic, White and Black, p. 317). The union of the two triangles typifies the male and female principles uniting in the formation of a new entity. The point in the center indicates where the generative principle is active, or where he builds the temple of a soul. The circle expresses the continuation of this process from age to age.

The following symbol is an ornament in the Royal Masonic Arch. "It symbolizes the world within the universe as well as the male and female trinities combined with each other, yet distinct." (Inman, Ancient Faiths, etc Vol. 1 p. 148).

In this form the double triangle symbolizes immortality as the result of regeneration, that is perpetual procreation (See Buck, Mystic Masonry, p. 244).

The evolution of the man is further symbolized by this six pointed star. The center field of these two triangles is a hexagon, the outline of the cube which is the symbol of the man in unconsciousness, the same as the rough ashler, the entered apprentice. The cube unfolded gives the cross or the square, the mark, measure, or 'sign' of a man. The cross or square symbolizes the conscious man, the one in whom consciousness of the power of generation has become a factor. It symbolizes the evolution of the Mason the perfect man from the entered apprentice, or the relationship of deity, nature and man in the generation and perfection of human life, and of the building of a temple for that life to dwell in. It is the "cubic stone" upon which the 'sacred law', the procreative instinct, is inscribed.

This double triangle with its mystic name inscribed, and all engraved upon a plate, was, according to the traditions of the Rabbis and of Freemasonry, deposited under the foundation of the first temple, by King Solomon and Hiram Abiff. When the temple was rebuilt by Zerubbabel, some workmen found this plate but could not read the mystic name. They therefore take it to Zerubbabel for interpretation. This is the tradition upon which Royal Arch Masonry is based. (See Heckethorn, Sec. Soc. Vol. 2 p. 32). The Royal Arch degree is essential to complete the idea of the third degree. In the third degree the 'word' is lost and a substitute is recovered. In the Royal Arch degree the lost word is recovered.

Among the Hebrews the double triangle and the five pointed star figured as symbols especially as amulets. They are called the "Shield of David," and "Solomon's Seal." They doubtless were derived in form and idea, from the eastern cults, with which Judaism came more or less in contact. The Rabbis endeavored to harmonize the Hebrew scriptures with the ideas of the phallic cults, and in doing so, departed from the true sense of scripture. Solomon was supposed to owe his sovereignty over demons to the possession of a seal on which was engraved the "most great name of God." With this seal he, according to the Rabbis could work mighty wonders. He abated the waters of the sea that arose in the foundation diggings for the temple, by casting a plate with this name engraved thereon, into the trench.

26

This name was the word which Hiram Abiff possessed, the male and female principles in their androgynous aspect, and by which he was building the temple, and for the possession of which, the three ruffians slew him.

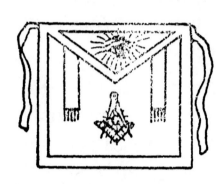

The Lambskin or White Leather Apron. Masonic authorities differ as to the ornamentation of the apron. Mackey contends that it should be perfectly plain, without any embroidering or emblematic decoration. But others think differently. Sickels gives the following description as the regulation form of the apron in the Master Mason's degere. The emblematic decorations which he gives as essential simply intensify the symbolization of the plain apron. He says: "The apron is a white lambskin, square at the corners, thirteen by fifteen inches, with flap triangular in shape, five inches deep at the point, lined and bordered with blue. On the flap is delineated an eye, irradiated; on the area the square and compass and the letter G irradiated, with flat Masonic tags suspended

on either side from under the flap." (Ah.
R. p. 220).

This apron is, in its plain form, a union
of the rectangular square and triangle. This
symbolizes the union of the male and female
principles essential to the generation of life.
One of the ancient symbols of life, or of immortality, that is of life to come, was this
△. "The union of two sexes and the spagy-
▢ rization of matter by triads are necessary
to develop the generative force, that prolific
virtue and tendency to reproduction which
is inherent in all bodies." (Ragon, Potency
of the Pythagorean Triangle).

This life symbolization as above stated,
is intensified by the emblems delineated upon the apron. In the triangular flap, the
symbol of the female principle, is the 'irradiated all seeing eye', the symbol of the creative principle in its androgynous aspect
and universal presence in the female element. It symbolizes the specific place where
the Great Architect operates and the process
by which he builds a temple for the indwelling of an immortal spirit, out of the material
substance of woman, and that is the universal and divine method. The tags sus-

pended from under this trangular flap are the symbols of the two pillars that support or uphold the temple in which the creative principle dwells, the thighs. The irradiated square and compass with inscribed letter G on the rectangular square, signifies that this Great Architect builds the temple of humanity by means of the male and female principles which are his creative powers, and by the reproductive organs which are his specific work tools. The apron in its entire symbolization signifies that by means of the sex principles and the sex organism in which these principles inhere, the Great Architect the god in Freemasonry is perpetually reproducing life, perpetually rebuilding the temple of humanity, and that these mysterious life processes go continually on in the region of the temple over which this apron is worn as a veil. It is in this phallic sense that the Masonic apron is a badge of immortality, or of 'life to come'.

This idea of immortality is further symbolized by the blue border and lining, blue being the color of the Master Mason as it was of Osiris, and signifies immortality. But this Masonic immortality is not that 'life and immortality brought to light by Jesus Christ through the gospel'. Masonic immortality is the notion or doctrine that the life of the parent reappears in the life of the child, a kind of permutation or transmigration of souls.

Sickels says: "The apron in ancient times was a universally received emblem of truth. Among the Grecian mysteries the candidate was invested with a white robe and apron." (A. R. p. 74). Going back to these mysteries and cults of the ancients we can get some idea of the significance of the apron and of the "truth" of which it is an emblem. Sickels does not tell all. The truth of which the apron was a symbol was the exact expression in symbolic language of the known facts in the generation of life. The apron worn in those processions of the mysteries had attached to it an artificial phallus of enormous size. The apron was worn like the Masonic apron, over the phallus, so as both to conceal and to reveal the thought to be set forth. On the Masonic apron there is no artificial phallus but a conventional symbol thereof, and so it also conceals and reveals the thought intended to be conveyed, namely that the phallus is the seat of life, the seat of immortality, of life to come. In the Masonic sense this is true, and of this truth the apron is a symbol, of this kind of immortality and of life to come, the Masonic apron is a badge.

Besides the wearing of aprons as phallic symbols, Tertullian, Clement, Diodorus, and other contemporary writers, declare and certify that in these Grecian mysteries the phallus was honored and exhibited as a sacred member, and that in it their divinity was enshined. "In the Baal cult of the Canaanites the rites consisted in exposing to the idol that part of the body which all persons usually take the utmost precaution to conceal." (Jewish Ency., Art. Baal Peor). Freemasons expose in their apron a conventional symbol of that part of the body. Yes, the white leather apron is the badge of a Mason. He is "to wear it with pleasure to himself and honor to the craft." Its great antiquity is emphasized in the ritual, and in its phallic use, it is more ancient than the golden fleece or the star and garter. It is in this sense that Freemasons claim Adam and Eve wore Masonic aprons, and that Freemasonry existed in the Garden of Eden. From the Christian viewpoint, the Masonic apron is a badge of shame, an offense to all sense of decency and propriety. This apron is a disguised obscene emblem.

The white leather apron "suggests the preservation of the garments from the defilements of labor, and morally, the guard of the soul from the defilements of sin. It is therefore the distinguishing badge of a society whose great aim is to prepare the soul for that spiritual building, that house not made with hands, eternal in the heavens." (Rob. Morris, Dict., Art. Apron). This is the usual Masonic explanation, but we believe this language, like many other Masonic explanations, is veiled, and means something else than that which it says. If it is to be taken at its face value we would raise this query. If the Masonic apron is to guard the soul from the defilements of sin, why not wear it over the heart, the seat of the soul in common imagery, like the Christian's breastplate of righteousness? Judging from its being worn over the phallus, we ask, do Masons locate the soul in that region? If not there is a striking incongruity in this language and the position of the apron.

Clement and other church fathers declare that as a part of the ceremony of initiation in the mysteries was the act of exposing female nakedness. This is also a part of the Masonic ceremony. This Master Mason's apron is a symbol of male and female nakedness. The triangular flap, with its two pendant tags projecting from beneath it, are a disguised outline of the female genital region, the tags representing the thighs. The indecencies transacted in the mysteries are repeated in Freemasonry, but in a disguised and emblematic manner.

The Collar and Jewel.—This emblem is worn by the officials. In form it should be triangular and terminate on the breast in a point. To it is attached the jewel, the square. This collar and jewel is in its symbolism identical with the crux ansata of the Egyptians. Worn around the neck it means not only that the Master Mason has come through the door of life into possession of Masonic immortality, but that he as an official or god in the lodge can also impart it to others. As the gods in the Egyptian cults were designated and given power of life by holding its symbol in their hand, so the Masonic official is designated as the giver of Masonic life by his collar and jewel. "The jewel in the lotus" in the symbolic language of Buddhism, "the circle and tau," "the linga and yoni", "the square and compass" and "the collar and jewel," all are symbols of life, symbolizing by what means that life is generated.

The collar and the jewel is doubtless worn in imitation of the jewel worn around or suspended from the neck of Hiram Abiff, and concerning the disposition of which Masonic tradition is very conflicting. When the body of Hiram was discovered, there was found upon its bosom a jewel which was removed and brought to King Solomon who recognized it as the jewel of the grand master Hiram Abiff. But in the traditions of Hiram it is said that he "threw the jewel into a well" before he was assassinated. It is in imitation of Hiram, the mysterious architect, that the collar and jewel are worn. This explanation or tradition that Hiram threw the 'jewel' into a deep 'well' before he was assassinated is a veiled expression whose meaning is readily determined by the principle guiding us in this interpretation.

The Dedication Emblem.—In this emblem the circles is the symbol of the sun. "The point denoting an individual brother," that is a Mason, and specifically the Master of the lodge, also symbolizes the generative principle in him as a creator of Masons. The parallel lines symbolize the parallelism 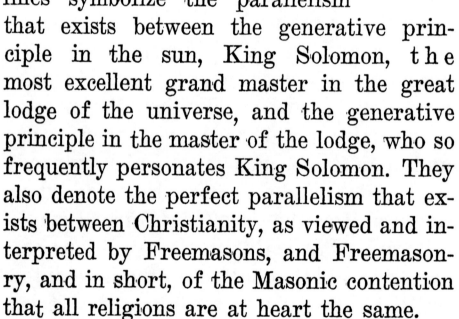 that exists between the generative principle in the sun, King Solomon, t h e most excellent grand master in the great lodge of the universe, and the generative principle in the master of the lodge, who so frequently personates King Solomon. They also denote the perfect parallelism that exists between Christianity, as viewed and interpreted by Freemasons, and Freemasonry, and in short, of the Masonic contention that all religions are at heart the same.

The holy book in this emblem in the aspect of resting upon the vertex of the circle, symbolizes the life essence that goes forth in the generative principle. It is to Christianity what the sun is in Freemasonry, the bearer of light and life. In the aspect of its position between the parallel lines, and the two Saints John, it is a veil to conceal the phallic character of the emblem, and esoterically means that there is a perfect parallel between Christianity, sun worship, light worship and Freemasonry, when these are rightly understood. It is an emblematic way of enjoining every Mason to regard every religion as his own. It is an ideograph expressing the parallelism which Masonry contends exists in all religions, and that at heart all religions are alike.

The Bee Hive.—The bee hive figures as an emblem in Freemasonry, and whether or not so designed in this institution, the bee is also an emblem in the phallic cult that prevailed in Asia Minor, especially at Ephesus. The distinctive features of the Anatolian religion is the idea that the divine power and the divine life is revealed in the nature of the bee. The life of the queen bee (See Ency. Brit.) is the best explanation of the Atys legend. In the fertilization of the queen bee, the drone is deprived of his organs of generation, and thus mutilated, is left to perish on the ground. The description applies with striking exactness to the relation between the mother goddess and the god, who exists merely to be her consort. The god consorted with the goddess by stealth and violence; the goddess was angry at the outrage; she mutilated the assailant, or caused him to be mutilated.

Now the queen bee was the symbol of the goddess in the Ephesian cult. The image of this goddess, Diana, is moulded far more after the form or shape of the bee than that of the shape of a woman. What are supposed to be breasts upon her body, represent eggs. In this cult, the Essenes were the drones, and the Melissae were the female working bees. (See W. M. Ramsay Relig. of Greece, Hast Bib. Dict. Extra Vol. p 116 seq).

With the light that this conception of the divine nature as held by the Ephesians, throws upon the symbolization of the bee, we naturally conclude that the emphasis laid upon the bee hive in the lecture is to be understood in the phallic sense.

The Coffin and the Grave.—In the Phrygian mysteries the grave was viewed as a temple of a deified dead man, and was jealously guarded against desecration. In the ancient cults of Asia, images of the linga were laid upon the grave to indicate the hope of existence beyond the tomb. They defended this symbolic teaching on the ground that the symbol left so much unexplained that it stimulated the intellect and trained to profound thinking. In the light of these customs among those cults from which Freemasonry claims derivation of its ideas, customs, and rites, we can interpret its symbolism. In the mysteries the coffin and the grave had a phallic signification, and this is likewise true of them in Freemasonry. The dead Mason in the coffin, and the coffin with its contents, lowered into the grave, that is into the bosom of mother earth, Demeter, is viewed as a conception which results in his birth into the Grand Lodge above. The sprig of acacia, thrown into the grave, a remnant of tree and plant worship, symbolizes the female principle, which uniting with the Mason as the male principle, generates the immortal life. The apron, itself a symbol of perpetual life generation, immortality, is laid upon the phallic region of the coffin, and symbolizes substantially the same idea. The formation of a circle around the grave by the lodge, again indicates the phallic idea. The whole ceremony of Masonic burial is phallic in its conception and signification.

The grave of a Mason is usually marked by an image of the square and compass, lying upon it, or by this emblem inscribed upon the grave stone. It protects the grave from desecration, and gives it sanctity in the eyes of the brethren.

The Anchor and the Ark.—This emblem is also phallic. The ark is feminine, the anchor masculine. The reader, from the principles herein before elucidated, can readily interpret its meaning.

The scythe, the sword, scimiter, and similar objects symbolize the destroying principle, the Typhon of the Egyptians, the Siva of India, and the ruffians of Freemasonry.

CHAPTER XV.

THE MASONIC MYSTIC NAMES AND WORDS, AND THEIR MEANING.

BESIDES symbols and emblems Freemasonry also employs a number of mystic names and words which have a secret meaning, or refer to some secret force or element in nature which it conceives as an emanation of the deity, or as the deity himself going forth from himself to give life and form unto a new entity or creature. These mystic words and names occur in the ceremonies, and are designated by certain characters inscribed upon their emblems and jewels, and thus constitute a component element in a number of the Masonic ideographs. The meaning of these mystic names and words is essential to a correct understanding of the ceremonies and emblems in which they occur.

The Word.—A word or utterance of God is the expression of his will relative to the thing spoken of. It is a bearer of his creative power, and a medium of his creative energy. The "word" is therefore something divine, an energy of God vocalized, going forth from himself to give life or to originate form and being, in another entity, whose form or being is that involved in the idea of which the word is the expression.

This notion of the "word" was prevalent in Jewish thought and philosophy as a suitable expression for the intermediary between God and the world, and also in Christian theology as a designation for the divine mediator between God and man. Thus it stands written "by the word of the Lord were the heavens made." "He spake, and it was done, he commanded and it stood fast." The fiat of God was the mediary through which, in which and by which the purposes of God were expressed, and made perpetually operative. The 'word' is the expression of his will, and accomplishes that whereto it is sent. Thus the procreation of the race continues by virtue of the word "Be fruitful and multiply and replenish the earth." Generation is a communication of being, and this perpetual self-identity of being is maintained through the eternal fiat "after his kind." By this "word" the procreative instinct, power and energy were implanted in the first pair, and continually recurring in their offspring and will so continue until He recalls that word.

And so in Christian theology the Word or the Word of God denotes the revelation of God's will and grace as we have it set forth in the Old and New Testament scriptures. That Word is the bearer of God's grace to them who hear and receive it. The Word of God is the form and content of revelation, and its greatest expression in concrete form is in the Person of Jesus Christ of Nazareth.

Among other nations of antiquity notions somewhat akin to this Jewish idea prevailed, namely, that words were bearers of magical powers and that by the right use of a word, or of a proper formula of words, great deeds could be wrought. Thus Isis is said to have raised Osiris from the dead by a magical formula. In many and probably in all the primitive ethnic cults the word was regarded as a magical power in itself. The primary idea in the ritual formulas was assimilation to the deity brought about by the power of the words themselves.

27

In Egypt it was believed that by the use of the proper words the most powerful gods could be made subservient to the will of man, and among all these magical words the most sacred was the 'name' which was regarded as an integral part of the deity himself, and containing within it all the attributes and powers of the deity.

In Freemasonry this idea also finds a place. In this cult the term "The Word" or the "Word of God," does not denote the revelation of God, neither its content, nor the form, nor the person Jesus Christ. The term is a glyph or veil or mask for something else. Pike says: "The Universe is the only uttered word of God." Mackey says: "The word itself is but a symbol for divine truth." In Freemasonry the 'word' denotes the seminal principle disseminated throughout the world. It is the 'life fire' of the generative principle, the vital force in its several aspects, inhering in nature. It is that in which the life essence is sent forth into new forms or living entities, containing also within itself the originating and destroying forces. Its several aspects then are viewed and conceived of in Freemasonry as the lost word, the omnific word, and the ineffable name.

The Lost Word.—"I think," says Garrison (Fort, 465), "there can be no doubt at least to any thoughtful Mason, that the keynote to much of our symbolism, and the true spirit of it all, are to be found in the traditions and meditations of the old searchers after the lost word." To discover this 'keynote' and this 'spirit' we need but turn to the ancient cults in whose rituals and myths there have come down to us from very remote ages the traditions and meditations of these ancient searchers for unity with the divine. In these traditions and cults there is a common feature the story of a god suddenly or violently deprived of his power of generation. It is found in the story of Osiris, of Zeus, of Sabazius, of Atys, of Mithras, and of Hiram Abiff. A very limited knowledge of the history of primitive worship and mysteries is necessary to enable any person to recognize in the Master Mason, Hiram, the Osiris of the Egyptians, the Mithras of the Persians, the Bacchus of the Greeks, the Atys of the Phrygians of which these people celebrate the passion, death and resurrection.   (See Reibold's Hist. of Freemasonry, p. 372).

The 'word' in Masonry is the seminal principle. The 'lost word' is a veil for the lost generative power, the seed producing power, the power of which the god was deprived by death or mutilation, or by the exhaustion of his generative powers in the creative act, so that he could not generate or create another entity. This 'word' in Freemasonry denotes the essence of life, the central life fire, the procreative principle, the seed essence of living entities, the possession of which is essential to the perpetuation of the life of the creatures in offspring. It is therefore the 'word' by which the temple of humanity is built, upheld and preserved from falling into decay. If lost it must be recovered, else the temple can not continue in course of building.

When this word is lost as in the case of Hiram Abiff's assassination, there is great mourning and lamentation, for without its recovery the temple of humanity can not be completed, but must fall into decay. "Even Solomon the Wise also bewailed the loss of Hiram because he knew that the vital and principal support of his typical universe had been lost by the master's assassination." (Fort, 409). In order then that the temple may be completed, the word must be recovered, or a substitute secured which is to be used until future generations discover the right word.

This tradition of the lost word as it appears in the third degree, Freemasons explain by referring to the Hebrew name of God JHVH whose correct pronunciation was lost through the very precautions taken to preserve it. This name was held in such reverence by the Jews that they seldom pronounced it, but substituted another name for it, namely Adonai. It is with this fact of Hebrew history concerning the sacred name of God JHVH, that Freemasons explain their legend of the lost word, so as to conceal more completely the underlying phallic idea. The lost name or word, JHVH in Freemasonry, is a mask for this lost generative power which figures so prominently in this institution.

To justify its course and to give warrant for this procedure, it gives a phallic interpretation to this covenant name of Jehovah.

Pike says, "the true word of a Mason is to be found in the concealed and profound meaning of the ineffable name of deity communicated by God to Moses, and which meaning was lost in the very precautions taken to conceal it. The true pronunciation of that name was in truth a secret in which was involved the far more profound secret of its meaning." (Morals and Dogma, p. 700). The secret meaning involved in this name JHVH, according to Pike, Clavel, Mackey and other high Masons, is that not only were the male and female principles originally in God, but that this idea is also expressed etymologically in the name itself as the root idea. This name is then in Freemasonry a secret or mystic name for the generative principle. In other words these Masons teach that the deity worshiped by the Jews was the generative principle and identical with the Great Architect, and that the true word of a Mason is his generative power. The lost word in Masonry is not the lost pronunciation, of the covenant name of God JHVH but the lost generative power of the architect of the temple, Hiram Abiff. It conceals this secret under this name, and

justifies it by giving this name of Jehovah
an arbitrary phallic interpretation.

The Omnific Word.—Freemasonry designates this word or seminal principle in its
generating, preserving or destroying aspects
as the omnific word. "The god Thoth gave
to Isis the word which caused her dead
husband to live again." (Budge, Hist. of
Egypt, p. 68). This husband of Isis, Osiris,
lived again in his son Horus. "Isis raised
the prostrate form of him whose heart was
still, she took from him his essence. She
conceived and brought forth a child, she
suckled it in secret, and none knew the place
thereof." (Budge, Relig. of Egypt. p. 56).
"This word was considered by Pythagoras
as the root and principle, the cause and
maker of all things." (Sickels, A. R., p. 91).
"He is celebrated as the discoverer of the
holy tetractys, the fountain and root of ever-
living nature." This root and principle the
cause and maker of all things was in the
Kabbalah the Foundation, the genital in the
archetypal man. In the Kabbalistic view
the Holy Aged exhausted his generative
powers through giving off the successive
sephira, but in the 'Foundation' it is recov-

ered, from which all subsequent and successive generations of creatures go forth. There the lost word is found. The meaning of the omnific and lost word is thus positively determined.

As a wonder working word it need only to be uttered. Thus Moses is said by the Rabbis and by Freemasons to have slain the Egyptian by simply uttering the secret name JHVH. So also they account for the miracles wrough by Christ, namely that he learned the correct pronunciation of this name in Egypt, and endowed his disciples with similar powers by teaching them how to pronounce it. This word if spoken to the dead would awaken them. It was seldom applied to the living.

The Egyptian word applied to the dead was Maa Kheru, meaning triumphant. This word made them who knew it, masters over all things necessary to their service.

In Freemasonry this word in the third degree is Mahabone, or as some Masons contend, Ma Adonai, or Macbenah, probably corrupted forms of Maa Kheru. This word spoken into the ear of the resurrected candidate transforms him into a Mason by its omnific power, and sets in action a process of spiritual transformation that continues throughout his whole Masonic career. This substitute generates in the Mason a spiritual and moral life, as the 'lost word' when conceived, generates the physical life in the matrix.

The Ineffable Name.—This omnific word or name of the deity, being so powerful if uttered by human lips, is a dangerous weapon to place in the hands of the indiscreet. It must therefore be veiled, concealed and kept secret. Among all magical words the most sacred was the 'name' of the deity, which in the primitive thought was regarded as an integral part of the god, his ego, his very self. "In all the religions of ancient Asia the mysterious name was considered a real divine being, who had a personal existence and exclusive power over both nature and the world of spirits." (Lenormant, Chald. Mag., p. 104). "This doctrine of the ineffable name is the common property of savage and cultured faiths." (Brinton, Relig. of Prim. People, 98).

In the Christian system the "name" of God stands not only for the appellation of

God, but also for the entire revelation which God has made of himself, of his will and grace. That name is hallowed when the word of God is taught in its truth and purity, and we lead holy lives in accordance with it. But in Freemasonry the term stands for something quite different. The ineffable name embodies the idea of the male and female principles in the highest and most profound sense, and that the generative power or spirit, and the productive matter, the female principle were originally in the deity. (See Pike, M. & D., 700). This is the profound truth hidden in the ancient allegory from the general view by a double veil. This is the secret involved in the Masonic use of this name, and must never be divulged. "I am certain", says Garrison (Fort, 467), "that any attempt to understand the principles of speculative Masonry without some knowledge of the history of the doctrines which have been connected with the sacred name, will simply be waste effort, as the one rests on and is at every point, interwoven with the other." "The ineffable name," says Buck, "is spelled in many ways, yet the word is the same."

Drawn from the Kabbalah and taking Jewish or Christian verbiage or symbols, Freemansory but discerns in them universal truths which it recognizes in all religions. (See Mystic Masonry, 113).

The Mystic Name.—The life essence, or generative principle, with which the deity was endowed, was designated by a mystic or secret name, which none but the priests were supposed to know. It was the secret name of deity, and generally designated by four letters. The tetragrammaton of Pythagoras referred to this generative principle, and was the mystic name of the deity in his system. In the cults of India, the Brahma, Vishnu and Siva coalesce to form the mystic Aum or Om, which designates the totality of all the powers in the essence of life. The Essenes had a mystic name for the sun, designating the generative principle in that luminary, and which they worshiped, probably as identical with Jehovah, for under the influence of the eastern cults, the Essenes associated the lost name JHVH with this generative principle and viewed it as resident in the sun. The thing referred to by these mystic names in these cults is the generative or the creative principle. The tetragrammaton of Pythagoras, the Aum of the Hindoos, the On of the Egyptians, the JHVH of the Essenes, the GAOU of Freemasonry are all representations or designations of substantially the same thing, the creative or generative principle with which the deity is endowed.

This essence or principle is not the soul of nature, but that mysterious constructive principle or artificer in the life essence which creates or builds up matter into the tabernacle for the indwelling life. The meaning of this mystic name was kept concealed from the vulgar populace by the priests, for its unveiling would have endangered, they contended, the well-being of the universe. So Masons claim that the unveiling of their secrets would destroy their institution.

The mystic name given to the sun, or to the deity, in the phallic cults, was doubtless designed to distinguish between the sun as an external object, and his generative power; and between the deity, as an objective existence, and his generative or creative power. The name of the deity designated him as a being, the mystic name designated his creative or generative power. The priests worshiped the generative power, the mysterious essence, the populace the external object.

The mystic name and the ineffable name are two aspects of substantially the same thing. The mystic name being the glyph representing the creative principle, the ineffable name being the sound representing the same. The one is the sign to the eye, the other is the sound or sign to the ear.

To give its system the appearance of scripturalness, Freemasonry applies the Hebrew name JHVH to this creative or generative principle, in its ceremonies, lectures and prayers, and under a biblical mask conceals its heathen and phallic ideas. By this syncretism of names, based upon an assumed identity in meaning and designation, it mixes the service of Jehovah with the heathen cults, and confuses the Mason so that he thinks there is no difference between them. By this method alone can Freemasonry make it plausible that the Great Architect of the Universe and Jehovah, are but different names of the same divine being.

Divine Truth.—The whole design of speculative Freemasonry is the investigation of the relation of deity, nature and man, of the nature, origin and destiny of the human soul, and of the mysteries involved in the generation and perpetuation of life, and to teach to its disciples the truth it professes to posses concerning these things. The doctrines and speculations of the ancient cults, and which it contends are demonstrably correct, constitute the knowledge which it claims to possess. This knowledge objectively stated is its divine truth.

Divine truth in the Christian system generally refers to the biblical teachings concerning God and the salvation he has promised. Truth is the perfect conformity of the statement with the fact. Divine truth in the Christian usage is the exact fulfillment in Christ of the promises of God made to Israel. But with this truth Freemasonry has nothing whatever to do.

In Freemasonry the term truth or divine truth refers to the exact conformity in statement, ritual and symbol with the facts, processes and acts involved in the generation of life. Freemasonry assumes that the human nature is an emanation of the divine nature, and as complex as the divine; that as the original androgynous divine nature separated into the two sexes in order to propagate the divine life, and by their reciprocal action that life is generated, so also does human nature continually separate itself into the male and female, through whose reciprocal action, human life is propagated. The generative acts are therefore not only viewed as divine, but as the acts of the divine nature through the human nature and the means by which the human comes into union with the divine. It views sexual passion only as an expression of the divine force, desirous of propagating the divine life, a repetition in the human nature what is conceived of as having occurred in the divine nature. Divine truth then in this cult is the exact conformity in symbolic, emblematic, ritualistic and monitorial expression with the known facts involved in the generation of life; the statement in esoteric terms what Freemasonry believes to be the relation of deity to man and man to deity.

CHAPTER XVI.

SYMBOLIZATION OF THE TEMPLE, THE LODGE, AND THE LODGE OF MASONS.

IN Masonry frequent reference is made to "The Temple" and in such a way as to leave the impression that the temple at Jerusalem, erected by King Solomon, is meant. But such is not the real meaning. In Freemasonry "The Temple" is a glyph for the universe, the macrocosm, and for the microcosm, sometimes referring to the one and sometimes to the other. The details given in the ritual concerning Solomon's temple, its artizans, apprentices, fellow-crafts, masters, pilasters, etc., are related to conceal the real Masonic meaning, or to give an apparently rational explanation to the ceremony. These things are the rubbish of the temple under which the real Freemasonry is concealed.

The Temple.—"The real temple referred to from first to last in Masonry, as in all ancient initiations is the tabernacle of the human soul." That is the human body, or the human race. This temple of humanity is built indeed without the sound of any ax or hammer, or any tool of iron. It is like that other spiritual temple not made with hands eternal in the heavens, for the old philosophy (Kabbalah) teaches that the immortal spirit of man is the artificer of the body, and its source of life. (See Mystic Masonry, p. 111).

"The temple ever building and never finished" is the continous course of natural reproduction. The Masonic symbol for the temple unfinished is the weeping virgin delineated upon the broken column, etc. (See Rit., p. 185, Sickels, A. R., p. 179). The woman alone, like the man alone is the temple of humanity incomplete. Each needs the other to build, to complete the temple and to prevent it from falling into decay and irretrievable ruin.

Buck says: "To rebuild the city and temple of the Lord," an expression occurring frequently in Masonic literature, "is a glyph that has many meanings." (Mystic Masonry, p. XXIII). "To 'build a city' means to establish a doctrine" to 'build a temple' means to establish a lodge, to make

28

converts to Masonry, and to procreate human beings with a view that they may become Masons. The expression then means the propagation of Masons and of the Masonic organization and religion.

The "old temple fallen into decay" is not Solomon's temple at Jerusalem, but the old phallic cults that have disintegrated under the influence of Christianity, and the older generations of Masons who have been cut down by the remorseless scythe of time. This temple is to be rebuilt. "Though the old temple be destroyed we must labor in building the new," says Mackey. The old phallic cults, the mysteries, must be restored, and new generations begotten among whom their doctrines may flourish, and in whom as a temple, the Great Architect, the generative principle, may dwell and be adored and worshiped. "To rebuild the city and temple of the Lord," is a veiled plea for re-establishing the ancient mysteries and the ancient phallicism.

And this is what the celebrated Belgian Mason Ragon contends is the task of Freemasons. He chides the British Masons for their mistaken ideas that Freemasonry is derived from the building of Solomon's temple at Jerusalem, and denies that the craft originated from that event. He contends that the task of Freemasons is to restore the ancient mysteries. (See his Maconnerie Orthodoxe, p. 44). The appeals made to the craft by Masonic writers "to destroy clericalism," and to remove the "rubbish of the church" from the temple of humanity, and to advance the cause of Freemasonry, evidently are to be understood in the same sense.

Masons claim to be "engaged in erecting a structure in which the God of Israel shall dwell forever, fitting immortal nature for that spiritual building not made with hands, eternal in the heavens." (Sickels, A. R., 71). This "God of Israel" is not Jehovah as viewed by Christians, but as Masons view him, the generative principle. The structure they are erecting, is the temple of the body, which the generative and nourishing principle is building out of woman's substance, as a dwelling place for this principle. This structure is upheld by the pillars of wisdom, strength and beauty, the generative, nourishing and renewing powers of nature, through sex agencies. On this temple no women work. They are the gross matter which the spirit, the masculine principle takes and shapes into living stones for this structure, for out of woman's substance every human being is built by this inherent artificer in man, through the impulse given by the masculine fecundating principle. This explains also why no women are admitted into the lodge, but why they are none the less loved and cherished by these workmen on the temple. This building of the temple concerning which Freemasons have so much to say means simply the propagation of the human race, and the promulgation of the Masonic doctrine.

Solomon's Temple.—"Solomon's temple is one of the most sublime symbols in the order of Freemasonry." (Masonic Library, p. 200). "In the ritual of Masonry King Solomon's temple is taken as a symbol. There is in the ritual a play upon the words. Solomon represents the name of the deity in three languages Sol-om-on, and the biblical history is doubtless an allegory or myth of the sun god." (Mystic Masonry, p. 82). These statements from Masonic authorities make it clear that the term King Solomon's temple refers especially to the universe, which is viewed as the temple of the Great Architect, its indwelling spirit and its support, while the term "the temple" refers specifically to humanity. On this point Blavatsky says: "If there are yet Masons who persist in regarding Solomon's temple as an actual structure, who of the students of esoteric doctrine will ever consider this mystic temple otherwise than an allegory, embodying the secret science. The building of Solomon's temple is the symbolical representation of the gradual acquirement of the secret wisdom, or magic, the erection and development of the spiritual out of the earthy; the manifestation of the power and splendor of the spirit in the physical world through the wisdom and genius of the builder." (Isis Unveiled, Vol. 2: p. 391).

The Lodge Room.—Section III of the lecture of the first degree concerning the form, dimensions, support, boundaries, covering, furniture, ornaments, lights, jewels, situation and dedication of the lodge, and Sickels' explanation and comments thereon, show plainly that the lodge room in the entered apprentice degree is a symbol of the macrocosm, or the universe. It is a symbol of that great world in which the various life forces of nature are inherent and continually operative. These cosmic and vital forces and especially the parts or organism through which they operate, or in which they are conceived as inhereing are represented by the accessories and "furniture" with which the lodge room is supplied. The mystic forces which hold the universe in poise, the vital forces which animate it, the sources from which they are derived, and the means or organs through which they are perpetuated, all are symbolized by certain objects in the lodge room. In this degree the floor of the lodge represents the surface of the earth or the floor of the universe, designated in the ritual as the grand pavement of King Solomon's temple.[1]

The Masonic teaching is that in the second degree the lodge room is a representa-

---

[1] The Masonic conception of the universe as symbolized by the lodge room, is substantially the same as that of the ancient Egyptians, namely a rectangular box, the roof of which is bedecked with stars, and supported by columns, while the earth constituted the floor. (See Maspero's Dawn of Civilization, p. 16.)

tion of the 'middle chamber of King Solomon's temple.' Mackey admits that the passage 1 Kings 6:9, is the slender material upon which the philosophical myth of the middle chamber is formulated. (See Sickels, Ah. R., p. 159). Freemasons have been very solicitous to find in the account of the temple of Solomon as related in the Bible, sufficient detail to furnish veils and glyphs for their phallic religious ideas. Its winding stairs, porch, columns, its holy of holies, ark, architect and builder are all appropriated as masks in order to conceal more completely the peculiar Masonic religion.

This "philosophical myth of the middle chamber" is told to explain the ritualistic acts of the second degree, but with the design of misleading the candidate. The middle chamber in Solomon's temple was an apartment above the temple for the priests, and not a part of the temple proper. The term in Freemasonry is doubtless a substitute for the holy of holies, for in some rituals it is stated that the lodge room in the second degree represents the holy of holies in Solomon's temple. The symbolization of Solomon's temple as given by Josephus and eminent biblical scholars, namely that it symbolized the universe, the holy of holies symbolizing the highest heavens, the holy place the heavens, and the forecourt the earth or God's footstool, is not adopted by Freemasonry. It adopts the symbolization of the Egyptian temples.

Broadly and exoterically speaking, the lodge room is a symbol or type of the universe, but specifically and esoterically, it is a symbol or type of the matrix of nature, that part of the universe in whose inscrutable recesses the mysteries of generation, of development, of birth, of growth, of death and resurrection are continually going on. Freemasonry like many of the ancient cults from which it derives its 'thought', views the earthly sphere as embodied in the female element, and the heavenly or celestial sphere as embodied in the masculine element. In those cults, Isis, Cybele and Demeter were nature in the aspect of the Great Mother. In the Indian cults, Brahma is the great hermaphrodite, the father and mother blended into one. In these cults the adytum of their temples was the symbol of the matrix of mother earth or of mother nature.

Of this matrix the Masonic lodge room is a symbol also.

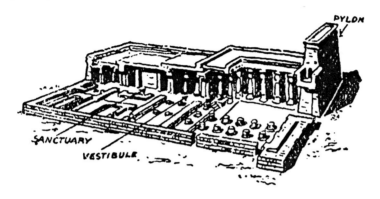

SECTIONAL VIEW OF TEMPLE OF EDFU.

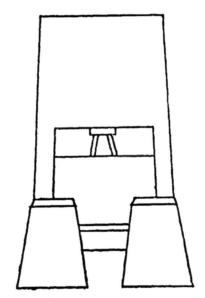

OUTLINE BIRD'S EYE VIEW OF EGYPTIAN
TEMPLE.

In the ancient Vedic cults the altar was modeled after the form of a prostrate woman (See Sacred Books of the East, Vol. XII, p. 62). There is abundant evidence for believing that the typical Egyptian temples were not only symbols but also conventional models of a woman in a supine position, and especially of the female generative organism. This gives a rational explanation for their peculiar architectural style. A glance at the appended drawings, will make this plain. In the holy of holies, or adytum were pictured the mysteries of birth together with the symbols of generation. In this adytum the female generative or reproductive principle was conceived as dwelling in a state of repose, awaiting fertilization by the masculine principle, the sun, the great Osiris, who at dawn darted his rays through the door and the holy place into the adytum and quickened life and activity. Before the temple stood the obelisk, the symbol of the masculine principle, either in the form of a ray of the sun, or of the phallus. "No account of the Egyptian religion can be regarded as fair which is silent upon the subject of the general idolatry and polytheism, of the existence of indecent rites and of constant occurrence of indecent emblems in the religious representations." (Rawlinson Hist. An. Egypt, Vol. 1, p. 425).

The Masonic lodge room is a convention-al copy of the adytum of these ancient temples, and like the adytum it is a symbol of the matrix of nature. Here, like in the adytum of the Egyptian temples we find not only the symbols of life and its generation, but also the mysteries of generation, of birth, of death and resurrection celebrated in mimic rites, according to the peculiar Masonic view of these things.

In the Phrygian cults the rites were usually celebrated in a cave, which answered to the adytum of the Egyptian temple. The cave was viewed as the matrix of the great mother.

In the Masonic lodge room and temple we have a revival in disguise of the ancient phallic temples, with their rites, symbols and religion reproduced but so disguised that not one Mason in a thousand suspects the fact, or discerns the meaning.[1]

The Dedication of Lodges.—The ritual says that "Lodges were anciently dedicated

[1]The ceremony of "placing" the newly made entered apprentice in the northeast corner of the lodge, is evidently a remnant of the practice in the ancient cults of burying or placing a living human being, man, woman or child, under the foundation stone of a building, especially of temples.

to King Solomon because he was our first Most Excellent Grand Master, but in modern times they are dedicated to St. John the Baptist, and St. John the Evangelist, who were eminent patrons of Masonry; and since their time there is represented in every regular and well governed lodge a certain point within a circle, the point representing an individual brother. The circle representing the boundary line of his duty to God and man, beyond which he is never to suffer his passions, prejudices or interests to betray him on any occasion. The circle is embroidered by two perpendicular parallel lines representing St. John the Baptist and St. John the Evangelist, who were perfect parallels in Christianity as well as in Masonry; and upon the vertex rests the book of holy scriptures which point out the whole duty of man. In going round this circle we necessarily touch upon these two lines, as well as upon the holy scriptures, and while a Mason keeps himself thus circumscribed it is impossible that he could materially err." (pp. 59-60).

This is the official statement concerning the matter of the dedication of lodges, and the exoteric explanation of the dedication emblem. We find however, that Masonic writers in commenting on the meaning of this emblem, offer quite a variety of explanations for it, which shows that either there is no particular meaning in this emblem, or that Masons generally do not understand that meaning, or that these different explanations are given for the sole purpose of misleading the candidate and the non-mason. As Masonry is an esoteric institution the latter is doubtless the most reasonable explanation for this diversity of interpretations.

Undoubtedly there is a secret or hidden meaning in this dedication statement and in the exoteric explanation of the meaning of this dedication emblem, which will yield only to a phallic key, its real meaning.

This dedication of lodges is simply the formal devotion of the lodge to the three-fold aspect of phallicism, the worship of the generative principle in the sun, in light and in man, as the Great Architect of the Universe.

The Ancient Dedications.—King Solomon, the most excellent grand master to whom lodges were anciently dedicated, is the sun, the grand master of the universe, and in whom the generative principle is viewed as residing and ever going forth in life generating activity, being borne to earth in the rays of light, and where it re-appears as the generative principle in man, the master of the microcosm, or Masonically viewed, in the master of the lodge. This circle in the emblem represents the sun, the solar disk of the ancient Egyptian Aten worship, and the same in meaning as the disk in the winged Egyptian, Persian and Assyrian symbols. The point within the circle represents this generative principle in the sun in its first going forth into generative activity. The parallel lines represent rays of light bearing this generative principle to earth, and doubtless mean the same as the wings attached to the disk in the Egyptian and eastern sun symbols, denoting the swiftness with which its potency moves. The dedication of lodges to the sun still prevails in Freemasonry. The idea and purpose has not changed, only the mode of expressing it. Mackey concedes the phallic origin of this emblem, but contends that the Masonic meaning is comparatively modern.

The Modern Dedication.—The statement that lodges in modern times are dedicated to the holy Saints John, because they were patrons of Masonry, and symbolized by the parallel lines because "they were perfect parallels in Masonry as well as in Christianity" is not to be taken at its face value. It is a mere pretense and a snare, and is designed on the one hand to conceal the phallic character of the dedication, and on the other to lead the candidate and the Mason of tender conscience into the belief that the lodge is a Christian institution, and that these saints were Masons. These saints as known to us in the scripture, and through the early testimony of the church were not Masons, nor did they hold or promote any doctrines in harmony with Freemasonry. Upon its face this dedication statement is untrue, and in direct conflict with the sober facts of history. But in the sense in which Masons speak of them, or rather in the light of what Masons contend these men taught, the statement is in a measure true.

It is a fact that the guilds of operative masons in the middle and later ages, usually invoked one of the saints as their particular patron, and dedicated the guild to his honor. It is a further fact that the revivers of Masonry organized the first Grand Lodge on St. John the Baptist's day, June 24, 1717. This custom of dedicating lodges to the saints, and the organization of the first Grand Lodge on St. John's day lent itself doubtless as a suitable means for disguising the real religious sentiments of the institution, for diverting suspicion from its real nature, and above all to commend it to the favorable consideration of Christians. The statement that they were eminent patrons of Freemasonry and perfect parallels in it, refers to this custom of lodges invoking them as their patron saints. In this respect the two saints were parallels, and in a sense parallels in Christianity as well as in Masonry, that is in operative masonry, for these saints were also invoked as patrons of Christian churches. This is the most charitable construction we can place upon these statements in the ritual, so as not to impeach its veracity.

This declaration concerning these saints is variously explained by Masonic writers. The two saints are St. John the Baptist, and

St. John the Evangelist. Buck states that
"one was the author of the Gnostic gospel,
and the other, the seer of Patmos was the
author of the Gnostic Apocalypse, which
many an uninitiate has vainly endeavored
to interpret." But Mr. Buck is somewhat
in error in his statements concerning both
the authors and character of these two
books of the New Testament. John the
Baptist was beheaded long before the gospel
was written, and left no literary remains.
Neither can it be shown that either of these
books are Gnostic in their teachings, except
by the Masonic method and principles of interpreting the scriptures.

It is upon the Masonic assumption that
these New Testament books are Gnostic
that the claim is made for the patronage
and parallelism of these saints in Freemasonry. Gnosticism was a form of phallicism, and an esoteric system. "Gnosticism,"
Heckethorn declares, "permeates every
vein of Freemasonry." It is one of the pre-
cursors of Freemasonry, a prototype of the
modern institution, and it is upon this baseless assumption that these saints were Gnostics, and the further baseless assertion of

29

the Baptist's authorship of the gospel, and upon the unwarranted declaration that the fourth gospel and the Apocalypse are Gnostic in their teaching, that this pretended dedication of Masonic lodges to the Saints John is defended and upheld. Speculative Masonry can erect more wonderful structures than operative masonry ever did. By such cunningly devised fables does this sublime moral institution lie in wait to deceive the unwary.

The Lodge of Masons.—The lodge assembled for work is a symbol or type of the microcosm, the universe of man, living, moving and acting in the great world or macrocosm. This microcosm, like the macrocosm, has within itself the self-reproducing, self-preserving and self-destroying forces. In the macrocosm the sun is viewed as the source and engenderer of the life forces on earth, through the changing processes of day and night, and of the seasons. Over against this celestial life engenderer, there are in the lodge the three officials, representing the sun in the east, in the south and in the west, who engender the Masonic life in the candidate. Over against the androgynous generative principle conceived as inhering in the macrocosm, there are on the altar the symbols of this generative principle inhering in man, and of the organs through which the life of the microcosm is perpetuated. The initiatory ceremonies are symbolical representations of the life-generating, life-preserving, life-destroying and life-renewing processes, ever going on in both macrocosm and microcosm. Over against the sun as the master in the macrocosm, stands the worshipful Master of the lodge. Over against the generative principle in the sun, to which the lodge is dedicated and which is symbolized by the point within the circle, stands the Master of the lodge, to whom the square, the symbol of the masculine principle in man, is dedicated. The 'furniture' of the lodge symbolizes the organs of generation, which are the furniture of the microcosm, for the perpetuation of itself. Because of the complex character and diversified operations of the vital forces in nature, the symbols representing them are varied, and frequently duplicated to emphasize these activities. The lodge at work is a symbol of the life forces and life functions in operation in the microcosm.

The furniture and accessories of the lodge are the visible objects which symbolize the invisible cosmical and vital forces in the universe. Thus the Bible, square and compass constitute the essential furniture of the lodge. The square and compass symbolizing the male and female generative principles and the organs in which those principles are conceived of as residing, while the book represents the seminal or life principle, by which life is transmitted and enkindled. These are the essential furniture for the preservation of the race, the real temple. They stand as the representatives of the life forces in the microcosm over against the androgynous generative principle in the macrocosm, and especially in the sun. What the sun is to the macrocosm, the phallus is to the microcosm.

The Pillars or Columns.—Pillars or columns figure prominently in the symbolism of Masonry. There are a number of them fundamentally symbolizing one and the same idea, but denoting its different aspects in the various operations of the lodge. They may be grouped into three classes according to the offices which they symbolically fulfill.

The Two Pillars.—In the second degree two columns figure in the symbolism. They are designated Boaz and Jachin, in imitation of the two pillars which stood before Solomon's temple and denote according to the ritual 'strength' and 'establishment'. "These pillars were cast in the clay grounds on the banks of the Jordan between Succoth and Zeredathah, by Hiram Abiff, the widow's son. They were cast hollow the better to serve as a safe depository for the archives of Masonry against all conflagrations and inundations." They were adorned with globes on their tops representing the terrestrial and celestial spheres. All this and more is said about these two columns in the ritual.

From between these two pillars the candidate starts upon his ascent of the winding stairs, consisting of three, five and seven steps.

What do these columns mean or symbolize in Masonry? That there is a double meaning conveyed by them we believe to be demonstrable. The first is, they symbolize

the female thighs from between which every
human being enters upon his career in this
world.   This career is symbolized by the
winding stairs, with its stages of infancy,
youth and manhood.   As such pillars they
also uphold the temple the female generative organism, in which the deity is viewed
as dwelling.   As "hollow columns in which
the archives of Masonry are preserved"
they symbolize the phallus the place where
the   generative   principle i s   preserved
against the destroying forces of nature.
Supporting the globes on their tops they
symbolize the   intelligent   and   material
worlds in which the Great Architect is constantly manifesting himself.   The references in the ritual to the sciences of geo-
graph, astronomy and navigation are simply intended to divert the candidate's attention from the underlying phallic ideas.

The Three Columns.—There are many
allusions in the ritual to the columns representing the different orders of architecture
that prevail in operative masonry.   Several
pages are devoted to the subject in the 'lecture' in the fellow craft degree.   But these
like so many other things in Masonry do not

mean what they so much show. With all the efforts of Masons to conceal the phallic nature of the religion of Freemasonry, it still speaks out plainly and distinctly. Of the five orders of architecture the Doric, the Ionic, and the Corinthian are the most esteemed by Masons (Ah. R. 142). These alone show invention and particular character. The Doric was formed after the shape of a robust *man*. The Ionic is said to have been formed after the model of an agreeable young *woman,* of an elegant shape, dressed in her hair, while the Corinthian is a masterpiece of art. (A. R. 140 Rit., p. 100).

Here then we have a recognition of the fact that the Doric column is a symbol or representative of a man, of the masculine principle, and that the Ionic is a symbol of a woman, or of the feminine principle, two of the 'pillars' that uphold and support this temple of humanity. The third pillar, the Corinthian, evidently symbolizes the union of these two as essential to the completion of the temple. Thus the three columns of Freemasonry designated Wisdom, Strength and Beauty, and which uphold the universe or temple in which the Great Architect, the creative principle, dwells, are the masculine, the feminine, and the hermaphroditic principles.

"In the British and other mysteries these three pillars represented the great emblematical triad of deity, as with us they refer to the three principal officers of the lodge. The delivery from between them was termed a new birth. The corresponding pillars of the Hindoo mythology were also known by the names Wisdom, Strength and Beauty." Sickels practically identifies these mystic columns with the phallic triad, Brahma, Vishnu and Siva. (A. R. 205).

The doctrines of the Kabbalah help to interpret the meaning of these three columns or pillars Wisdom, Beauty and Strength, or the Doric, Corinthian and Ionic, for this is the proper order in which they should be named. MacKenzie in the Royal Masonic Cyclopedia p. 407 shows that there is an analogy in the three pillars of the Kabbalah to the three pillars of Freemasonry. Garrison shows the same thing and greatly emphasizes this fact. Pike drew largely from the Kabbalah to illustrate the 'analogies of faith'. Buck assigns great authority to the Kabbalah as an infallible light for the correct interpretation of Masonic art speech and symbols, so that we have official Masonic authority and warrant for looking to this system of oriental and Jewish theosophy for light upon Masonry.

In the Kabbalah the masculine emanations, which constitute the right side of the Adam Kadmon, form the Wisdom column, and was called Jachin, the pillar of mercy. The feminine emanations which constitute the left side of the Adam Kadmon, form the Strength column, and was designated as the pillar of judgment, or Boaz. The duo-sexual or hermaphroditic emanations constitute the central column and was termed the middle pillar or Compassion. By these three mystic pillars of Freemasonry, Wisdom, B e a u t y and Strength, symbolized respectively by the Doric, Corinthian and Ionic orders of architecture and termed Jachin, Compassion and Boaz in the Kabbalah, the masculine, hermaphroditic and feminine princples, the universe of man or microcosm is supported and sustained. In the Kabbalah this Adam Kadmon with his three pillars or branches constitutes the 'tree of life'.

There exists then in these 'pillars' of Masonry and the Kabbalah more than an analogy. It is an identity of ideas. The pillars of Freemasonry are identical in meaning and design with the pillars of the phallic cults.

The Broken Column.—"Masonic tradition informs us that there was a marble column erected to Hiram Abiff's memory upon which was delineated a beautiful virgin weeping, before her lay a book open. In her naked right hand a sprig of acacia, and in her left an urn, and behind her stood Time with his fingers unfolding the ringlets of her hair. (Rit., p. 185). This emblematic picture is explained as follows: "The broken column denotes the untimely death of our grand master Hiram Abiff. The beautiful virgin weeping, the temple unfinished, etc." Here the broken column represents the slain Hiram, and what Hiram means in Masonry we shall explain in another place.

This weeping virgin delineated upon the broken marble column denotes the female nature in which the ancients not only conceived the universe to be embraced, but also as containing the masculine principle. She is the same as the weeping Isis, Demeter, and Cybele, who while they were viewed as mothers, were nevertheless also viewed as virgins. The female nature in which the universe was conceived as embraced, was always regarded in those ancient cults as a virgin. This also is the idea in Freemasonry, and this virgin is weeping because of the loss of the impregnating principle through the untimely death of Hiram. She is a symbol of the temple unfinished, for the woman without the man is not humanity complete.

We think the demonstration complete therefore that the pillars in Freemasonry are symbols of the mysterious generative forces that animate and uphold the living universe, and are essentially phallic symbols, because these mysterious forces are inseparably associated in the Masonic speculations with the generative organs and functions.

The Altar.—In the primitive Vedic religion the altar with its base was a linga in yoni, symbolizing a union of the sex principles. The altar itself as a whole was viewed as feminine and the fire as masculine. "Their union in covenant and worship gave life." For the underlying thought of the Vedic altar symbolism, the reader is referred to Vol. XII p. 62 of the Sacred Books of the East.

In the Baal cult the altar stood in the midst of a grove or upright poles. The altar was considered masculine, and the ashera or trees, as feminine. On or at the side of the Baal altar were placed a conical stone, a symbol of the female breast, and a slender stone the symbol of the phallus. Their meaning is obvious. In the Kabbalah the altar was considered masculine and the shekinah as feminine. In each and all of these cults the phallic idea is dominant.

The Masonic altar is a square and in some cases either a cylindrical or a triangular pedestal. It stands in a 'triangle of lights' which Buck says "has a profound meaning or else the whole ritual is a meaningless farce." It also stands in the triangle of the Masonic officials, who are the pillars of the lodge. Upon this altar lie the square, the compass and the holy book, the essential 'furniture' of the lodge. It is at this altar, standing in the 'triangle' of lights, and from out of the 'triangle' of officials that the neophyte is born into Masonry, born into the lodge. The triangle of lights and of officials form the 'door' through which every Mason is born into the world of Masonry, and the deacons and stewards are the attendants who assist the institution in giving birth to the worshipful progeny.

The floor of the lodge is a rectangle. The positions of the three officials form a triangle, so here we have the union of the two sex principles again expressed, namely that the lodge is a place where men come to Masonic life, light and immortality. The lodge floor is therefore holy ground.

There is no fire upon the Masonic altar, but instead we find the holy book, the square and the compass. The 'holy book' is the symbol of the 'divine fire', the 'central flame', the seminal essence which kindles life. The square and compass symbolism is obvious. By their union the fire of life is kindled. By these sacred objects, and at this altar, the candidate enters into solemn covenant with Masonry. With one hand under and the other resting upon these phallic symbols,[1] he solemnly covenants with his brethren in this phallic faith.[2]

If we look at the lodge room from the view point of the Kabbalah, we find so many parallels and correspondences that the conclusion is irresistible that this identy of ideas is not accidental but designed. The emblems of deity the Great Architect, suspended in the lodge room or portrayed upon the wall in the east, correspond to and symbolize the "crown" of the Kabbalistic man, the first emanation from the inscrutable En. Soph. This "crown" like these emblems, has its own absolute character, and

---

[1] In the entered apprentice degree the candidate has his naked left hand under the holy book and the right on the square and compass. The fellow craft has his naked right hand upon the holy book, square and compass, and his left elbow forming a right angle supported by the square. The Master Mason has both hands on the holy book, square and compass.

[2] The ancient custom of swearing was by placing the hand upon the phallus. (See Gen. 24:3; 47:29.) Of this the Masonic covenant is a remnant.

receives from above, from the En Soph what it communicates to that which is below. It contains like the Great Architect of the Universe as in a totality all intelligences and all powers, and continually pours them forth into the emanations or entities flowing from it.

If we place the Kabbalistic man in a supine position upon the floor of the lodge, other striking correspondences appear. The head or "crown" correspond to the place of the worshipful master in the east, the feet or "kingdom" to that of the senior warden in the west and his extended left hand to that of the junior warden in the south. The "foundation" or genital corresponds to the blazing star in the center of the room, upon which are placed the altar and the triangle of lights. The indented tessel corresponds to the emanation called "kingdom" which incloses and embraces all the other emanations and within which they are continually active.

In the light of the Kabbalah, then, the Masonic altar is the symbol of the genital, the local dwelling place of the deity; the spot where all the wisdom of the ages are synthetized, and from which it ever goes forth into new entities; the object upon which all the speculations of the institution are centered, and the place where all Masonic life originates. Around this altar and that which it symbolizes, all Masonic religion, ethics and philosophy, revolve. It is the "foundation" of Freemasonry as well as the "foundation" of the Kabbalah.

The Blazing Star and Altar.—In the illustrations of the lodge given in Sickel's Ahiman Rezon, the altar stands upon this blazing star in the center of the lodge floor. The ritual states that "the blazing star in the center is commemorative of the star which appeared to guide the wise men from the east to the place of our Savior's nativity," and that this blazing star hieroglyphically represents our reliance upon divine providence for the blessings and comforts that surround us. (pp. 56, 57). It is evident that there is an esoteric meaning in this language, which is not readily discerned.

This blazing star is not a comet as some poorly informed Freemasons seem to think, nor is it the star of Bethlehem of Christian story, as the ritual would lead the inattentive Masons to believe. The ritual says that this star is commemorative, that is "tends to keep in remembrance" that star which appeared to guide the wise men from the east to the place of the Savior's nativity. This explanation is given to divert the candidate's and the interpreter's attention from the real meaning. The blazing star of Freemasonry has no reference whatever to the star of Bethlehem.

If we view Freemasonry as sun worship, this blazing star very aptly symbolizes the sun, and it may be that luminary under this misleading name. In view of the altar's position on this star, and the covenant made thereon, the statement that it "hieroglyphically expresses the Mason's reliance upon divine providence for the blessings and comforts of this present life," is in a measure satisfied. But there evidently is in it a deeper meaning hieroglyphically expressed.

This deeper meaning we shall now endeavor to unfold. As the emblems of deity suspended in the lodge room in the east are symbols of the "crown" of the Kabbalistic man, which crown is identical with the Great Architect of Freemasonry, so this blazing

30

star, is a symbol of the "foundation" of the Kabbalistic man, the Great Architect in the aspect of the generative principle, re-appearing in the totality of all the powers that were originally in the "crown," and which now continually go forth dividing into the male and female principles in the generation or emanation of new entities. The powers that were "lost" by the crown in its generation or emanation of new entities are "found" or recovered in this "foundation." The blazing star is a symbol of the Great Architect in the aspect of the generative, creative, nourishing and constructive powers, as they are manifested in the building of the temple of humanity.

The Masonic altar stands upon this blazing star, or seems to emerge from it, as does also the "triangle of lights." Through this altar and triangle of lights, the symbols of the reproductive organs, as the media, this generative or constructive principle generates the Mason, through the symbolic ceremony of initiation. He becomes a copy of the archetypal man, and the offspring of his god. In this blazing star and its superimposed altar and triangle of lights, is revealed and concealed the central idea of the Kabbalistic philosophy, or the emanation of man from the deity.

Yes we agree with Dr. Buck, that the symbolism of the altar in the triangle of lights, a linga in yoni, and the whole super-imposed upon the blazing star, has a profound meaning, and that the ritualism is not a meaningless farce. It is an intensified phallic service, but not one Mason in a thousand, suspects its meaning.

Hiram Abiff.—"The ceremonial of the degree of the Master Mason is unquestionably the most important, impressive, and instructive portion of the ritual of ancient Freemasonry. It transcends all others in the profoundness of its philosophy, in the wide range of ideas it aims to elucidate, and the dramatic interest with which it is invested." (Sickels, Ah. R. 195). The 'wide range of ideas' it aims to elucidate is here affirmed by Sickels. The complex character of its symbolism is also evident. It is a religious composite, which to separate into all its component parts, is an almost bewildering task. We can point out only some of the more prominent features.

Hiram Abiff, the widow's son, the so-called architect of Solomon's temple at Jerusalem, (2 Chron. 2:13, 14) is the historic personage behind and beneath whose name and office the several aspects of the generative principle are veiled and concealed, in the ceremonial of the third degree. This personage the candidate simulates, both in his historic and in his legendary career. But be it remembered that Hiram is only a cloak under which the phallic ideas are concealed, and a figure in which they are expressed.

Hiram as the Sun.—Buck says that Hiram has been shown to be identical with the sun gods of all other nations, and Ragon has demonstrated that he is a solar myth. Hiram according to Sickels (Ah. R., p. 196), is the same as Osiris. As a representative of the sun, he is a symbol of the fructifying or life generating principle in the sun.

Hiram as the Temple Architect.—As the architect of the temple Hiram is a symbol of the generative principle in man, the temple being humanity. As such he is also the symbol of the phallus. In the ceremonial of the third degree, he stands as the antithesis of King Solomon, the sun. As the sun is viewed as the generator of terrestrial life, and of the temple in which it subsists so Hiram is viewed as the generator of human life and architect of the temple in which it subsists. As in the Baal cults the phallus stood over against the sun, the generative principle in the temple of humanity over against the generative principle in nature, so Hiram stands over against King Solomon, in Freemasonry, and with an identical signification. Specifically Hiram the architect is not so much the generative principle, as that mysterious power or instinct in that principle, which builds the bodily form in which the life is to dwell, the invisible architect of the human body, and frequently referred to in Freemasonry as the divine artist.

Hiram as the Widow's Son.—Hiram is frequently spoken of as the widow's son. This sometimes refers to the Hiram of scripture, and sometimes it has a veiled meaning. Master Masons are also frequently spoken of as the widow's sons. In the aspect of the widow's son, he is the resurrected Hiram, the same as Horus, the son of his widowed mother Isis, in whom the slain Osiris re-appears and lives. Osiris is always the setting sun, Horus the rising sun. Hiram as the widow's son is the same as Sabazius the son of the widowed Cybele, the life of nature annually dying, but also annually born again. He is also Zeus, the son of Demeter, and Dionysus, the son of Kora, Demeter's daughter, in whom the life of Zeus re-appears as the life of humanity.

The several aspects in which Hiram appears as a symbol, are the setting sun, the risen sun, the generating principle in the sun, the phallus, the generative principle in the phallus, the fashioning force in the life principle, and the life of man.

The Assassination of Hiram Abiff.--This act in the initiatory ceremony of the third degree, is veiled and phallic. It is a symbolic act illustrating the deprivation of the god of his generative power. Hiram as a representative of the sun is slain by the three winter months represented by the three ruffians, by which he is deprived of his generative power. As the master builder, he is a symbol of the phallus, and his assassination refers to the mutilation of that organ, which is especially symbolized by the broken column. The 'word' lost through his assassination is the seminal principle, the fashioning principle in the life force. Hiram's assassination is a ceremony in which all the legends of antiquity concerning the mutilation and death of the god, and the various conceptions of these myths, are combined into one, and veiled under a legendary story connected with the architect of the temple at Jerusalem, erected by the Israelitish king.

The Resurrection of Hiram Abiff.— When the body of Hiram is discovered, the lodge not only laments his death, but the master resolves upon his resurrection, so that the "word," or a substitute for it, may be recovered. The master now impersonates King Solomon, the sun, the life giver. Three attempts are made, by the grip of the entered apprentice, of the fellow craft, and of the master Mason, the last of which is successful. The master says: "Yes my brethren I have a word, and though the skin may slip from the flesh, and the flesh cleave from the bones, there is strength in the lion of the tribe of Judah, and he shall prevail." The master then goes to the candidate's feet, places his right foot against them, takes him by the strong grip of a master Mason or lion's paw, and with the assistance of the senior and junior wardens, raises him erect. He then whispers the great Masonic word into his ear, and requires him to return it in the same manner. This resurrection ceremony which is Egyptian and antedates the resurrection of Jesus Christ by two thousand years, is represented by certain Masons in order to conceal its phallic nature, as a symbol of Christ's resurrection. Whatever is lost through the death of Hiram Abiff, this 'resurrection' symbolizes its recovery. Says an anonymous Masonic writer: "What this means, in all its fulness, can never be known to any but those who have traveled the path, received the instruction, done the work, made the demonstrations, and had the personal experiences. To others than these the most that can be given is a mere word picture. Under the most favorable conditions this can convey but an imperfect conception of the great truths of which the picture itself is but an inadequate reflection."

It seems to mean what the Upanishads

enjoin, namely that phallic worship is a step leading to the knowledge of the absolute. (See the Aitareya and Taittirya Upanishads).

The Exclusion of Woman. — There are many reasons assigned by Masonic writers and apologists why woman is not received into the order. Some eminent Masons favor her admission, but the general sentiment is against it. These apologists say she is not excluded because of ignorance, nor because she can not keep a secret, nor because of any intellectual, moral or spiritual inferiority to man, and that with these reasons for her exclusion she should be satisfied. Positive reasons are assigned in that it was thought proper at first to exclude her, and customs do not change readily; that the dangers to which she would be exposed because of the prejudice existing against the institution, necessitate her exclusion; that because Solomon employed no women on the temple, they can not be admitted into the order, and that she is excluded because Masonry is Masonry. (See Calcott's Disquisitions, p. 248).

The true reason is to be found in this last statement. Woman can not be admitted because of the fundamental philosophy of the institution. She can not be made a Mason because she can not be made a man. The true reason is to be found in the fact and function of her sex. The Mason is a representative of his deity, the generative principle, and must be a man. He must possess the generative virility.

In the mysteries, the mother earth the female principle, was viewed as passive, while the male principle was viewed as the active principle in the generation of life. In order therefore, that the unity and harmony of the symbolism may be maintained, woman must of necessity be excluded from the order. The philosophical basis of Masonry excludes woman for the same reason that a young man in his youth, a hermaphrodite, an old man in his dotage, or a eunuch is excluded. All this palaver about women not being employed upon the temple, of the dangers they would be exposed to if entrusted with the secrets of the institution, is nothing but ignorance of the true nature and genius of Masonry, or deliberate deception in order to conceal the true reason. A woman can not be made a Mason for the same reason she can not be a father. The function and fact of her sex preclude it.

As sex is a physiological difference in which is involved and upon which the propagation of human life depends, and as the masculine generative principle is ineffectual without the feminine nourishing power, so both phallic emblems square and compass are essential to the completion of the symbolism of Masonry. But as Freemasonry is a strictly masculine organization the complete symbolization of 'the necessities of human nature' also requires a feminine organization. Hence the establishment of androgynous Masonry. In this, woman also can symbolize her office in the procreative work.

The Antiquity of Freemasonry.—The great antiquity of Masonry put forward by so many Masonic writers, we are disposed to concede, if understood in the sense in which we are persuaded these claims are made. Oliver contends that Freemasonry existed before the creation, and his language plainly indicates that he means the creative principle, which was already active before the creation of man. Sickels in explaining why Freemasons have a calendar peculiar to themselves, which dates from the year of light, says: "This fact has a symbolic reference, not because they believe Freemasonry is, but that the principles and light of the institution are coeval with creation." (Ah. R. 388). This principle which is coeval with creation, is the creative or generative principle, and in the Christian view of the world inheres in every creature, not by emanation but by virtue of the divine fiat, and is itself a product of the Almighty Divine Creator, instead of being the creator himself. The 'light' they profess to have, is the specific knowledge relative to these facts and theories of creation, which the institution claims to possess.

These claims of Freemasons for the antiquity of their institution, are to be understood in a phallic sense. Phallicism is the oldest form of idolatry. It is not only one of the most ancient but also the most universal of religions, and it prevailed among all nations of antiquity. It has been handed down to the present in both dead and living forms. "The mysterious principle of life, as transmitted by the seed of man, is the earliest object of veneration." (Sam'l Johnson, Oriental Relig., India, 205). It was in the reproduction of life that men found the most wonderful exhibition of the divine activity, and so the function of reproducing life became a sort of sacrament, a divine mystery, and the organs of reproduction, symbols, and in a sense representations of the divine power in primitive times the world over. Dalcho's statement that Adam was the first Grand Master and that he initiated Eve into the same mystery is evidently made in a phallic sense, namely that he was the first to procreate life. The wife is by nature the sole and sacred path to man reproducing himself in the son, so that he who marries a wife not only initiates her into the mystery of life, but opens a door through which unborn generations troop.

In a phallic sense the claims to antiquity made by Masons are not only conceded, but they are true.

PART IV.

The Ethics of Freemasonry

(479)

CHAPTER XVII.

THE BASIS OF MASONIC ETHICS. ITS MORAL LAW.

"Morality is one of the precious jewels of Freemasonry."—*Mackey*.

WHILE not all Masons are agreed that Freemasonry is a religion, some even emphatically denying its religious character, they are however unanimous in the claims that it "is a moral institution, possessing sublime moral precepts which it inculcates and enforces among its disciples;" that "it is a progressive moral science," a "moral philosophy," a "philosophy of life," and that "the work of the lodge unfolds a perfect code of morals, based upon the three postulates, namely the existence of God, the immortality of the soul, and the brotherhood of man." They claim that "Masonry concerns itself almost solely with the spiritual illumination and moral or ethical education of individuals," and that "it is therefore a great school for the moral education of its members."

With these claims concerning the moral character of Freemasonry, the official definitions of the institution agree; that is, that "Freemasonry is a system of morality," and some say a peculiar and a particular system of morality, "veiled in allegory and illustrated by symbols," and that "it is a course of ancient hieroglyphical and moral instruction taught according to ancient usage by types, emblems and allegorical figures." (Rit., p. 23).

As Freemasonry is a moral institution, a "school of ethical science," and as it veils its ethical principles under allegories and illustrates them by symbols, which mean something very different from their ordinary sense, it is in keeping with our design to devote some space to the discussion and interpretation of this veiled system of ethics, that it may become intelligible to the non-masonic reader.

Masonic apologists lay great stress upon this moral character of the Masonic institution, and upon its "sublime moral precepts and practices." They claim for it not only the possession but also the inculcation and enforcement of these among its members, and that these moral precepts and principles transcend those of any other institution, not excepting Christianity, and in order to safeguard these precious possessions and prevent them from becoming known to the "profane," it obligates its members by solemn and irrevocable oaths to perpetual secrecy concerning them.

If these claims can be sustained, then Masonry deserves the support of every friend of morality and virtue, and every effort should be made to extend and commend it to mankind. If these claims were true we would not utter a word against the institution.

But we take issue with these claims of Masonry to a superior kind of moral principles, precepts and practices. In this discussion it is our purpose to show not only that these claims are absolutely without foundation, but also that the ethics of Masonry when the veil is removed, is decidedly immoral, and subversive of the divine order; that if these principles were to animate mankind, the state, the family and the church, and all the moral relations, ties and duties now universally recognized as right and proper would be overthrown and broken down, and society again would wallow in the sties of paganism.

We admit that this is a serious charge, but we make it only after a prolonged and careful study of the 'covenant', and of the language of Masonic authorities. We make this charge against Masonry, and not against Masons as individuals, but with the conviction that when men assume a name they also assume the obligations of that name. Men can not honestly accept or subscribe a confession, or enter into a covenant unless they believe its contents and agree to live and practice its principles. A Mason therefore is one who has assumed the covenant with all that it involves, accepts and stands for its principles, and is supposed to do what that covenant logically inculcates and enforces. We hold, therefore, that if a Mason is a moral man, he is such not because of the covenant, but in spite of it, for some men are better than the system to which they adhere. We therefore ask our readers to consider carefully what we have to offer in this work, as an interpretation of the veiled ethics of Freemasonry.

The foundation of true morality is the true religion, and the foundation of the true religion is the recognition and worship of the true God who has revealed himself and his will in nature and especially in his Word. From the Christian viewpoint any departure from this recognition and worship of the true God as God, is heathenism. Paul shows very clearly in Romans I that all the abominations, vices and unnatural crimes so common among the heathen, even in their most highly civilized and intellectual advancement, grew out of this departure from, and a refusal to worship the true God as God, and the history of religion sustains Paul's position.

The foundation of Christian morality, or of Christian ethics, is the Christian religion. Christian ethics is the scientific statement of the clearly established duties of man which the doctrines of Christianity with more or less distinctness enjoin. The ultimate and supreme standard of right and wrong in Christianity, is the Word of God. That standard expressed in mandatory form, as a moral law, is the decalogue.

The final analysis of the question of morals brings us into the presence of a supreme Will, as expressive of God's nature, and to which every finite will must bow. The philosophy of ethics brings us into the presence of an infinite Personality of supreme authority, whose enactments as a law can alone be the test of action. Thus moral philosophy and Christianity both reach the same results, and place the supreme moral law in the decalogue. The whole body of ethical truth purged of all obscuring errors, has been set forth in the clearest light in the moral teachings of Jesus Christ. He stood upon that law, was subject to it and interpreted it in its true sense and spirit, both in his words and in his acts. Christian morality, or rather the principles and practices of Christian morality are founded upon this law, and by it Christianity claims all other systems of morality are to be tested. Of this law one jot or tittle can not pass. It is of divine enactment, and no human power or institution can lawfully amend, annul or revoke it, or supplant it with another. It is founded upon the holiness of God, the infinite Personality.

"Moral science, like religion, works with the ideas of law, duty, right, wrong; but its standard is the law in reason, in conscience; it does not bring deeds into the light of God's judgment, or regards them in their turpitude as offenses against Him. Religion on the other hand, views moral law itself as emanating from God, and having its ground in his essential being; it brings conduct, and behind conduct, the state of the heart, into the light of the divine holiness; it judges by the quality of the deed by its contrariety to the divine purity, and by its enormity as disobedience to the divine will. We can not therefore speak properly of sin except in the sphere of religion; and only that religion can yield an adequate idea of sin which like the biblical is based on a right conception of God as the all holy and all good." (Orr's Image of God in Man, p. 213).

The foundation of Masonic morality, or of Masonic ethics, is not the Christian religion, but the Masonic religion. Masonic ethics is the statement of the clearly defined duties of the Mason to his fellow Masons, and to the "profane", as the doctrines of Freemasonry with more or less distinctness, enjoin. The Masonic ethics arise "from and are supported by the recorded facts of nature and the relation of all these to man, through experience or the demonstration of science." (Buck in Life and Action, Vol. 2, No. 2, p. 133). The ultimate standard of right or wrong in Freemasonry is not the decalogue, but that which they term the law of nature. This law of nature is the operation of the so-called divine nature, as it is discerned by human reason, or human experience, which Masons have demonstrated, classified, and systematized, and apply to individual conduct. This law of nature Freemasonry accepts as the sole revelation of the will of the deity, and has adopted it as its moral standard. The chief moral precepts and practices, deduced from this law of nature, are set forth in the 'lectures', are expressed in obligatory form in the 'oath or covenant', and in mandatory form in the 'charges'. They are veiled under symbols of the work-tools of a builder's craft, and in geometrical figures and terms. The foundation of Christian ethics is entirely distinct and different from the foundation of Masonic ethics. The former is traced back to the holiness of God, the supreme Personality; the latter is traced back to the operations or experiences as discerned by human reason, in the law of nature, which is best expressed in the free life of nature. It claims to have derived its credentials as a progressive school of morals from the parent school of India. Masonic ethics deal with actual facts and experiences and not with metaphysics and speculation. Its practice is symbolized by the square and compass, but the real Masonic meaning of the square and compass, and not their ordinary meaning, determines the real character of this Masonic ethical teaching. Its real sentiments are veiled under these symbols and concealed in their names.

That Masonic ethics may be rendered intelligible to our readers we must judge, estimate and interpret it not by the decalogue, but by the Masonic standard of morals, the law of nature. We must study and interpret the lectures, the covenant, the charges, the allegories, the symbols and the geometrical veils, and note what these mean in this institution, rather than what they say in the ordinary value of the expressions. Masonry on its ethical side is a "peculiar system of morals veiled in allegory and illustrated by symbols." The symbolic illustrations are double veils; they conceal rather than reveal the true ethical ideas. Masonry employs to some extent the terms of Christian ethics under which to hide its peculiar moral ideas. In its ethical expressions the words do not mean what they say. It is esoteric in its ethics as well as in its religion.

This much we have deemed necessary to say in order that the reader may be prepared for the discussion that follows. We first invite his attention to

THE MORAL LAW IN FREEMASONRY.

The decalogue given at Sinai, and which is so clearly explained by Jesus Christ, is rejected and repudiated by Freemasonry, but it conceals this rejection and repudiation by retaining and employing the term the moral law, as though the decalogue were meant. This Sinaitic law is too narrow and restricted in what it enjoins and permits, and too broad in what it forbids, to serve as a rule of action for the members of this institution. As Masonry supplants Jehovah with its Grand Architect of the Universe, so also it supplants Jehovah's law by another which it designates 'the law of nature'. In support of our contention we submit the language of the foremost authority among Masons. ''Every Mason, say the old charges of 1722, is obliged by his tenure to obey the moral law. Now this moral law is not to b' considered as confined to the decalogue of Moses, within which narrow limits the ecclesiastical writers technically restrain it, but rather as alluding to what is called the *lex naturae* or the law of nature. This law of nature has been defined by an able but not recent writer on this subject, to be the Will of God relating to human actions grounded on the moral differences of things; and because discoverable by natural light, obligatory upon all mankind. This is the moral law, to which the old charge already cited, refers, and which it declares to be the law of Masonry. And this was wisely done for it is evident that no law less universal could have been appropriately selected for the government of an institution whose prominent characteristic is its universality. This law of nature is therefore the only law suited in every respect to be adopted as the Masonic code." (Mackey's Jurisprudence, p. 502). Again the same writer says: "The ten commandments are not obligatory upon a Mason as a Mason, because the institution is tolerant and cosmopolite, and can not require its members to give their adhesion to any religious dogmas or precepts, excepting those which express a belief in the existence of God and the immortality of the soul. No partial law prescribed for a particular religion can be properly selected for the government of an institution whose great characteristic is its universality." (Ency. p. 205).

This language of Mackey certainly settles the question. The moral law to which Masons are obligated, is not the decalogue, but the law of nature. Freemasonry has a moral law distinct and different from that of Christianity. The basis for its ethics is not the decalogue. The church's interpretation of that law Freemasonry rejects and repudiates.

What is this law of nature upon which Masons lay so much stress, and of which they speak as being their moral law? It is not identical in its objective form and essence with that 'law of nature', spoken of by the theologians, nor with the moral law of Christianity. Freemasons tell us it is the "Will of God grounded upon the moral differences of things." In other words this law of nature is simply the natural inclination of human nature acting without let or hindrance as expressed or exhibited in the free life of nature. This law of nature is not a command, nor a series of commandments, but uniformities of action as exhibited by intelligent creatures. It is not addressed to creatures, but exists rather as instinct. It is substantially identical with the 'divine nature' as conceived of in the Phrygian and other ancient mysteries, the ancient Freemasonry, to whose ethical ideas and symbolism Masonic writers frequently refer as illustrations and warrants for their moral ideas and practices. This divine nature in these institutions was regarded as expressed in the life processes in nature, and constituted the model according to which the human life is to be arranged and conformed. What man has to do is to imitate the divine life and actions, and practice these divinely revealed methods. In this ancient Freemasonry the moral law was characterized by a negation of the moral distinctions and family ties that exist in the more developed society, but do not exist in the free life of nature. The only immorality recognized was a departure or violation of the ritual, and the actions of the gods and goddesses, Zeus and Demeter, Sabazius and Cybele, formed the basis of the ritual, while the stories related of the gods aimed to explain it. The individuals made their lives right by conforming their lives and actions to the lives and acts of the gods, which was the divine plan, and whose examples they cited in defense of their own gross and incestuous lives. They treated all that veiled, or modified, or restrained, or directed these processes as impertinent outrages upon the divine simplicity. Such is the light which the ancient Freemasonry throws upon what the law of nature is, and of the morality it inculcates. In how far it harmonizes with the moral law of Freemasonry, and the moral practices it enjoins, the reader will perceive as we pursue our interpretation.

In order that we may get a clear idea of the principles and practices of this Masonic moral law, this law of nature in Masonry, we must go to the English deists, who are the accepted authorities on morals in Masonry. Deism was in flower when modern Masonry took its rise, and its principles and precepts were incorporated in this institution. It was deism that transformed the Masonic guilds from an operative into a speculative fraternity. The deistic principles were widely published and extensively accepted, and the deists appealed to the law of nature as a warrant and justification of their practices. The Masonic institution under the powerful influences of this intellectual movement, adopted this law of nature as its moral law, and doubtless for the same reasons that the deists took refuge behind it. To ascertain therefore the teachings of this law of nature, we go to its greatest expounders, the men who professed to be guided by natural light alone.

That the Masonic fraternity was powerfully influenced by the deists is conceded by eminent authorities. Findel, a high Masonic authority, says: "The most decisive agent in accomplishing the transformation of Masonry was that intellectual movement known under the name of English deism which boldly rejected all revelation and religious dogmas and under the victorious banner of Reason and Criticism, broke down all barriers in its path. It can not be denied that there is to be found a certain spiritual connection between this movement and the fraternity o f Freemasons, as it afterwards a p p e a r e d." "This intellectual revolution must necessarily have exercised an important influence upon the fraternity of Masons, and we can not doubt that it contributed essentially to its final transformation from an operative to a universal speculative society." (Quoted in Frost's Secret Societies of the European Revolution, Vol. 1, p. 25). Findel refers particularly to Mr. Toland's work Pantheisticon, as a proof of the connection of Freemasonry with deism. This work was chiefly a liturgical service made up of passages from heathen authors, in imitation of the Church of England service. Frost who gave much attention to the origin of Freemasonry concurs in this opinion of Findel. This makes it plain to whom Masonry is indebted for its moral principles and for its ideas of the moral law.

We give here a summary of the moral teachings of the deists, to show how exquisitely they harmonize with the ethics of Freemasonry, as we shall hereinafter show. These ethics are based upon the law of nature by which both deists and Freemasons profess to be governed.

Lord Herbert taught that men are not hastily or on small grounds to be condemned who are led to sin by bodily constitution; that the indulgence of lust and of anger is no more to be blamed than the thirst occasioned by dropsy, or the drowsiness produced by lethargy. Mr. Hobbes taught that every man's judgment is the only standard of right and wrong; that every man has a right to all things, and may lawfully get them if he can. Lord Bolingbroke resolved all morality into self-love as its principle, and taught that ambition, lust of power, sensuality and avarice may be lawfully gratified if they can be safely gratified; that the

32

chief end of man is to gratify the appetites and inclinations of the flesh; that modesty is inspired by mere prejudice; that polygamy is a part of the law of nature. He also intimates that adultery is no violation of the law of nature, and that there is no wrong except in the highest lewdness. Dr. Tindal maintained that the morality of the law of nature is perfect, and is in no need of a revelation. David Hume taught that adultery must be practiced if men would obtain all the advantages of life; that if generally practiced it would cease to be scandalous, and if practiced secretly or frequently, it would by degrees come to be thought no crime at all. Both Voltaire and Helvetius, French deists, advocated the unlimited gratification of the carnal appetites; and the latter held that it is not agreeable to policy to regard adultery as a vice in a moral sense. Rousseau made the feelings the standard of morality. (See Horne's Introduction to the Scriptures, Vol. 1, p. 31, Edinburg Edition 1825, where the deists' moral teachings are summarized).

Such are the moral precepts and ethical principles deduced from the law of nature by the men who professed to be guided solely by the light of nature. Such are the "sublime moral precepts" which are discerned in nature, when the mind is unenlightened by a supernatural revelation. Such are the practices that are advocated by these prophets and apostles of deism, the spiritual mother and sponsor of modern Freemasonry. Who for a moment will contend that these moral principles and precepts accord with the teachings of Jesus Christ. The views of these deists on ethics are also supported by the moral teachings set forth in the mysteries, the ancient Freemasonry as they are deduced from the fragments of the ritual that have come down to us, and from the positive statements of contemporary writers. The ritual constituted the body of ethics, and any violation of the ritual was a great offense. But the ritual was based upon the incestuous acts, the deceptions and frauds of Zeus, practised upon his mother Demeter, and upon her daughter and his, Kora. These acts were enacted before the initiate, to impress him with the moral teachings of the mysteries. The law of nature was best illustrated in the free life of nature, and in the lives and actions of the gods and goddesses upon which the religion of the ancient Freemasonry was based.

Notwithstanding the boastful claims of Masonry, there is no such thing as a law of nature which can serve as a sufficiently clear rule of action. That there was such natural law impressed upon man's moral nature originally, we concede, and so the scriptures teach. (Rom. 2:14-15). But that law became obscured by reason of sin, and can no longer be a sufficiently clear guide for human actions. The moral law of God, promulgated at Sinai is the only moral law for man, and it is obligatory upon all men, Masons not excepted. The Masonic claim of the existence of another moral law, the law of nature, can not be sustained. The final analysis of the question of morals, is against it. The results of moral philosophy, which aims to give a reason why certain actions are right, and others are wrong, is against it. The history of the moral degeneration of nations, such as Babylon, Egypt, Rome, and others is against it. The moral consciousness is against it, and above all the Word of God is against it.

This law of nature, constituting the moral law of Freemasonry, consistently interpreted with the covenant language, with the utterances of standard Masonic authorities, and with the accepted Masonic aphorisms, warrants the following statements as expressing the ethical principles, ideas and sentiments inculcated by the institution: It negatives the moral distinctions and family ties that exist in Christian society; that that which is immorality from a Christian viewpoint, is from the Masonic view-point merely an innocent contravention of the arbitrary standards of society; that marriage is a restriction of the rights vouchsafed by the law of nature, imposed by creed-bound religionists upon the race contrary to the consent of society; that alliances formed without the marriage bond are no more immoral than those within it; that woman, yielding to the impulse of her nature, is absolved from shame; that a Freemason is one who has renounced for himself, all these artificial standards set up by creed-bound teachers, and solemnly covenanted with others of like views, to act in accord with his natural inclinations. In other words, this moral law of Freemasonry permits, enjoins and justifies outside of a restricted sphere everything that the Decalogue forbids.

CHAPTER XVIII.

THE MORAL PRINCIPLES, PRECEPTS AND PRACTICES OF FREEMASONRY.

"It is no doubt highly convenient for persons who do not pretend to a rigid observation of the duties of religion and morality to have spiritual guides who diminish the guilt of transgression, disguise the deformity of vice, let loose the reins of all the passions, nay even nourish them by their dissolute precepts and render the way to heaven as easy and as agreeable and as smooth as possible."—*Mosheim.*

In the preceding chapter we have shown that Freemasonry makes the law of nature the basis of its moral principles, precepts and practices, and that it designates this law of nature as the moral law of Masonry. We purpose to show in this chapter what the Masonic moral ideas are, as they are indicated in its covenant and precepts.

1. *Its Oaths.* The oath is the covenant, the obligation that makes the Mason. It is the central thing in the ceremony of initiation. It is the formal imposition of the principles, the faith, the religion and the ethics

of Masonry upon the individual, and his solemn promise to exhibit them in his Masonic life. This oath is, from the Masonic standpoint, irrevocable and supercedes all other relations, whether to family, to state, or to the church. "No law of the land can affect it, no anathema of the church can weaken it." "Its obligation is perpetual." "It never can be repudiated or laid aside."

If we take this covenant in its natural or ordinary sense and analyse it, we shall find that the principles it contains, and the practices it enjoins are absolutely irreconcilable with Christian ethics. We therefore contend that from the Christian viewpoint, neither Masonry as an institution, nor the Masonic officials as the ministers of Masonry, have the right or power to impose the oath, or the authority to inflict the penalty assented to by the candidate, if it be violated; that Freemasonry has no such right, authority or power within itself, nor has it derived it from the state or from God, and therefore, that all such oaths are illegal, unlawful and profane, and of no binding force whatever. These principles and practices have been analyzed and discussed by anti-masonic writers so frequently and so thoroughly that it is not necessary to reproduce the arguments.

We purpose in this chapter to examine and interpret this covenant on the same principles that have guided us in this work, namely that its language and covenant acts the 'due form' in which the candidate must be placed, are veiled, and that when correctly understood the moral principles therein involved and the practices and precepts thereby enjoined are from the Christian viewpoint as reprehensible as they are in their exoteric sense, and phallic as is the religion of Freemasonry. We shall show that these ethical principles and practices are a logical outgrowth of the religion of Freemasonry, in perfect harmony with it, and unquestionably an attempt to sanction their indulgence under the name and the authority of religion. Between the exoteric and esoteric ethics of this institution there is no great difference, save only that the esoteric sense betrays its phallic character.

When the candidate enters into the solemn engagements with the Masonic institution, he is placed in 'due form' to be made a Mason. He kneels at the Masonic altar, and places one hand under the holy book and the other on the square and compass resting upon that book, and all resting upon the altar. After the oath is administered, he kisses the holy book in token of his sincerity of purpose to be steadfast. He also invokes the deity to help him in this purpose. The reader will observe that there is in all this a semblance of great reverence for the Bible, and for God and his name. But what does all this mean? It is all allegorical and symbolical, and does not mean what it so solemnly expresses. The Bible, square and compass, and also the altar, are symbols and stand for other objects. They are substitutes for the real objects venerated by Masonry. There is a secret meaning conveyed by these which few Masons apprehend, and which the candidate does not understand. That secret sense, or meaning, or idea, veiled under these symbolic objects, constitutes the essence of the oath, the subject matter of the covenant. The real Masonic moral ideas are concealed beneath these external objects, and in the allegorical acts of the candidate.

"We must bear in mind," says J. D. Buck, M. D. a 32° Mason, "the principle that a symbol is not the thing symbolized. Hence it is important to determine for what great truth or eternal principle does the Bible as a symbol or the Great Light in Masonry stand.   How does the work of the lodge unfold, exemplify and demonstrate the meaning of this symbol?" (Life and Action, Indo-Amer. Magazine, July-Aug. 1910, p. 135). The Bible, square and compass on the altar, and the altar itself, are symbols, and distinct from the thing symbolized by them.   And it is also plain that the candidate is solemnly bound in his oath, not by these symbols, but by the thing or things of which these are symbols.   It is not then reverence for the Bible that is here expressed, but reverence for that which the Bible on the Masonic altar symbolizes.   It is not the square and the compass that he swears by, or upon, but the thing which those instruments stand for.   It is not the name and authority of God as these are regarded in the Christian religion, that is appealed to and invoked, but the thing this term means in Freemasonry.   It is not so much the altar that gives sanctity to this ceremony and covenant, but the thing for which the altar stands and designates. Let this be borne in mind by the reader. What then is the essence of this covenant; what is the objective thing that binds the Mason to the institution and to his brethren?

The reader has learned in previous chapters of this work that the square and the compass are symbols of the male and female generative organs, and the Bible of the seminal or life principle, and that it is by these as sacred objective entities that the Freemason is bound in this covenant. It is a disguised, veiled and allegorical form of the ancient phallic oath, in which men swore by placing the hand upon the phallus. The ancient cults viewed the phallus as the abiding place of the deity, and as a symbol of his generative power. It was the sacred shrine and to it the parties of the covenant appealed as a token of their sincerity and honesty of purpose. The candidate, though ignorant of this esoteric meaning, binds himself by his life generating power to be true to the Masonic covenant, and to this phallic religion and ethics of Freemasonry. It is this peculiar covenant that makes the Mason.

The penalties which the candidate agrees to have inflicted upon himself in case he prove "so vile a wretch as to violate this his Masonic oath," if inflicted are mortal, and in keeping with the essence of the oath. He swears by his life generating power, and consents to forfeit his life as a penalty if unfaithful to his compact.

Thus under a veil of reverence for the Bible, and of the 'name' of God, Freemasonry practices the ancient phallic custom of swearing its disciples to fidelity to the institution, to each other, and to a phallic religion. Under an allegorical ceremony which seems reverent and solemn, it sets forth a phallic oath, whose covenant principle tends, if logically carried out, to demoralize and debauch its adherents. Masonry is a particular and peculiar system of morality veiled in allegory and illustrated by symbol.

The candidate is solemnly assured before taking the oath, that "the solemn engagements which he is required to make before he can participate in the labors and privileges of Masonry, are made in the name of God, and when once taken they can never be repudiated or laid aside.'' (Rit., p. 30). The expression "in the name of God" means by the authority of God. Here the institution pretends to have authority from God, to make this covenant, and bind the parties by these horrible penalties, and to inflict them upon the unfaithful. The oath concludes with an appeal to God to help the candidate to be steadfast. This is not the ethics of Christianity.

The 'God' whom Masons 'reverence and serve', is not Jehovah, the God and Father of our Lord Jesus Christ. It is the generative principle, a force in nature. This generative principle Masonry veils under the names and appellations of the God of revelation, and worships it as its chief good. Freemasonry has forged the name of Jehovah to its oath and covenant, and symbolizes and conceals this phallic deity and its operations under Christian verbiage, and veils its frauds under the pretense that the Bible is the great light in the institution. The poor blind candidate is wickedly imposed upon by this 'school of progressive moral science'. It truly 'unfolds a system of moral culture'.

These principles which the candidate accepts and which he solemnly promises and swears to observe, and which make him a Mason, a different order of man, are to guide him in his relation and duties to his fellow men, to Masons and to the profane. They involve among other things the duties of veracity, of honesty, and of chastity. We therefore take the oath, this covenant, as the official Masonic application of these principles of the Masonic moral law, to these relations in society. From it we deduce the peculiar Masonic ethics. If these principles logically and consistently deduced from the covenant are from the Christian viewpoint corrupting and immoral, it is because of the fundamental principles, religious and ethical, in Freemasonry. We must test it by its covenant.

2. *Concerning Veracity.* The moral law makes it the duty of every one to speak the truth. It forbids all lying, deceit and dissembling, whether in action or word. It forbids every form of lying whether of silence, or through mental reservation, pre-

varication, or equivocation, with the intention of misleading. Not only does it require this but the maintenance of the proper active relations of human beings with one another demands it.

Nor can any class of men be exempt from these obligations. They are equally binding upon each and all alike. Any ethical system that encourages, sanctions or teaches that these duties are not obligatory upon each and all persons alike, is essentially immoral. No man or class of men, can by any act or resolution exempt themselves either from this law, or from any of its commands; no more can they do this than they can exempt themselves from the law of gravitation.

But Masonry does not so teach. It does not regard its devotees bound by these principles of Christian ethics. Masons, the institution teaches, are exempt from these duties because Masonry has another moral law, and consequently another system of morals, which is not to be tested by the decalogue. It has a moral realm which is not identical with the moral realm of Christianity. It encourages, sanctions and inculcates deceit, dissembling and lying, and justifies the same on the ground that the existence of the institution is dependent upon these things. The fact that Masonry is secret, is oathbound, and exclusive, requires, from the nature of the case, that these things be practiced. We therefore contend that Masonry not only fosters deceit, falsehood, dissembling and lying, that the whole institution is an organized lie, but also that it teaches, encourages, sanctions and enforces these things upon its disciples. Its whole system of rites, language, lectures and symbols does not mean what it says.

The candidate in the covenant solemnly swears that he 'will forever conceal and never reveal' the secrets of Masonry. He also swears never to reveal the secrets of a brother Mason entrusted to him, not even excepting his crimes. In the case of murder or treason, he is left to his own discretion. In the higher degrees, there are no exceptions made. These things make it plain that the Mason must, in order to be true to his covenant, frequently dissemble, deceive and lie, in order to keep his promise,

33

and the ethics of the institution justify such a course.

In the charge delivered to the candidate in the first degree we find this language. "Neither are you to suffer your zeal for the institution to lead you into argument with those who through ignorance may ridicule it." (Rit., p. 39). If among the profane, he must conceal the honors, beauties and valuable things of the order. He must pretend not to be a Mason for the sake of the honored institution. "The public has no right to know that a man is a Mason" is one of their dicta.

In the discussions upon the virtues of Masonry occurs the following: "The virtue (prudence) should be the peculiar characteristic of every Mason, not only for the government of his conduct, while in the lodge, but also when abroad in the world. It should be particularly attended to in all strange and mixed companies, never to let fall the least sign, or token, or word, whereby the secrets of Masonry might be unlawfully obtained." (Rit., p. 63, Sickels, A. R., 96). The chief aim and the essence of these virtues is to keep safely the secrets of

Masonry. Temperance is enjoined, not for its own sake, but for the reason that when a Mason is intoxicated, he might unwittingly reveal the secrets of Masonry. (Rit., 62, Sickels, A. R. 96).

Mackey says: "You shall be cautious in your words and carriage and sometimes you shall divert a discourse and manage it prudently for the honor of the worshipful fraternity." (Jurisprudence, 61).

From these quotations it is plain that Masonry teaches and swears its members to study the science and practice the art of deception. To be a loyal Mason one must endorse these tenets. Not to endorse them and still adhere to the lodge, is disloyalty to the institution.

The fraternity encourages, yes teaches, that if the circumstances render it necessary it is the duty of the Mason to perjure himself as to his civil oath in order to protect the honor of the institution. His oath as a Mason is paramount. It teaches that such violation of his oath as a witness or as a citizen, is not perjury. If a Mason be so placed that his duty as a witness in court, or as a citizen of the land conflicts with his

duty as a Mason or as a citizen of the state
of Masonry, he must be true to his order.

Besides these precepts concerning the
duty of Masons to conceal the secrets of the
institution, it deals with lies, and legends in
its lectures and statements, which are so
glaring that the wonder is that Masons can
look each other in the face while reciting
them, except upon the assumption that they
are veils for other things.   To give these in
detail would be to transcribe a large portion
of the ritual. Its statements concerning the
honor of the lambskin apron, of the middle
chamber of King Solomon's temple, of Hiram Abiff, of the hollow columns where the
archives of Masonry were kept, of the pillars, and a host of other things equally du-
bious, are in their natural sense falsehoods,
palmed off upon the gaping candidate as
veritable history and authenticated facts.
Masonry has very little regard for truthful-
ness.   It binds its members to be true to
each other, but leaves them to deal and to
speak with the profane as their judgment
and the circumstances may dictate. The exoteric language or sense is in the main a deception.   Its natural sense is not the sense

intended to be conveyed. The only palliation is, that these expressions are veiled. But the candidate does not know this and is none the less deceived.

Masons contend that those Masons who have divulged the secrets of Masonry, or published expositions of the craft, are perjurers. Then again, that these expositions do not set forth the real secrets of the order. Now there is a falsehood at some point. If from the Masonic viewpoint these seceding Masons who have exposed and divulged the ritualism of the craft, are perjurers, then that which they have published, must be the facts; and further, if they are perjurers from the Masonic viewpoint, then that which they have disclosed is Masonry, that is, exoteric Masonry. Heckethorn gives much of the ritual work of the craft. He says "the objects that modern Masonry professes to pursue, are brotherly love, relief and truth. Surely the pursuit of these objects can not need any secret rites, traditions, and ceremonies." (Vol. 2:17). "The true regeneration of mankind, need neither secret signs nor passwords to recognize each other. Liberty consists in publicity." (Vol. 2:18).

"Masons have been very indignant with me for making these statements, but honest members of the craft know, and occasionally admit, I am right." (Vol. 2:109).

"The more I study Masonry, the more I am repelled by its pretences. Are not its pretensions groundless? Is not its present existence a delusion and an anachronism? Is the holding out of the communication of secrets not a delusion, and the imposition of childish oaths a farce?" (Vol. 2:106).

There is that which we may very properly term the morality of language. "It is a first element of truth with which no right private or public can conflict, that names shall honestly represent things," and that words be used so as to express the ideas of which they are the legitimate signs. To use names and words otherwise is to make language commit suicide. By these esoteric methods and the dishonest use of words every distinctive biblical doctrine and fact can be fused and dissipated, every ethical duty annulled, and all moral standards thrown into hopeless confusion. The Masonic institution is esoteric, and its names do not mean what they say. The names and terms which it employs, even in its most solemn ceremonies do not honestly represent things. These names and terms have a value in Freemasonry, different from their value in common usage, which value the fraternity refuses to disclose. This fact is not generally known, either to Masons or to non-Masons. It calls things by their opposites. It substitutes legends for facts, expresses legendary lore and pagan myths in the language of holy scripture. It calls heathen deities by biblical names of God, heathen rites by Christian phrases, and Masonic doctrines in phases and terms of Christian theology. The whole system is not what it appears or pretends to be. It is a pretence, a delusion, a fraud, a lie. It hides its moral and religious ideas under veils, glyphs, ideographs and expresses them in art speech, emblems, and types, which have a semblance of the true but really refer to the untrue. It inculcates moral and religious ideas which from the Christian viewpoint are absolutely vicious and immoral. It enjoins practices which from the scripture standpoint, are damnable. It makes the crime, the vice, the sin consist, not in the act but in being found out. What immorality then is more patent than the pretence that membership in this institution is something which authorizes a a man to make his whole life a falsehood? The institution itself is a deception. It conceals its real sentiments, even in its solemn instruction and lectures in the lodge. It does not mean what its language most expresses. It has a secret system of principles and moral ideas which aims to subvert the present order of things, and an open system which professes to support it. But all this must be concealed, and to conceal it, it teaches its disciples to practice the art of dissembling, prevarication, deception, and falsehood, in word, in act, and in profession. Masonry is from the standpoint of Christian ethics, a stupendous, organized lie. It holds down the truth in unrighteousness, upholds falsehood under the garb of truth, and by this trick of substitution and juggling with language it deprives the Bible and especially its ethics of all vitality so that the adherents of the craft can safely regard that book with contempt. In its most solemn utterances it does not speak frankly and openly.

Over against all these indisputable facts, the institution solemnly professes to be guided solely by truth, by an earnest desire to learn the truth, to discover it and teach it to its disciples. It professes that all its statements conform exactly with the facts, and in order to convince the neophyte and non-mason of its honesty of action, the sincerity of its purpose, and the guilelessness of its motives, it solemnly affixes the name of Him who is absolute Truth, who can not lie, to the institution as a seal, and solemnly pretends to invoke Him to add His blessings.

If this charge of deception is brought against the institution its defenders reply that these statements are not understood by the profane; that there is a secret meaning conveyed by these expressions which only craftsmen discern. It therefore evades the charge of falsehood by esoteric speech.

Whatever may be the meaning of Masonic expressions it is certain that they practically operate as if the worse sense were the real one, and their mischievousness is not diminished but aggravated by their obscurity and double meaning. They do the work of positive error, and yet can not be reached as candid error can. One of the greatest hallucinations and under which most Freemasons are laboring is the idea that truth may be expressed in ambiguous formulas, understood by different persons in different senses.

Freemasons contend that Pythagoras was one of its prophets. He instituted an esoteric system in which words meant not what they do ordinarily. His followers, the Pythagoreans, taught that it is not only lawful but even praiseworthy to deceive, and even to use the expedient of a lie in order to advance the cause of truth and piety. (Mosheim, Ecc. Hist., Vol., 1:198). The Buddhist sacred books define a falsehood thus: "A statement constitutes a lie when discovered by the person to whom it is told to be untrue." So Masonic statements are to be considered true until discovered by Masons to be untrue. That is, the essence of the falsehood consists not in the teaching or motive of the one who utters it, but in the wit of the fellow who discerns that untruth. This tends to keep the Mason from prying too deeply into the esoteric language. It is plainly evident that in their ethical ideas concerning veracity, there is a striking harmony between the Pythagoreans, Buddhists and Freemasons.

3. *Concerning Honesty.*—The obligations to honesty and honest dealings with others is set forth in the covenant as follows: "I solemnly promise and swear that I will not cheat, wrong or defraud a lodge of master Masons, or a brother of this rank, knowing them to be such, but will give them due and timely notice that they may ward of all approaching danger." (Rit., 149). This simply means that the master Mason as a Mason is bound by the covenant not to cheat, wrong or defraud either a master Mason lodge or a master Mason, if he knows them to be such. The obligation to honesty applies to only these two things and that obligation contingent upon his knowledge of their Masonic character. Masons of the two lower degrees and all other classes and conditions of men are not included. They are lawful prey for the dishonest procliv-

ities of the master Mason. And if these never discover that they have been wronged, cheated or defrauded, no crime has been committed. If they do discover it, the master Mason is not guilty, for he acted wholly within the limitations of his covenant and his moral law.

These principles included in the explanation to the commandment "Thou shalt not steal," would make it mean we should so fear and love God as not to rob our neighbor if he be a master Mason and we know him to be such, of his money or property, or bring it into our possession by unfair dealings or fraudulent means, but rather assist him to improve and protect it, but all others are lawful victims provided we can keep the act concealed from them and from all others.

4. *Concerning Chastity.*—The law of God says "Thou shalt not commit adultery." This means in other words that we should fear and love God, and be chaste and pure in our thoughts, words and deeds, each one also loving and honoring his wife or her husband. Jesus in commenting upon this law says, "But whoso looketh upon a woman

to lust after her, hath committed adultery with her in his heart." According to Jesus the essence of this sin lies in the unlawful and impure desire in the heart, rather than in the outward act. Christ's interpretation shows that while men are ever prone to look upon the outward appearance and the outward act, God looks at the heart. The Christian system therefore aims to purify the heart, for out of it are the issues of life. The command is absolute and every moral creature is embraced in its injunctions and prohibitions. There are no exceptions, and one's obligation to this law can not be transferred to another law. One can no more evade its requirements than he can evade the omniscience of God.

But it is quite different in the Masonic system. Instead of aiming to purify the heart so that the life may be pure, it aims to legalize the indulgence of the passions, and find accommodations for their indulgence by restricting them within certain spheres. The essence of vice in the Masonic system is not in its indulgence, but in failing to keep it concealed. The crime is not in the act, but in the failure to prevent discovery. So long as the indulgence in a vice is kept concealed, especially from the world, it is a virtue. It is a vice only to the Christian, or to those who hold to the decalogue, but not in Masonry, except in a very few cases. What makes these things vices in the estimation of the public, is its erroneous position on the moral law, which position Masonry proposes to correct. The ethics of Masonry are irreconcilable with the ethics of Christianity. They are mutually antagonistic. Christianity denounces all vice, all sin. Masonry finds accommodation in its system for some of the most heinous and dastardly and legalizes them by its own moral law. Follow our discussion, reader, if you are in doubt of this.

To ascertain the Masonic ethics on chastity we go to the covenant. The reader will bear in mind that "it is the covenant that makes the Mason." There is something in that covenant which when taken or entered into, makes the man of a different moral order, and marks him as guided by a system of ethical principles and precepts, different from those which marked him before, especially if he was a Christian. He is now a different order of man. He has chosen and is by his covenant bound by a different system of ethics. He now has certain rights, lights, and liberties which the ordinary constitution of society, and the law of God, do not grant him. He has entered into a new and a unique religious and moral realm, by having abjured the God of revelation, and covenanted to make the generative principle under the name of the Great Architect, his god, and the law of nature his ethical standard.

In the examination of the Masonic teachings concerning chastity, we take that part of the master Mason's oath relating to this virtue. It is as follows: "I solemnly promise and swear that I will not violate the chastity of a master Mason's wife, mother, sister or daughter, knowing her to be such." (Rit., p. 149). The law of God says "Thou shalt not commit adultery." It speaks to all alike, man, woman, married or single. It has no restriction, exception or qualification. This is the "narrow code of Moses and the ecclesiastics." But the Masonic moral law is broad. It insists upon chastity, which the decalogue makes incumbent upon all, in a very limited sphere, but outside of that restricted sphere it makes lawful what the decalogue absolutely forbids. Let us take this covenant and analyze it and note:

I. *What this master Mason's Covenant forbids.*

a. It forbids adultery with the chaste wife, mother, sister or daughter of a master Mason. The master Mason solemnly covenants with his brother Masons of the same degree, that he will respect the chastity of their female relatives within these specific degrees of relationship.

b. This prohibition however is too broad, so he adds a qualification. He agrees to respect the chastity of such above named female relatives provided he knows them to be so related. The prohibition limits itself to adultery with a master Masons' wife, mother, sister, or daughter if the master Mason is cognizant of such relationship. According to this principle the Masonic interpretation of the commandment forbidding adultery, would be "Thou a master Mason shalt not commit adultery with a master Mason's wife, mother, sister, or daughter, knowing her to be such."

c. But assuming that the master Mason observes this covenant and respects the chastity of the female relatives of a master Mason as set forth in the covenant, why does he do so? Is it because he respects female chastity? Is it because the commandment says "Thou shall not commit adultery"? No. Is it because he is virtuous himself? No. Is it because of the holiness of God? No. It is simply for the oath's sake, because he has covenanted to respect the chastity of the female relatives of the master Mason, and for the master Masons' sake, who were present when he covenanted with them, and for the institution's sake. The fear, love and trust in God, out of which all true moral virtues and duties spring, have nothing whatever to do with it. If there is virtue in such obedience to a covenant, it is based upon an oath unlawfully taken, and not upon the fear, love and trust in God. Such virtue and honor thieves, thugs and cut-throats have, when they swear to be true to one another. Such

34

virtue Herod had when for his oath's sake he ordered John the Baptist beheaded.

The claim of a high Mason made to the writer some years ago, that Masonry deals only with the second table of the moral law, is not only sustained by the covenant, but also explained by it. It deals with these commandments with a high hand. It qualifies, restricts and changes them, and places the credit for their observance in their eviscerated forms, upon the institution. Christianity places the subjective ground of obedience to the moral law in the fear, love and trust in God, and the objective ground in the holiness of God. Masonry puts it in the institution. God alone has the right to amend his law. If there could be any change in it God alone has the right, authority and power to make such change. But this prerogative of God, Masonry has usurped, and changed the commandment which says "Thou shalt not commit adultery" into "Thou, a master Mason, shalt not commit adultery with a master Mason's wife, mother, sister, or daughter, if you know her to be so related." It views the decalogue as no more sacred than a syllabus.

But we have some further observations to make concerning this covenant. Let us notice in the next place

II. *What it permits.*

a. It permits the master Mason to commit adultery with the unchaste wife, mother, sister, or daughter of a master Mason. An unchaste woman has no chastity to be respected or protected. It matters not whether the master Mason knows the relationship of such or not. His oath binds him only in respect to the question of chastity in such cases.

b. It permits the master Mason to commit adultery with the prescribed class of female relatives of a master Mason, provided he does not know them to be so related. In this case his covenant binds him only with respect to his knowledge of the woman's relationship. And his licentious desires would hardly permit him to make inquiry concerning this point.

c. It permits the master Mason to commit adultery with the female relatives without restriction, of an entered apprentice or fellow craft. A Masonic oath is not retroactive in its injunctions. This feature tends to stimulate those of the lower degrees to work up into the higher, so that their female relatives may enjoy the protection (?) offered by the higher degrees.

d. It permits the master Mason to commit adultery with any woman, who is not related in the prescribed degrees to a master Mason.

e. It permits the master Mason to commit adultery with the female relatives of a master Mason farther removed than wife, mother, sister, or daughter, even if he knows them to be so related.

f. It permits the master Mason to be an adulterer so long as he does not infract upon those circumscribed relationships set forth in the covenant, or if he do infract upon them he succeeds in keeping it concealed from the institution.

g. This covenant while it proposes to protect female virtue, in fact undermines it. It makes the guilt of adultery, if there be any guilt possible, rest upon the woman instead of upon her seducer, except she be

the wife, mother, sister, or daughter of a
master Mason, and he knows her to be such.
In all other cases, he is not guilty. As a
master Mason he is a privileged character
in this respect. The only adultery recognized by this covenant, is the master Mason's carnal knowledge of a master Mason's
wife, mother, sister, or daughter, known by
him to be such. In all other cases, from the
standpoint of the Masonic moral law, it is
not adultery and he is absolved from guilt.
It is simply following the dictates and inclinations of the lex naturae, and the examples of the deities worshiped by the
ancient Freemasons. It makes the essence
of adultery lie in the relationship of the
female to a master Mason, in the man's
knowledge of that relationship and in not
keeping the fact concealed.

The Masonic writers inform us that the
institution not only inculcates the moral
principles of the order, but that it also enforces them among its members. We have
shown what these moral principles are, with
respect to chastity, and that they are very
corrupt. Now if Freemasonry enforces
them among its members, then it tends to

corrupt the morals of every Mason; then no man can be a good and true Mason unless he accepts and practices these principles and precepts; unless he indulge in all these infractions upon the law of God so long as he can do so with safety. The institution is a debauching one. It perverts the morals of its members.[1] This is the conclusion to which we are driven by a logical analysis of its covenant and the application of its teachings.[2]

Let us notice in the next place

III. *What this Covenant assumes.*

a. It assumes that females generally have a very exalted opinion of Masonic dignity and honor, and that these are shared by all women who come under its influence.

b. It assumes that the master Mason is holy, and hallows everything he touches.

Note 1. Mormonism legalizes and inculcates adultery and aims to make it respectable under the institution of "plural marriage", and no man is a good Mormon unless he has plural wives. Masonry legalizes adultery by making its ethics provide for it as a logical deduction of the law of nature.

Note 2. In some of the ancient religions it was required that every woman at least once in her life, yield her person to the carnal knowledge of a stranger. Is this covenant a remnant of these ancient religions?

He is an incarnation of his god. He can do no wrong.

c. It assumes that womanly chastity is a light thing and that women readily sacrifice it to the honor of the worshipful fraternity and that in doing so they be absolved from shame. No wonder that eminent women who have studied the moral principles and precepts of Freemasonry have declared that every Masonic lodge is a standing insult to the womanhood of the community. It can not be otherwise if Masons mean what they covenant in the matter of chastity.

d. It takes no account of the chastity and moral acts of the master Mason. He may debauch womanhood outside of the sphere circumscribed by the Masonic covenant, and still be a moral man. He does not violate his covenant, nor go beyond the bounds of the Masonic law of nature, in doing so. The law of the ten commandments does not apply to him. "It is partial, and too narrow for so cosmopolite an institution." His covenant has supplanted it, and this is what makes him a Mason. He is a different order of man. He is holy. All things are now lawfully his if he can get them, and all things outside of the Masonic circle are lawful to obtain if he can. He is not governed by the decalogue. As a Mason he is not under that law. He can violate its precepts with impunity. The standard of Masonic morality is the law of nature, and so long as he obeys it, he is a moral man. He may steal, lie, deceive, and commit adultery outside of the circumscribed sphere of the fraternity, and not be guilty of any immorality, Masonically viewed. He is under a different moral government, bound by a different moral law, and guided by a different system of ethics. Masonry by its covenant makes the essence of morality consist in the relation of the individual to Masonry.

"It is the covenant that makes the Mason," is the proud boast of Masonic writers. "The oath is the covenant." "When once taken it can never be repudiated nor laid aside." "Once a Mason, always a Mason," "Its obligations are perpetual." When asked "What makes you a Mason" the reply always is "My Obligation." It is plain then, that the Mason is a different

order of man,[1] governed by ethical principles different and at variance with Christian ethics. He is under a different government, which is restricted to the narrow circumscribed sphere of the lodge. Outside of
that sphere he is free to do as he chooses, and
is not amenable to the institution. Things
unlawful for the "profane" become lawful
for him, provided he indulges his passions
outside of the institution, for immorality in
the Masonic view is simply an act in contravention of society's accepted standards,
but which standards Freemasonry rejects.
The covenant partially protects the female
relatives of the master Mason from the
adulterous designs of his brother master
Masons, but from no one else. It protects
no other females from designing Masons.

This covenant does not forbid adultery.
It aims only to restrict it as advocated by the
English deists. It legalizes it in every
sphere, save one, and that a very limited
one, and makes it safe and honorable. It is

Note 1. An order is a class of men so closely linked
together that they form, or profess to form, a separate class
in the community. That which links them is a particular
principle or opinion which is not shared by the community.

an institution in which an adulterer is regarded as a chaste man.

If Masonry is unchangeable as its proud boast is, then men can become no better by joining it. If these principles animate and pervade it, then good men become bad by joining it, and by being governed by them. A covenant which not only permits but inculcates and enforces dishonesty, deception, unchastity, and all kinds of vice, is bad, immoral, unchristian, heathenish, and will inevitably produce the bitter fruits of Sodom. Does it not seem that the corrupt men who originated this shameless system, did so in order to secure themselves against the licentiousness of each other? And yet in the face of these vicious, immoral principles, there are men who make claim to respectability, yes ministers of the gospel, who defend the institution as a "grand moral organization" and attempt to identify its teachings with those of Christianity. This strange infatuation, we can explain only on the grounds that the god of this world has blinded their eyes and dulled their powers so that they should believe a lie.

Masonry as a moral institution, as an ethical system, is unchristian. "Its principles are derogatory to the principles of morality." (Judge Whitney). They are such as to permit the strangest medley of good and bad men to be united in a brotherhood whose covenant principles defeat every effort at discipline. But however such moral dishonesty may be condoned, it must be plain to every reflecting man that such an institution is an organized lie, with a priesthood, service, and association, united to sustain the lie. Corruption in doctrine works best when it is unfettered by any explicit statement of that doctrine. Error loves ambiguities. It does not desire to state its position clearly, either because it has no distinct position to state, or if stated, it would stand convicted of iniquities in the eyes of all honest and God fearing men. It might as well be assumed that the Bible is a compromise with the devil, and that the Holy Ghost was excluded from aiding in its production as to assume that Masonry is a Christian institution, or that the spirit of Christ pervades its ethics.

A Freemason according to the derivation of the word by some Masonic authorities, is a Mason who is free to go wherever he chooses to pursue his avocation. A Mason is a builder. In this cult he is a laborer upon the temple of humanity. A Freemason is one free to labor on this temple. The term then in its Masonic sense means one who is free from all the moral and civil restraints that organized society imposes upon its members. He is one who insists upon the right to follow the law indicated in the free life of nature.

IV. *As it relates to the Marriage Covenant.* From the Christian view point marriage is the union of one man and one woman for life. The essence of marriage is in the consent of the parties joined together, mutually given, publicly acknowledged and approved, and their troth mutually and solemnly plighted until parted by death. This covenant based upon and warranted by the Word of God, is indissoluble. Neither party to the marriage has the right, or the authority to violate it by those acts which destroy the marital union. God joins them in marriage by that word which constitutes the marriage institution, and no man has authority to put them asunder.

This marriage covenant imposes upon husband and wife certain mutual duties and invests each with certain inalienable rights, relative to those things, conditions or associations which would foster infidelity to the marriage vow, or tend to jeopardize the marriage covenant. These duties and rights are guarded by a holy conjugal jealousy which can not from the nature of the marital relation, brook any interference with or corruption of the conjugal love and trust. Each one has a right to know what associations the other may form, lest the one or other be tempted to infidelity through them. They twain are one flesh, and their mutual duty is to be pure and chaste, each one loving and honoring the other, so that neither may be tempted from the path of rectitude. Therefore neither of them can enter lawfully into a covenant with other persons, which infringes upon any of the rights, duties or obligations conferred or imposed by the marriage covenant, or which would jeopardize or invite an abrogation of any of the obligations of the conjugal tie.

With this marriage covenant, and with the rights and duties of the married pair, involved in it, this Masonic covenant concerning chastity, comes into direct antagonism and conflict. The ethical principles involved in the one are incompatible with those involved in the other. They are mutually destructve, so that if the master Mason accepts the principles involved in his covenant with his brother Masons, and logically and consistently carries them out in practice, as they evidently are designed to be, he vitiates the marriage tie with his wife. This covenant aims in its effect, to protect adultery and make it Masonically lawful, and is therefore a blow at the institution of marriage and if it were generally accepted would doom the home as an institution in society. If there is any meaning in language, an analysis of this Masonic covenant and of its provisions, plainly warrant this conclusion.

The wife, according to all principles of fairness and Christian ethics, has an inalienable right to know the nature of the covenants her husband makes with other persons, if those covenants involve principles

or authorize acts which weaken or annul his
duty of purity and chastity. Whatever
questions there may be relative to her rights
in other matters, there certainly can be none
as to this. In the matter whether the husband will be unchaste, or form alliances with
other women, he is not free to act as he may
elect, and be guiltless. There is a divine
law here which he can neither evade nor circumvent. He is her husband, and the standards of Christian society, the law of the
state, and the law of God require and demand that he be pure and chaste, and true
to his marriage vow. To this he solemnly
agreed at the nuptial altar. That agreement is a matter of record in the court, and
every sense of right and sentiment of justice
demand that he keep his plighted troth and
honor. He has no right to do otherwise.
He has no right to go beyond the sphere of
his marital obligation, or deceive his wife
under the plea and pretext of a higher law.
God has fixed that sphere in the law "Thou
shalt not commit adultery." He must obey
that law, as he demands his wife to do, or
else she can not remain his wife, for her
honor as a true and virtuous woman requires

that he too be pure and chaste. The law of God precludes his right to make any covenant which aims or claims to supplant the marriage covenant, as this Masonic covenant pretends and assumes to do.

This marital requirement that the husband be pure and chaste is annulled and superseded by the provisions of the master · Mason's covenant. That covenant imposes positive duties, but limits and qualifies them with exceptions. It recognizes exceptions in his duties concerning chastity. It therefore by virtue of these exceptions, authorizes him to be impure and unchaste, if he so elects, and keep the thing concealed from his wife, or justifies his acts, on the grounds of a higher law. It virtually says no matter what your wife's ideas or the standards of society, or the biblical teachings are in respect to the marriage covenant, this Masonic covenant is paramount. It therefore logically denies to the master Mason's wife any marital right which he is bound to respect. It denies her right to inquire or to know about his chastity, or to know anything about these covenant privileges, or to apply the accepted standard of ethics to his actions. This covenant vitiates and essentially abrogates the marriage covenant, because it provides for and authorizes the master Mason to commit adultery, without affecting his Masonic moral character, and in entire defiance of the biblical standards.

This covenant not only authorizes the master Mason to be unchaste, but it jeopardizes the chastity of his wife. She and her chastity, are a part of the subject matter included in its provisions. It relates to the wives of master Masons, and their chastity. By it he places his wife in a relation to his brethren which virtually authorizes them with his consent, in case they may not know she is his wife, to debauch and seduce her from virtue. It is a compact in which these men agree and covenant to respect the chastity of each other's wives, if they so know them, but otherwise not. It involves mutual consent to the infidelity of their wives under certain contingencies, and that the woman thus seduced be absolved from all shame, and moral guilt.

This covenant is made without the wife's knowledge or consent, though she be an object included in its provisions. It therefore

*35

assumes that the wife has no voice, right or power over her own chastity, and therefore, absolved from all shame and guilt if she yields to seduction. She is not consulted in the matter, neither by the lodge nor by her husband, for though she may consent to his becoming a Mason, neither she nor he is presumed to know the nature of that covenant in advance. She is mere chattel. She is ignorant of the nature, provisions and principles of that covenant, and of its logical sequences, and is therefore unaware of the danger to which she is thereby exposed although assured that it gives her protection.

Finally, this covenant with the principles involved in it and the practices it authorizes, from the Christian viewpoint, abrogates the marriage covenant, and from the Masonic viewpoint, supercedes it. It is paramount to all others. In the Masonic view, marriage is a restriction of the rights vouchsafed by the law of nature, a restriction which has been foisted upon the race by the Bible and Christian creeds, and therefore it is in conflict with and subordinate to the Masonic covenant which aims to restore these rights of the law of nature to the master Mason, and to allow and protect him in forming alliances without the marriage bond, which shall not be construed as immoral. It authorizes him to do as he chooses only that he act with prudence in doing so, because of the false sentiment and erroneous ideas still prevalent on these matters in society. When these doctrines are once sanctioned by the people, then they become right and lawful to all, as they are now right and lawful to Masons. "This covenant is perpetual." "It cannot be repudiated or laid aside." It is paramount, hence the Mason needs fear nothing, for the institution guarantees protection to him in all his assumed rights. "No law of the land can affect it, no anathema of the church can weaken it."

These are the principles and practices of morality as we find them expressed or implied in the moral law of Freemasonry as it is expressed in its covenant, and stated in aphoristic forms by Masonic writers, over against those of Christianity, which Freemasons contend were arbitrarily imposed upon the enslaved human intellect in the days when men were dominated by the creeds, "blind adherence to which it is one of the aims of Freemasonry to destroy." If "Morality is one of the precious jewels of Freemasonry" the reader can form some idea of the nature of these "precious jewels."

5. *Its penal features.*

In analyzing the god-idea of Freemasonry and tracing it back to the sources from which it claims derivation, we discover the three ideas common to those oriental cults, the creative, the preservative and the destructive. The first permeates the initiatory features of the institution; the second the secrets; the third the penal features. It is this latter that now demands our attention. It is a veritable Typhon spirit.

From the Christian viewpoint Masonry is animated by a spirit and characterized by principles that are the antitheses of Christianity. Christianity preserves and propagates itself by openly proclaiming its fundamental truth, the truth as it is in Jesus Christ and thereby win adherents. Freemasonry aims to preserve and propagate itself by keeping secret its doctrines and fundamental truths, the truth as it is in the facts of the generation of life, and by so doing, gain adherents through the fascination of its mysteries. It does not rely upon any power in this truth, if it possesses any, to win adherents and defenders. It does not present its claims openly and frankly to men that they may know it and test it. Neither does it meet its opponents in open and fair discussion, and convince them of error through the powers of logic, reason and truth. It can not upon its own confession flourish in the open. It therefore teaches in its long catalogue of oaths and covenants, destroy your enemies, employ every means to injure them in their property, in their business, in their reputation and in their person. Discomfit and consume them. And the inference is, that in so doing, they are rendering service to the Great Architect of the Universe, who evidently in their judgment approves of their execution, for they appeal to him for help to be true and steadfast in all the features of the covenant. The spirit of Masonry is a murderous spirit.

We offer the following in support of this proposition:

a. The barbarous and horrible penalties which the institution threatens to inflict upon the unfaithful brother, and to which he consents in the covenant. This reveals the spirit that pervades and animates the institution. It is not a loving, but a bloody, destroying spirit. It enforces obedience and secures fidelity by the threats of an awful, atrocious and ignominious death, in case of unfaithfulness.

Now these oaths with their horrible penalties affixed, either express the spirit of Masonry, or they do not. If they do, then it is a murderous, bloody spirit that animates it. If they do not, then it lies and deceives when it imposes them.

That Masons believe that these penalties will be mercilessly inflicted upon them, should they betray its secrets, we know to be true in many cases. The convictions of those who have exposed the ritualism of the order, that they took their lives into their hands in doing so, is proof. The numerous confessions made to the writer, on the part both of Masons and ex-Masons, is further proof. If Masonry does not seriously intend to inflict them it at least succeeeds in making its members believe that it will. In either case it is murderous.

That Masonry makes these threats in good faith is evident from what it has done in the past. And as it never changes, this murderous spirit must still animate it. The French, Italian and Spanish Masons, a number of years ago, cited before their tribunals, the Emperor Napoleon III, the Emperor of Germany, the Crown Prince, the Pope, and Marshal Prim. These persons paid no attention to the citations. They were however condemned by the order, to assassination. Marshal Prim was assassinated, but whether in obedience to this Masonic decree we know not. (See Heckethorn, Vol. 2: p. 108). These acts betray its spirit. And as the institution is one the world over, it must also be animated by the same spirit the world over.

That William Morgan was murdered in obedience to a Masonic decree, is in the opinion of all non-Masons who have carefully and impartially examined the evidence, proven beyond a doubt, and that his murderers were protected from summary justice, by the institution, is equally proven.

We do not deem it necessary to go into details concerning this crime. We simply refer to it as an instance in which the murderous spirit of the institution became active and operative. Another instance is the case of Judge Whitney, of the Belvidere Lodge in Illinois, who escaped assassination at the hands of master Masons, through their fear of public vengeance. Sickels states that one of the powers of a lodge is to exercise penal authority.

The basis of the initiation in the third degree is a dramatic tragedy, a murder symbolically acted out. The candidate is theoretically murdered by three ruffians, by inflicting upon him the penalties of the first, second and third degrees. These ruffians when apprehended are theoretically executed by having the penalties of the three degrees inflicted upon them respectively. This is done to impress the candidate with the seriousness of Masonic intentions, and the summary vengeance that speedily follows a breech of Masonic covenants. Blood, vengeance, death, against unfaithful members and its enemies, is the spirit that permeates the whole institution.

b. It approves murder. The knight of Kadosh swears to take revenge on the traitors of Masonry, to sacrifice the traitors of Masonry. This is a deliberate promise on the part of the candidate to murder. In the oath the candidate acquiesces in his own murder, should he betray its secrets. It takes the powers of life or death into individual hands, without a shadow of authority.

The action of the murderers of Ellen Slade, in Boone County, Illinois, in resisting the law, was tacitly approved by the action of the Belvidere Lodge, and of the Grand Lodge of Illinois. The testimony of Judge Whitney on this point is as follows: "The resistance of the law by Masons, in the case of the death of Miss Slade, was well known to the Grand Lodge and their committee, and they have approved it, and this lodge (Belvidere No. 6 F. A. M.) has quietly acquiesced; and having their charter restored by the present Grand Master, several of the most culpable of the members have been elected to the most important offices of the lodge." This action under the full knowledge of the facts in the case, can be construed as nothing else than an official vindication of the men who murdered Miss Slade, and who resisted the law of the state and escaped from its justice through the machinations of Masons.

. c. It is merciless. President C. G. Finney, himself a Mason, characterizes Masonry as follows: "Freemasonry knows no mercy, but swears its candidates to avenge violations of Masonic obligations, even unto death. Masonic oaths pledge its members to commit the most unlawful and unchristian deeds; to conceal each other's crimes; to deliver each other from difficulty whether right or wrong; to unduly favor Masonry in business transactions; its members are sworn to retaliate, and persecute unto death the violators of Masonic obligations."

Because of the excitement produced by the murder of Morgan; of the facts that were brought to light by the testimony of witnesses before the courts; of the action of the New York Legislature; and of the defense of Masonry by the Grand Lodge of Rhode Island, the scholarly John Quincy Adams was led to make an impartial examination and investigation of Masonry. He did so from purely patriotic motives. We give his views as they are expressed in letters and in his "Address to the People of Massachusetts." He says: "I saw a code of Masonic legislation adapted to prostrate every principle of equal justice and to corrupt every sentiment of virtuous feeling in the soul of him who bound his allegiance to it. I saw the practice of common honesty, the kindness of Christian benevolence, even the abstinence of atrocious crimes, limited exclusively by lawless oaths and barbarous penalties, to the social relations between the brotherhood and the craft. I saw slander organize into a secret, widespread and affiliated agency, fixing its invisible fangs into the hearts of its victims, sheltered by the darkness of the lodge room, and armed with the never ceasing penalties of death. I saw self-invoked imprecations of throats cut from ear to ear, of hearts and vitals torn out and cast off and hung on spires. I saw wine drank from a human skull with solemn invocation of all the sins of its owner upon the head of him who drank it. I saw a wretched mortal man dooming himself to eternal punishment, when the last trump shall sound, as a guarantee for idle and ridiculous promises. Such are the laws of Masonry; such are their indelible character, and with that character perfectly corresponds the history of Masonic lodges, chapters, encampments, and consistories, from that day to the present. A conspiracy of the few against the equal rights of the many; anti-republican in its sap from the first blushing of the summit of the plant to the deepest fiber of its root." Notwithstanding these horrid oaths and penalties of which a common cannibal would be ashamed, the General Grand Royal Arch Chapter of the U. S. forbade their abandonment. That Masonry sanctions these barbarities, is therefore proven beyond a question.

The experience of Elder David Bernard, an esteemed and influential minister of the Baptist Church, is a confirmation of what we contend is involved in the Masonic covenant. He had spoken against the principles of the institution and consequently was requested to attend a lodge meeting to give an account of himself. He says: "At the next meeting of the lodge, by request of the Master, I attended. Here a scene passed which lan-

guage can not describe. Several hours were
occupied in abusing and making charges
against me, the principal of which were, I
had spoken against the institution. Many
questions were asked and insults offered me.
I told them frankly I had spoken against the
principles of the order; that the right of
opinion, the freedom of speech and the liberty of the press were privileges given me
by God, purchased by the blood of my
fathers; that I had inhaled them with my
first breath and I would only lose them with
my last; that if they could remove my objection to the institution, which I then exhibited, well, if not, they must suffer the consequences. My objections were not removed,
and I requested permission to withdraw.
Soon after I left them, they expelled and immediately commenced a most wicked persecution against me. The professed ministers
of Christ, infidels and drunkards from Buf-
falo to Albany were united to destroy my
character. I was admonished by oral and
epistolary communications to be on my
guard, to carry arms; and so great was my
personal danger, that my friends would not
suffer me to ride alone from one town to

another. In short, they opposed my interest, deranged my business, pointed me out as an unworthy and vicious vagabond, an object of contempt, and transferred this character after me and it would seem that they intended to do it during my natural life. The united efforts of the fraternity to injure me have, however, proved unavailing." (Bernard's Light on Freemasonry p. 5). Toward the close of his eventful life he wrote: "And Freemasonry is the same now, in letter and spirit, in its nature and tendencies, in its objects and aims, that is was when I published its secrets to the world." (Id. Pref. p. 1). And as Masonry never changes, this must still be its spirit. This is in perfect harmony with Buck's statement: "The penalty of revealing the secrets of Masonry in modern times is the execration of all honest men and Masons." (220). "The oath is the covenant" and "the covenant makes the Mason." That oath or covenant is barbarous, bloody, and breathing the spirit of murder, of atrocious acts, of vengeance.

From these opinions and testimonies of competent and trustworthy witnesses, and facts which are indisputable as well as from the oaths themselves, it is plain that the spirit of Masonry is an unclean, dark, malignant, murderous spirit, and that the institution can not acquit itself of this charge. It does not attempt to defend itself. It takes refuge in silence and secrecy. It swears its subjects not to discuss these things with the profane. It enjoins prudence lest the secrets might leak out. It remains silent under these charges, in the hope that men will believe that they are malicious and false. It can not reply to them without incriminating itself. It therefore has no other alternative but to hide in the darkness and avoid the light. It can not come to the light without having its evil deeds made manifest.

In our charge that Masonry is murderous, we however, discriminate between principles and men. Some men are worse, and some are better than their principles. But we do not see how in holding to these murderous principles and sanctioning these atrocious sentiments by adhering to the institution that imposes them, men can escape from being guilty before God. The institution enjoins its devotees to hate the enemies of Masonry, and hatred is the essence of murder. It is this spirit that we condemn and not the poor deluded victims of the system. We pity, we commiserate these poor deluded souls, and pray that they may be brought from their darkness into the true light of the gospel of Jesus Christ. It is to this end that we labor.

The only just way of judging what Masonry is, is to examine its own official statements, its ritual, and the utterances of its recognized authorities. This we have done, and if these do not speak as we have testified that they speak, then there is no meaning in them.

Masonry is a system of ethics and religion in which there is some truth, though eviscerated and mutilated; and moral precepts, which in their negative limited exoteric form, appear beyond criticism. It is a system held and defended by many men; men of learning, of wealth, of social influence; men of strong and magnetic personality; men of kindly and liberal tendencies; men who have piety in their peculiar religious consciousness; men who have taste for the artistic, the beautiful, the sublime, men who in the eyes of the world of their fellow crea-

tures are gods of power and graciousness.
And yet this system is capable without in
the least straining a single principle, of the
vilest and most dastardly acts which man can
do to his fellow creature; acts of treachery
and of advantage dastardly taken over innocence, guilelessness, and reposed confidence, such as the annals of humanity can
scarcely surpass; and if not approved by
the system, is at least protected and defended
by it. Not only can it do this, but its spirit
and principles foster it, and it does it. And
when such acts are committed by its adherents, the system shields the perpetrators, and
assures them that there is no wrong in them,
though for reasons of convenience and ex-
pedience, these acts must be kept secret.

These indulgences in which its adherents
may engage are a pleasure which they especially may enjoy, but which must not be
spoken of, a thing never to regret, but ever
to conceal; the only wrong in them is in being found out. The value of its secrets lies
in this. Thus at one stroke it ravishes virtue, destroys all belief in virtue, and denies
all need of repentance and reformation. And
the palpable object of all this is not that its

adherents believe in this strange system of ethics, for that would seem impossible for rational and moral beings to do, but simply to avert the consequences which would prevent them from continuing the diabolical deeds. No system can be more devilish, and no character more hateful and diabolical than that fostered and produced by such principles. No ethics can be more subversive of all true morality, virtue, chastity, sobriety, veracity and godliness than this, which makes the wrong, the crime, consist in being found out. It is woven out of the warp of heaven and the woof of hell. The institution standing for and protecting this system of ethics may stand high and beautiful in the eyes of men, but in it are chambers giving license to the passions, in which human souls are ruined, and virtue stabbed, and all the genius, kindliness, truth and secrecy it contains, shall not avail before Him who sitteth upon the throne of righteous judgment.

O Almighty, Merciful and Gracious God and Father, with our whole heart we beseech Thee for all who have forsaken the Christian faith, all who have wandered far from any portion thereof, or are in doubt or temptation through the corruptors of Thy Word, that Thou wouldest visit them as a Father, reveal unto them their error, and bring them back from their wanderings that they in singleness of heart, taking pleasure alone in the pure truth of Thy Word, may be made wise thereby unto everlasting life; through Jesus Christ Thy Son our Lord. Amen.